A Man of Sark

A MAN OF SARK

A MAN OF SARK

CARETTE

A
MAN OF SARK

BY
JOHN OXENHAM
Author of "Barbe of Grand Bayou," "The Long Road," etc.

ILLUSTRATED BY W. T. BENDA

NEW YORK
THE BAKER AND TAYLOR COMPANY
1907

The Plimpton Press Norwood Mass. U.S.A.

FOREWORD

SERCQ is a small exclusive land where the forty farm-holdings to-day are almost identical with those fixed by Helier de Carteret in the time of Queen Elizabeth; where feudal observances which date back to the time of Rollo, Duke of Normandy, are still the law of the land; and where family names and records in some cases run back unbroken for very many generations.

To obviate any personal feeling, I desire to state that, to the best of my belief, no present inhabitant of Sercq is in any way connected with any of the principal characters named in this book.

The name Carré is still an honoured one in the island. It is pronounced Caury.

The numbers on the map refer to the farms and tenants in the year 1800 — the approximate date of the story. As this map has been specially compiled, and is, I believe, the only one of its kind in existence, it may be of interest to some to find at the end of this volume a list of the holdings and holders in Sercq about one hundred years ago.

CONTENTS

CONTENTS

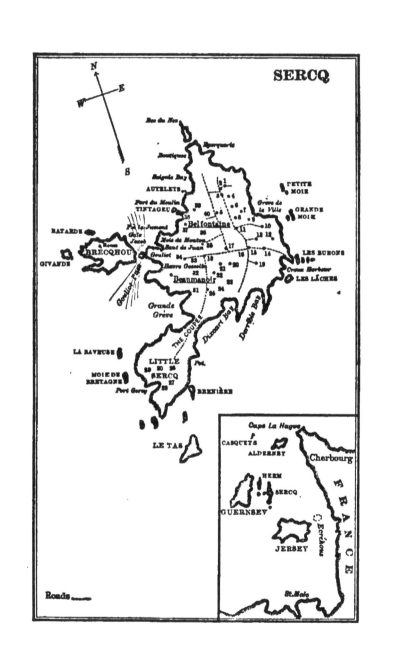

A MAN OF SARK

CHAPTER I

HOW PAUL MARTEL FELL OUT WITH SERCQ

To give you a clear understanding of matters I must begin at the beginning, and set things down in their proper order, though, as you will see, that was not by any means the way in which I myself came to learn them.

For my mother and my grandfather were not given to overmuch talk at the best of times, and all my boyish questionings concerning my father left me only the bare knowledge that, like many another island man in those times — ay, and in all times — he had gone down to the sea and had never returned therefrom.

That was too common a thing to require any explanation, and it was not till long afterwards, when I was a grown man, and so many other strange things had happened that it was necessary, or at all events seemly, that I should know all about my father, that George Hamon, under the compulsion of a very strange and unexpected happening, told me all he knew of the matter.

This, then, that I tell you now is the picture wrought into my own mind by what I gathered from him and

1

from others, regarding events which took place when I was close upon three years old.

And first, let me say that I hold myself a Sercq man born and bred, in spite of the fact that—well, you will come to that presently. And I count our little isle of Sercq the very fairest spot on earth, and in that I am not alone. The three years I spent on ships trading legitimately to the West Indies and Canada and the Mediterranean made me familiar with many notable places, but never have I seen one to equal this little pearl of all islands.

You will say that, being a Sercq man, that is quite how I ought to feel about my own island. And that is true, but, apart from the fact that I have lived there the greater part of my life, and loved there, and suffered there, and enjoyed there greater happiness than comes to all men, and that therefore Sercq is to me what no other land ever could be, — apart from all that, I hold, and always shall hold, that in the matter of natural beauty, visible to all seeing eyes, our little island holds her own against the world.

My grandfather, who had voyaged even more widely than myself, always said the same, and he was not a man given to windy talk, nor, indeed, as I have said, to overmuch talk of any kind.

And for the opening of my eyes to the rare delight and full enjoyment of the simple things of Nature, just as God has fashioned them with his wonderful tools, the wind, the wave, and the weather, I have to thank my mother, Rachel Carré, and my grandfather, Philip Carré, — for that and very much more.

It has occurred to me at times, when I have been thinking over their lives as I knew them — the solitariness, the quietness, the seeming grayness and dead levelness of them — that possibly their enjoyment and apprehension of the beauty of all things about them, the small things as well as the great, were given to them to make up, as it were, for the loss of other things, which, however, they did not seem to miss, and I am quite sure would not have greatly valued. If they had been richer, more in the world — busier they hardly could have been, for the farm was but a small one and not very profitable, and had to be helped by the fishing — perhaps they might not have found time to see and understand and enjoy those simpler, larger matters. But some may look upon that as mere foolishness and may quote against me M. La Fontaine's fable about the fox and the grapes. I do not mind. Their grapes ripened and were gathered and mine are in the ripening.

Sercq, in the distance, looks like a great whale basking on the surface of the sea and nuzzling its young. That is a feature very common to our islands; for time, and the weather, and the ever-restless sea wear through the softer veins, which run through all our island rocks, just as unexpected streaks of tenderness may be found in the rough natures of our Island men. And so, from every outstanding point, great pieces become detached and form separate islets, between which and the parent isles the currents run like mill-races and take toll of the unwary and the stranger. So, Sercq nuzzles Le Tas, and Jethou Crevichon, and Guernsey Lihou and

the Hanois, and even Brecqhou has its whelp in La
Givaude. Herm alone, with its long, white spear of
sand and shells, is like a sword-fish among the nursing
whales.

In the distance the long ridge of Sercq looks as bare
and uninteresting as would the actual back of a
basking whale. It is only when you come to a more intimate acquaintance that all her charms become visible. Just as I have seen high-born women, in our
great capital city of London, turn cold, unmoved faces
to the crowd, but smile sweetly and graciously on their
friends and acquaintances.

As you draw in to the coast, across the blue-ribbed
sea, which for three parts of the year is all alive with
dancing sun-flakes, the smooth, bold ridge resolves
itself into deep rents and chasms. The great granite
cliffs stand out like the frowning heads of giants,
seamed and furrowed with ages of conflict. The rocks
are wrought into a thousand fantastic shapes. The
whole coast is honeycombed with caves and bays, with
chapelles and arches and flying buttresses, among
which are wonders such as you will find nowhere else
in the world. And the rocks are coloured most won-
drously by that which is in them and upon them, and
perhaps the last are the most beautiful, for their lichen
robes are woven of silver, and gold, and gray, and
green, and orange. When the evening sun shines full
upon the Autelets, and sets them all aflame with golden
fire, they become veritable altars and lift one's soul to
worship. He would be a bold man who would say he

knew a nobler sight, and I should doubt his word at that, until I had seen it with my own eyes.

The great seamed rocks of the headlands are black and white and red and pink and purple and yellow; while up above, the short, green herbage is soft and smooth as velvet, and the waving bracken is like a dark green robe of coarser stuff lined delicately with russet gold.

Now I have told you all this because I have met people whose only idea of Sercq was of a storm-beaten rock, standing grim and stark among the thousand other rocks that bite up through the sea thereabouts. Whereas, in reality, our island is a little paradise, gay with flowers all the year round. For the gorse at all events is always aflame, even in the winter — and then in truth most of all, both inside the houses and out; for, inside, the dried bushes flame merrily in the wide hearthplaces, while, outside, the prickly points still gleam like gold against the wintry gray. And the land is fruitful too, in trees and shrubs, though, in the more exposed places, it is true, the trees suffer somewhat from the lichen, which blows in from the sea, and clings to their windward sides, and slowly eats their lives away.

And now to tell you of that which happened when I was three years old, and I will make it all as clear as I can, from all that I have been able to pick up, and from my knowledge of the places which are still very much as they were then.

The front door of our island is the tunnel in the rock

cut by old Helier de Carteret nearly three hundred years ago. Standing in the tunnel, you see on one side the shingle of the beach where the boats lie but poorly sheltered from the winter storms, though we are hoping before long to have a breakwater capable of affording better shelter than the present one. You see also the row of great capstans at the foot of the cliff by which the boats are hauled as far out of reach of the waves as possible, though sometimes not far enough. Through the other end of the tunnel you look into the Creux Road which leads straight up to the life and centre of the island.

Facing due east and sloping sharply to the sea, this narrow way between the hills gets all the sun, and on a fine summer's morning grows drowsy with the heat. The crimson and creamy-gold of the opening honeysuckle swings heavy with its own sweetness. The hart's-tongue ferns, matted all over the steep banks, hang down like the tongues of thirsty dogs. The bees blunder sleepily from flower to flower. The black and crimson butterflies take short flights and long, panting rests. Even the late wild roses seem less saucily cheerful than usual, and the branching ferns on the hillsides look as though they were cast in bronze.

I have seen it all just so a thousand times, and have passed down from the sweet blowing wind above to the crisp breath of the sea below, without wakening the little valley from its sleep.

But on one such day it had a very rude awakening. For, without a moment's warning, half the population

of the island came pouring down the steep way towards
the sea. First came four burly fishermen in blue
guernseys and stocking-caps, carrying between them, in
a sling of ropes, a fifth man, whose arms and legs were
tightly bound. His dark face was bruised and dis-
coloured, and darker still with the anger that was in
him. He was a powerful man and looked dangerous
even in his bonds.

Behind these came Pierre Le Masurier, the Sénéchal,
and I can imagine how tight and grim his face would
be set to a job which he did not like. For, though he
was the magistrate of the island, and held the law in
his own hands, with the assistance of his two conné-
tables, Elie Guille and Jean Vaudin, they were all just
farmers like the rest. M. le Sénéchal was, indeed, a
man of substance, and had acquired some learning,
and perhaps even a little knowledge of legal matters,
but he trusted chiefly to his good common sense in
deciding the disputes which now and again sprang up
among his neighbours. And as for Elie Guille and
Jean Vaudin, they had very little to do as officers of
the law, but had their hands very full with the farming
and fishing and care of their families, and when they
had to turn constable it was somewhat against the
grain, and they did it very mildly, and gave as little
offence as possible.

And behind M. le Sénéchal came two or three more
men and half the women and children of the island,
the women all agog with excitement, the children dodging in and out to get a glimpse of the bound man.

And none of them said a word. The only sound was the grinding of the heavy boots in front, and the bustle of the passage of such a crowd along so narrow a way. There had been words and to spare up above. This was the end of the matter and of the man in bonds, so far as the island was concerned, — at least that was the intention. There was no exultation over the prisoner, no jibes and jeers such as might have been elsewhere. They were simply interested to see the end.

Behind them all, slowly, and as though against his will, yet determined to see it out, came a tall man of middle age, like the rest, half farmer, half fisherman, but of a finer — and sadder — countenance than any there. When all the rest poured noisily through the tunnel and spread out along the shingle, he stood back among the capstans under the cliff and watched quietly.

The bearers placed their burden in one of the boats drawn up on the beach, and straightened their backs gratefully. They ran the boat rasping over the stones into the water, and two of them sprang in and rowed steadily out to sea. The others stood, hands on hips, watching them silently, till the boat turned the corner of Les Lâches and passed out of sight, and then their tongues were loosed.

"So!" said one. "That's the end of Monsieur Martel."

"Nom de Gyu! We'll hope so," said the other. "But I'd sooner seen him dead and buried."

"'Crais b'en!" said the other with a knowing nod. For all the world knew that if Paul Martel had never

THE BEARERS PLACED THEIR BURDEN IN ONE OF THE BOATS

come to Sercq, Rachel Carré might have become Mistress Hamon instead of Mme. Martel — and very much better for her if she had.

For Martel, in spite of his taking ways and the polished manners of his courting days, had proved anything but a good husband, and he had wound up a long period of indifference and neglect with a grievous bodily assault which had stirred the clan spirit of the islanders into active reprisal. They would make of it an object-lesson to the other island girls which would be likely to further the wooings of the island lads for a long time to come.

Martel, you see, came from Guernsey, but he was only half a Guernseyman at that. His father was a Manche man from Cherbourg, who happened to get wrecked on the Hanois, and settled and married in Peter Port. Paul Martel had grown up to the sea. He had sailed to foreign parts and seen much of the world. He was an excellent sailor, and when he tired of a roving life turned his abilities to account in those peculiar channels of trade which the situation of the islands and their ancient privileges particularly fitted them for. The government in London had, indeed, tried, time after time, to suppress the free-trading, and passed many laws and ordinances against it, but these attempts had so far only added zest to the business and seemed rather to stimulate that which they were intended to suppress.

Martel was successful as a smuggler and might in time have come to own his own boat and run his own cargoes, if he had kept steady.

The government now and again had harsh fits which made things difficult for the time being in Guernsey, and at such times the smaller islands were turned to account, and the goods were stored and shipped from there. And that is how he came to frequent Sercq and made the acquaintance of Rachel Carré.

George Hamon, I know, never to his dying day forgave himself for having been the means of bringing Martel to Sercq, and truly he got paid for it as bitterly as man could.

Martel might, indeed, have found his way there in any case, but that, to Hamon, did not in any degree lessen the weight of the fact that it was he brought him there to assist in some of his free-trading schemes. And if he had guessed what was to come of it, he would never have handled keg or bale as long as he lived, rather than, with his own hand, spoil his life as he did.

For a time they were very intimate, he and Martel. Then Martel made up to Rachel Carré, and their friendship turned to hatred, the more venomous for what had gone before.

But even George Hamon admits that Paul Martel was an unusually good-looking fellow, with very attractive manners when he chose, and a knowledge of the world and its ways, and of men and women, beyond the ordinary, and he won Rachel Carré's heart against her head and in the teeth of her father's opposition.

Perhaps if her mother had been alive things might have been different. But she died when Rachel was eight years old, and her father was much away at the fishing, for the farm was poorer then than it became afterwards, and Martel found his opportunities and turned them to account.

I do not pretend to understand fully how it came about — beyond the fact that the little god of love goes about his work blindfold, and that women do the most unaccountable things at times. Even in the most momentous matters they are capable of the most grievous mistakes, though, on the other hand, that same heart instinct also leads them at times to wisdom beyond the gauging of man's intelligence. A man reasons and keeps tight hand on his feelings; a woman feels and knows; and sometimes a leap in the dark lands one safely and sometimes not.

To make a long story short, however, Paul Martel and Rachel Carré were married, to the great surprise of all Rachel's friends and to the great grief of her father.

Martel built a little cottage at the head of the chasm which drops into Havre Gosselin, and her father, Philip Carré, lived lonely on his little farm of Belfontaine, by Port à la Jument, with no companion but his dumb man Krok.

Rachel seemed quite happy in her marriage. There had been many predictions among the gossips as to its outcome, and sharp eyes were not lacking to detect the first signs of the fulfilment of prophecy, nor reasons for visits to the cottage at La Frégondée with a view to discovering them. And perhaps Rachel understood all that perfectly well. She was her father's daughter, and Philip Carré was one of the most intelligent and deep-thinking men I have ever met.

Her nearest neighbour and chief friend was Jeanne Falla of Beaumanoir, widow of Peter le Marchant, whose brother John lived on Brecqhou and made a certain reputation there both for himself and the island. She was old enough to have been Rachel's mother, and Rachel may have confided in her. If she did so, her confidence was never abused, for Jeanne Falla could talk more and tell less than any woman I ever knew, and that I count a very great accomplishment.

She was a Guernsey woman by birth, but had lived on Sercq for over twenty years. Her husband was drowned while vraicking a year after they were married, and she had taken the farm in hand and made more of it than ever he would have done if he had lived to be a hundred, for the Le Marchants always tended more to the sea than to the land, though Jeanne Falla's Peter, I have been told, was more shore-going than the rest. She had no child of her own, and that was the only lack in her life. She made up for it by keeping an open heart to all other children, whereby many gained through her loss, and her loss turned to gain even for herself.

When Rachel's boy came, she made as much of him as if he had been her own. And the two between them named him Philip Carré, after his grandfather — instinct, maybe, or possibly simply with the idea of pleasing the old man whose heart had never come fully round to the marriage — happily done, whatever the reason.

For Martel, outside business matters, which needed
a clear head and all a man's wits about him unless he
wanted to run himself and his cargoes into trouble,
soon proved himself unstable as water. The nature
of his business tended to conviviality. Successful runs
were celebrated, and fresh ones planned, and occasional
losses consoled, in broached kegs which cost little.
Success or failure found equal satisfaction in the flowing bowl, and no home happiness ever yet came out of
a bung hole.

Then, too, Rachel Carré had been brought up by
her father in a simple, perhaps somewhat rigorous,
faith which in himself developed into Quakerism. I
have thought it not impossible that in that might be
found some explanation of her action in marrying
Paul Martel. Perhaps her father drew the lines somewhat tightly, and her opening life craved width and
colour, and found the largest possibilities of them in
the rollicking young stranger. Truly, he brought
colour enough and to spare into the sober gray of her
life. It was when the red blood started under his
vicious blows that their life together ended.

Martel had no beliefs whatever, except in himself
and his powers of outwitting any preventive officer
ever born.

Rachel Carré's illusions died one by one. The
colours faded, the gray darkened. Martel was much
away on his business; possibly also on his pleasures.

One night, after a successful run, he returned home
very drunk, and discovered more than usual cause for

resentment in his wife's reproachful silence. He struck her, wounding her to the flowing of blood, and she picked up her boy and fled along the cliffs to Beaumanoir where Jeanne Falla lived, with George Hamon not far away at La Vauroque.

Jeanne Falla took her in and comforted her, and as soon as George Hamon heard the news, he started off with a neighbour or two to Frégondée to attend to Martel.

In the result, and not without some tough fighting, for Martel was a powerful man and furious at their invasion, they carried him in bonds to the house of the Sénéchal, Pierre le Masurier, for judgment. And M. le Sénéchal, after due consideration, determined, like a wise man, to rid himself of a nuisance by flinging it over the hedge, as one does the slugs that eat one's cabbages. Martel came from Guernsey and was not wanted in Sercq. To Guernsey therefore he should go, with instructions not to return to Sercq lest worse should follow. Hence the procession that disturbed the slumbers of the Creux Road that day.

CHAPTER II

"You paid off some of your old score up there, last night, George," said one of the men who had stood watching the boat which carried Martel back to Guernsey.

"Just a little bit," said Hamon, as he rubbed his hand gently over a big bruise on the side of his head. "He's a devil to fight and as strong as an ox"; and they turned and followed the Sénéchal and Philip Carré through the tunnel.

"Good riddance!" said a woman in the crowd, taking off her black sunbonnet and giving it an angry shake before putting it on again. "We don't want any of that kind here," — with a meaning look at the big fishermen behind, which set them grinning and winking knowingly.

"Aw, then, Mistress Guilbert," said one, lurching uncomfortably under her gaze, with his hands deep in his trouser pockets. "We others know better than that."

"And a good thing for you, too. That kind of work won't go down in Sercq, let me tell you. Ma fé, no!" and the crowd dribbled away through the tunnel to get back to its work again.

15

The Sénéchal was busy planting late cabbages and time was precious. The grave-faced fisherman, who had stood behind the crowd, tramped up the narrow road by his side.

"Well, Carré, you're rid of him. I hope for good," said the Sénéchal.

"Before God, I hope so, M. le Sénéchal! He has a devil."

"How goes it with Mistress Rachel this morning?"

"She says little."

"But thinks the more, no doubt. She has suffered more than we know, I fear."

"Like enough."

"I never could understand why she threw herself away on a man like that."

"It was not for want of warning."

"I am sure. Well, she has paid. I hope this ends it."

But the other shook his head doubtfully, and as they parted at the crossways, he said gloomily, "She'll know no peace till he's under the sea or the sod." And the Sénéchal nodded and strode thoughtfully away towards Beauregard, while Carré went on to Havre Gosselin.

When he reached the cottage at the head of the chasm, he lifted the latch and went in. He was confronted by a small boy of three or so, who at sound of the latch had snatched a stick from the floor, with a frown of vast determination on his baby face — an odd, meaningful action.

At sight of Philip Carré, however, the crumpled face

relaxed instantly, and the youngster launched himself at him with a shout of welcome.

At sound of the latch, too, a girlish figure had started up from the lit-de-fouaille in the corner by the hearth — the great square couch built out into the room and filled with dried bracken, the universal lounge in the islands and generally of a size large enough to accommodate the entire family.

This was Carré's daughter, Rachel, Martel's wife. Her face was very comely. She was the island beauty when Martel married her, and much sought after, which made her present state the more bitter to contemplate. Her face was whiter even than of late, at the moment, by reason of the dark circles of suffering round her eyes, and the white cloth bound round her head. She sat up and looked at her father, with the patient expectancy of one who had endured much and doubted still what might be in store for her.

Carré gripped the small boy's two hands in his big brown one, and the youngster with a shout threw back his body and planted his feet on his grandfather's leg and walked up him until the strong right arm encircled him, and he was seated triumphantly in the crook of it. Whatever the old man might have against his son-in-law, there was no doubt as to his feeling for the boy.

"He is gone," he said, with a grave nod, in response to his daughter's questioning look. "But I misdoubt him. You had much better come with me to Belfontaine for a time, Rachel."

She shook her head doubtfully.

"He's an angry man, and if he should get back —"
said her father.

"In his right mind he would be sorry —"

"I misdoubt him," he said again, with a sombre nod.
"I shall have no peace if you are here all alone."

But she shook her head dismally with no sign of
yielding.

"It has been very lonely," he said. "You and the
boy —"

And she looked up at him, and the hunger of his face
seemed to strike her suddenly. She got up from the
fern bed and said, "Yes, we will come. My troubles
have made me selfish."

"Now, God be praised! You lift a load from my
heart, Rachel. You will come at once? Put together
what you will need and we will take it with us."

"And the house?"

"It will be all safe. If you like I will ask George
Hamon to give an eye to it while you are away. Perhaps —" Perhaps she would decide to remain with
him at Belfontaine, but experience had taught him to
go one step at a time rather than risk big leaps when
he was not sure of his footing.

So, while she gathered such things as she and the boy
would need for a few days' stay, he strode back down
the sunny lane to La Vauroque, to leave word of his
wishes with Hamon's mother.

And Philip Carré's heart was easier than it had been
for many a day, as they wound their way among the

great cushions of gorse to his lonely house at Belfontaine.   And the small boy was jumping with joy, and
the shadow on his mother's face was lightened somewhat.   For when one's life has broken down, and
untoward circumstances have turned one into a subject
for sympathetic gossip, it is a relief to get away from it
all, to dwell for a time where the clacking of neighbourly
tongues cannot be heard, and where sympathy is all
the deeper for finding no expression in words.   At
Belfontaine there was little fear of oversight or over-
hearing, for it lay somewhat apart, and since his daughter's marriage, Philip Carré had lived there all alone
with his dumb man Krok, who assisted him with the
farm and the fishing, and their visitors were few and
far between.

Now that jumping small boy was myself, and Rachel
Carré was my mother, and Philip Carré was my grandfather.   But what I have been telling you is only what
I learned long afterwards, when I was a grown man,
and it had become necessary for me to know these
things in explanation of others.

CHAPTER III

WHEN George Hamon told me the next part of the story of those early days, his enjoyment in the recalling of certain parts of it was undisguised. He told it with great gusto.

As he lay that night on the fern-bed in the cottage above the chasm, he thought of Rachel Carré, and what might have been if Martel's father had only been properly drowned on the Hanois instead of marrying the Guernsey woman. Rachel and he might have come together, and he would have made her as happy as the day was long. And now — his life was empty, and Rachel's was broken, — and all because of this wretched half-Frenchman, with his knowing ways and foreign beguilements. The girls had held him good-looking. Well, yes, he was good-looking in a way, but it passed his understanding why any Sercq girl should want to marry a foreigner while home lads were still to be had. He did not think there would be much marrying outside the island for some time to come, but it was bitter hard that Rachel Carré should have had to suffer in order to teach them that lesson.

Gr-r-r! but he would like to have Monsieur Martel up before him just for ten minutes or so, with a clear field and no favour. Martel was strong and active, it was true, but there — he was a drinker, and a Frenchman at that, and drink doesn't run to wind and a Frenchman doesn't run to fists. Very well — say twenty minutes then, and if he — George Hamon — did not make Monsieur Martel regret ever having come to Sercq he would deserve all he got and would take it without a murmur.

He was full of such imaginings, when at last he fell asleep, and he dreamt that he and Martel met in a lonely place and fought. And so full of fight was he that he rolled off the fern-bed and woke with a bump on the floor, and regretted that it was only a dream. For he had just got Martel's head comfortably under his left arm, and was paying him off in full for all he had made Rachel Carré suffer, when the bump of his fall put an end to it.

The following night he fell asleep at once, tired with a long day's work in the fields. He woke with a start about midnight, with the impression of a sound in his ears, and lay listening doubtfully. Then he perceived that his ears had not deceived him. There was someone in the room, — or something, — and for a moment all the superstitions among which he had been bred crawled in his back hair and held his breath.

Then a hand dropped out of the darkness and touched his shoulder, and he sprang at the touch like a coiled spring.

"Diable!"

It was Martel's voice and usual exclamation, and in

a moment Hamon had him by the throat and they were whirling over the floor, upsetting the table and scattering the chairs, and George Hamon's heart was beating like a merry drum at feel of his enemy in the flesh.

But wrestling blindly in a dark room did not satisfy him. That which was in him craved more. He wanted to see what he was doing and the full effects of it.

He shook himself free.

"Come outside and fight it out like a man — if you are one," he panted. "And we'll see if you can beat a man as you can a woman."

"Allons!" growled Martel. He was in the humour to rend and tear, and it mattered little what. For the authorities in Guernsey, after due deliberation, had decided that what was not good enough for Sercq was not good enough for Guernsey, and had shipped him back with scant ceremony. He had been flung out like a sack of rubbish onto the shingle in Havre Gosselin, half an hour before, had scaled the rough track in the dark, with his mouth full of curses and his heart full of rage, and George Hamon thanked God that it was not Rachel and the boy he had found in the cottage that night.

Hamon slipped on his shoes and tied them carefully, and they passed out and along the narrow way between the tall hedges. The full moon was just showing red and sleepy-looking, but she would be white and wide awake in a few minutes. The grass was thick with dew, and there was not a sound save the growl of the surf on the rocks below.

Through a gap in the hedge Hamon led the way towards Longue Pointe.

"Here!" he said, as they came on a level piece, and rolled up the sleeves of his guernsey. "Put away your knife," and Martel, with a curse at the implication, drew it from its sheath at his back and dug it among the bracken.

Then without a word they tackled one another. No gripping now, but hard blows fell straight from the shoulder, warded when possible, or taken in grim silence. They fought, not as men fight in battle, — for general principles and with but dim understanding of the rights and wrongs of the matter; but with the bitter intensity born of personal wrongs and the desire for personal vengeance. To Hamon, Martel represented the grievous shadow on Rachel Carré's life. To Martel, Hamon represented Sercq and all the contumely that had been heaped upon him there.

Their faces were set like rocks. Their teeth were clenched. They breathed hard and quick — through their noses at first, but presently, and of necessity, in short, sharp gasps from the chest.

It was a great fight, with none to see it but the placid moon, and so strong was her light that there seemed to be four men fighting, two above and two below. And at times they all merged into a writhing confusion of fierce pantings and snortings as of wild beasts, but for the most part they fought in grim silence, broken only by the whistle of the wind through their swollen lips, the light thud of their feet on the trampled ground, and the grisly sound of fist on flesh. And they fought for love of Rachel Carré, which the one had not been able to win and the other had not been able to keep.

Martel was the bigger man, but Hamon's legs and arms had springs of hate in them which more than counterbalanced. He was a temperate man, too, and in fine condition. He played his man with discretion, let him exhaust himself to his heart's content, took with equanimity such blows as he could not ward or avoid, and kept the temper of his hatred free from extravagance till his time came.

Martel lost patience and wind. Unless he could end the matter quickly his chance would be gone. He did his best to close and finish it, but his opponent knew better, and avoided him warily. They had both received punishment. Hamon took it for Rachel's sake, Martel for his sins. His brain was becoming confused with Hamon's quick turns and shrewd blows, and he could not see as clearly as at first. At times it seemed to him that there were two men fighting him. He must end it while he had the strength, and he bent to the task with desperate fury. Then, as he was rushing on his foe like a bull, with all his hatred boiling in his head, all went suddenly dark, and he was lying unconscious with his face in the trodden grass, and George Hamon stood over him, with his fists still clenched, all battered and bleeding, and breathing like a spent horse, but happier than he had been for many a day.

Martel lay so still that a fear began to grow in Hamon that he was dead. He had caught him deftly on the temple as he came on. He had heard of men being killed by a blow like that. He knelt and turned the other gingerly over, and felt his heart beating. And then the black eyes opened on him and the whites of them gleamed viciously in the moonlight, and Hamon stood up, and, after a moment's consideration, strode away and kicked about in the bracken till he found the other's knife. Then he picked up his jacket and went back to the cottage with the knife in one hand and his jacket in the other, and went inside and bolted the door, which was not a custom in Sercq.

CHAPTER IV

GEORGE HAMON slept heavily that night while Nature
repaired damages. In the morning he had his head in
a bucket of water from the well, when he heard footsteps coming up the steep way from the shore, and as
he shook the drops out of his swollen eyes he saw that
it was Philip Carré come in from his fishing.

"Hello, George —?" and Carré stopped and stared
at his face, and knew at once that what he had feared
had come to pass. "He's back then?"

"It feels like it."

"Where did you meet?"

"He came in here in the middle of the night. We
fought on Longue Pointe."

"Where is he now?"

"I left him in the grass with his wits out."

"She'll have no peace till he's dead and buried,"
said Carré, gloomily.

Then they heard heavy footsteps in the narrow way
between the hedges, and both turned quickly with the
same thought in their minds. But it was only Philip
Tanquerel coming down to see to his lobster pots, and

at sight of Hamon's face he grinned knowingly and drawled, "Bin falling out o' bed, George?"

"Yes.   Fell on top of the Frenchman."

"Fell heavy, seems to me.   He's back then?   I doubted he'd come if he wanted to."

Then more steps between the hedges, and Martel himself turned the corner and came straight for the cottage.

He made as though he would go in without speaking to the others, but George Hamon planted himself in the doorway with a curt, "No, you don't!"

"You refuse to let me into my own house?"

"Yes, I do."

"By what right?"

"By this!" said Hamon, raising his fist.   "If you want any more of it you've only to say so.   You're outcast.   You've no rights here.   Get away!"

"I claim my rights," said Martel through his teeth, and fell suddenly to his knees, and cried, "Haro! Haro!   Haro!   à l'aide mon prince!   On me fait tort."

The three men looked doubtfully at one another, for a moment, for this old final appeal to a higher tribunal, in the name of Rollo, the first old Norseman Duke, dead though he was this nine hundred years, was still the law of the islands and not to be infringed with impunity.

All the same, when the other sprang up and would have passed into the cottage, Hamon declined to move, and when Martel persisted, he struck at him with his fist, and it looked as though the fight were to be renewed.

"He makes Clameur, George," said Philip Tanquerel, remonstratively.

"He may make fifty Clameurs for me. Let him go to the Sénéchal and the Greffier and lay the matter before them. He's not coming in here as long as I've got a fist to lift against him."

"You refuse?" said Martel, blackly.

"You had better go to the Greffier," said Philip Carré. "The Court will have to decide it."

"It is my house."

"I'm in charge of it, and I won't give it up till the Sénéchal tells me to. So there!" said Hamon.

Martel turned on his heel and walked away, and the three stood looking after him.

"I'm not sure —" began Tanquerel, in his slow, drawling way.

"You're only a witness, anyway, Philip," said Hamon. "I'm the oppressor, and if he comes again I'll give him some more of what he had last night. He may Haro till he's hoarse, for me. Till the Sénéchal bids me go I stop here," and Tanquerel shrugged his shoulders and went off down the slope to his pots.

"More trouble," said Carré, gloomily.

"We'll meet it — with our fists," said Hamon, cheerfully. "M. le Sénéchal is not going to be browbeaten by a man he's flung out of the island."

And so it turned out. The cutter had brought M. Le Masurier a letter from the authorities in Guernsey

which pleased him not at all.   It informed him that
Martel, having married into Sercq and settled on
Sercq, belonged to Sercq, and they would have none
of him, and were accordingly sending him home again.

When Martel appeared to lodge his complaint, and
claim the old island right to cessation of oppression
and trial of his cause, M. le Sénéchal was prepared for
him.   It was not the man's fault that he was back on
their hands and he said nothing about that.   As to his
complaint, however, he drew a rigid line between the
past and the future.   In a word, he declined to interfere in the matter of the cottage until the case should
be tried and the court should give its judgment.

"Hamon must not, of course, interfere with you any
further.   But neither must you interfere with him,"
said the wise man.   "If you should do so he retains
the right that every man has of defending himself, and
will doubtless exercise it."

At which, when he heard it, George smiled crookedly
through his swollen lips and half-closed eyes, and
Martel found himself out in the cold.

He reconnoitred at a safe distance several times
during the day, but each time found Hamon smoking
his pipe in the doorway, with a show of enjoyment
which his cut lips did not in reality permit.

He stole down in the dark and quietly tried the
bolted door, but got only a sarcastic grunt for his pains.

He tried to get a lodging elsewhere, but no one would
receive him.

He begged for food.   No one would give him a

crust, and everyone he asked kept a watchful eye on him until he was clear of the premises.

He pulled some green corn, and husked it between his hands, and tried to satisfy his complaining stomach with that and half-ripe blackberries.

He crept up to a farmsteading after dark, intent on eggs, a chicken, a pigeon, — anything that might stay the clamour inside. The watchdogs raised such a riot that he crept away again in haste.

The hay had been cut in the churchyard. That was No Man's Land, and none had the right to hunt him out of it. So he made up a bed alongside a great square tomb, and slept there that night, and scared the children as they went past to school next morning.

One of the cows at Le Port gave no milk that day, and Dame Vaudin pondered the matter weightily, and discussed it volubly with her neighbours, but did not try their remedies.

During the day he went over to Little Sercq in hopes of snaring a rabbit. But the rabbits understood him and were shy. When he found himself near the Cromlech it suggested shelter, and creeping in to curl himself up for a sleep, he came unexpectedly on a baby rabbit paralysed with fear at the sight of him. It was dead before it understood what was happening. He tore it in pieces with his fingers and ate it raw. They found its skin and bones there later on.

Under the stimulus of food his brain worked again. There was no room for him in Sercq, that was evident. He was alien, and the clan spirit was too strong for him.

He crept back across the Coupée in the dark, and passed a man there who bade him good-night, not knowing till afterwards who he was.

Next morning, when Philip Carré came in from his fishing and climbed the zig-zag above Havre Gosselin, he was surprised at the sight of George Hamon smoking in the doorway of the cottage.

"Why, George, I thought you were off fishing," he said.

"Why, then?"

"Your boat's away." And Hamon was leaping down the zig-zag before he had finished, while Carré followed more slowly. But no amount of anxious staring across empty waters will bring back a boat that is not there. The boat was gone and Paul Martel with it, and neither was seen again in Sercq.

For many months Rachel Carré lived in instant fear of his unexpectedly turning up again. But he never came, and in time her mind found rest. The peace and aloofness of Belfontaine appealed to her, and at her father's urgent desire she stayed on there, and gave herself wholly to the care of the house and the training of her boy. The name of Martel with its unpleasant memories was quietly dropped, and in time came to be almost forgotten. The small boy grew up as Phil Carré, and knew no other name.

I am assured that he was a fine, sturdy little fellow, and that he took after his grandfather in looks and disposition. And his grandfather and Krok delighted in him, and fed his hungry little mind from their own hard-won experiences, and taught him all their craft as he grew able for it, so that few boys of his age could handle boat and nets and lines as he could. And Philip the elder, being of an open mind through his early travels, and believing that God was more like to help them that helped themselves than otherwise, made him a fearless swimmer, whereby the boy gained mighty enjoyment and sturdy health, and later on larger things still.

But it was his mother who led him gently towards the higher things, and opened the eyes of his understanding and the doors of his heart. She taught him more than ever the schoolmaster could, and more than most boys of his day knew. So that in time he came to see in the storms and calms, more than simply bad times and good; and in the clear blue sky and starry dome, in the magical unfoldings of the dawn and the matchless pageants of the sunset, more than mere indications of the weather.

Yet, withal, he was a very boy, full of life and the joy of it, and in their loving watchfulness over his development his mother and grandfather lost sight almost of the darker times out of which he had come, and looked only to that which he might in time come to be.

CHAPTER V

I suppose I could fill a great book with my recollections of those wonderful days when I was a boy of twelve and Carette Le Marchant was a girl of ten, and far and away the prettiest girl on Sercq, — or on Guernsey or Jersey either, for that matter, I'll wager. And at that time I would have fought on the spot any boy not too visibly beyond me who dared to hold any other opinion.

My mother and my grandfather did not by any means approve my endless battles, I am bound to say, and I do not think I was by nature of a quarrelsome disposition, but it seems to me now that a good deal of my time was spent in boyish warfare, and as often as not Carette was in one way or another accountable for it. Not that herself or her looks could be called in question. These spoke for themselves, though I grant you she was a fiery little person and easily provoked. If any attack was made on her looks or her doings it was usually only for my provocation, as the knights in olden times flung down their gauntlets by way of challenge. But there were other matters relating to Carette, or rather to her family, which I could defend only with my fists, and not at all with my judgment

33

even at twelve years old, and only for her sake who had, of herself, nothing whatever to do with them.

For the Le Marchants of Brecqhou were known and held in a somewhat wholesome respect of fear, by all grown-up dwellers in the islands, from Alderney to Jersey.

It was not simply that they were bold and successful free-traders. Free-trade — or, as some would call it, smuggling — was the natural commerce of the islands, and there were not very many whose fingers were not in the golden pie. My grandfather, Philip Carré, was one, however, and he would have starved sooner than live by any means which did not commend themselves to his own very clear views of right and wrong. The Le Marchants had made themselves a name for reckless daring and carelessness of other people's well-being when it ran counter to their own, which gave them right of way among their fellows but won comment harsh enough behind their backs. Many a strange story was told of them, and as a rule the stories lost nothing in the telling.

But my boyish recollections of Carette — Carterette in full, but shortened by everyone to Carette, unless it was Aunt Jeanne Falla under very great provocation, which did not, indeed, happen often but was not absolutely unknown — my recollections of Carette, and of my mother, and my grandfather, and Krok, and George Hamon, and Jeanne Falla, are as bright and rosy as the dawns and sunsets of those earlier days.

All these seem to have been with me from the very beginning. They made up my little world, and Carette was the sunlight, — and occasionally the lightning, — and the moonlight was my mother, and the bright stars were Jeanne Falla and George Hamon, while my grandfather was a benevolent power, always kind but rather far above me, and Krok was a mystery man, dearly loved but held in something of awe by reason of his strange affliction.

For Krok could hear and understand all that was said to him, even in our island tongue, which was not native to him, but he had no speech. The story ran that he had been picked off a piece of wreckage, somewhere off the North African coast, by the ship in which my grandfather made his last voyage, very many years ago. He was very intelligent and quick of hearing, but dumb, and it was said that he had been captured by Algerine pirates when a boy and had his tongue cut out by them. This, however, I was in a position to contradict, for I had once got a glimpse of Krok's tongue and so knew that he had one, though his face was so covered with hair that one might have doubted almost if he even had a mouth.

He was said to be Spanish. He was said to be Scotch. Wherever he was born, he was by nature an honest man and faithful as a dog. My grandfather had taken a liking to him, and when he quitted the sea, Krok followed him and became his man and served him faithfully. He could neither read nor write at that time, and his only vocal expression was a hoarse

croak like the cawing of a crow, and this, combined
with ample play of head and hand and facial expression
and hieroglyphic gesture, formed his only means of
communication with his surroundings.

The sailors called him Krok, from the sound he
made when he tried to speak, and Krok he remained.
In moments of intense excitement he was said to have
delivered himself of the word "Gug" also, but doubts
were cast upon this. He was of a placid and obliging
nature, a diligent and trustworthy worker, and on the
whole a cheerful companion with whom one could
never fall out — by word of mouth, at all events.

He was short and broad, but very powerful, and his
face, where it was not covered with hair, was seamed
and meshed with little wrinkles, maybe from pinching
it up in the glare of the sun as a boy. His eyes were
brown and very like a dog's, and that was perhaps
because he could not speak and tried to tell you things
with them. At times, when he could not make you
understand, they were full of a straining anxiety, the
painful striving of a dumb soul for utterance, which
was very pitiful.

I remember very well quite breaking down once,
when I was a very little fellow, and was doing my best
to explain something I wanted and could not make
him understand. In my haste I had probably begun
in the middle and left him to guess the beginning.
Something I had certainly left out, for all I could get
from Krok was puzzled shakes of the head and anxious
snappings of the bewildered brown eyes.

"O Krok, what a stupid, stupid man you are!" I cried at last, and I can see now the sudden pained pinching of the hairy face and the welling tears in the troubled brown eyes.

I flung my little arms half round his big neck and hugged myself tight to him, crying, "O Krok, I love you!" and he fondled me and patted me and soothed me, and our discussion was forgotten. And after that, boy as I was, and as wild and thoughtless as most, I do not think I ever wounded Krok's soul again, for it was like striking a faithful dog or a horse that was doing his best.

But better times came — to Krok, at all events, — when my mother began to teach me my letters.

That was in the short, winter days and long evenings, when all the west was a shrieking black fury, out of which hurtled blasts so overpowering that you could lean up against them as against a wall and with no more fear of falling, and the roar of great waters was never out of our ears.

In the daytime I would creep to the edge of the cliff, and lie flat behind a boulder, and watch by the hour the huge white waves as they swept round the Moie de Batarde and came ripping along the ragged side of Brecqhou like furious white comets, and hurled themselves in thunder on our Moie de Mouton and Tintageu. Then the great granite cliffs and our house up above shook with their pounding, and Port à la Jument and Pegane Bay were all aboil with beaten froth, and the salt spume came flying over my head in great, sticky gouts and whirled away among the seagulls feeding in the fields behind. When gale and tide played the same way, the mighty strife between the incoming waves and the race of the Gouliot passage was a thing to be seen. For the waves that had raced over a thousand miles of sea split on the point of Brecqhou, and those that took the south side piled themselves high in the great basin formed by Brecqhou and the Gouliot rocks and Havre Gosselin, and finding an outlet through the Gouliot Pass, they came leaping and roaring through the narrow black channel in a very fury of madness, and hurled themselves against their fellows who had taken the north side of the island, and there below me they fought like giants, and I was never tired of watching.

But in the evenings, when the lamp was lit, and the fire of dried gorse and driftwood burnt with coloured flames and lightning forks, my grandfather would get out his books with a sigh of great content, and Krok would settle silently to his work on net or lobster pot, and my mother took to teaching me my letters, which was not at all to my liking.

At first I was but a dull scholar, and the letters had to be dinned into my careless little head many times before they stuck there, and anything was sufficient to draw me from my task — a louder blast outside than usual, or the sight of Krok's nimble fingers, or of my grandfather's deep absorption, which at that time I could not at all understand, and which seemed to me extraordinary and made me think of old Mother Mauger, who was said to be a witch, and who lost herself staring into her fire just as my grandfather did into his books.

My wits were always busy with anything and everything rather than their proper business, but my mother was patience itself and drilled things into me till perforce I had to learn them, and, either through this constant repetition, or from a friendly feeling for myself in trouble, Krok began to take an intelligent interest in my lessons.

He would bring his work alongside, and listen intently, and watch the book, and at times would drop his work and by main force would turn my head away from himself to that which was of more consequence, when my mother would nod and smile her thanks.

And so, as I slowly learned, Krok learned also, and very much more quickly, for he had more time than I had to think over things, because he wasted none of it in talking, and he was more used to thinking than I was. And then, to me it was still only drudgery, while to him it was the opening of a new window to his soul.

Why, in all these years, he had never learned to read and write, — why my grandfather had never thought to teach him, — I cannot tell. Perhaps because my mother had learned at the school; perhaps because Krok himself had shown no inclination to learn; perhaps because, in the earlier days, the scanty little farm and the fishing which eked it out took up all the men's time and attention.

However that might be, now that he had begun to

learn Krok learned quickly, and the signs of his knowledge were all over the place.

He knew all that wonderful west coast of our island
as well as he knew the fingers of his hand, and before
long the ground all round the house was strewn about
with smooth, flat stones on which were scratched the
letters of the alphabet, which presently, according to
the pace of my studies indoors, began to arrange themselves into words, and so was I encompassed with
learning, inside and out, as it were, and sucked it in
whether I would or no.

Well do I remember the puzzlement in old Krok's
face when the mischief that dwells in every boy set me
to changing the proper order of his stones, and the
eagerness with which he awaited the evening lesson to
compare the new wrong order of things with his recollections of the original correct one, and then the mild
look of reproachful inquiry he would turn upon me.

But my mother, catching me at it one day, sharply
forbade me meddling with Krok's studies, and showed
me the smallness of it, and I never touched one of his
stones again.

Both my mother and my grandfather could read
and speak English, in addition to the Norman-French
which was the root of our island tongue, and that was
something of a distinction in those days. He had
learned it perforce during his early voyagings. He
had been twice round the world, both times on English
ships, and he was the kind of man, steady, quiet,
thoughtful, to miss no opportunities of self-improve-

ment, though I do not think there ever can have been a man less desirous of gain. His wants were very few, and so long as the farm and the fishing provided us all with a sufficient living, he was satisfied and grateful. He saw his neighbours waxing fat all about him, in pursuits which he would have starved sooner than set his hand to. To them, and according to island standards, these things might be right or wrong, but to him, and for himself, he had no doubts whatever in the matter.

You see, long ago, in Guernsey, he had come across Master Claude Gray, the Quaker preacher, and had been greatly drawn to him and the simple high life he proclaimed. Frequently, on still Sabbath mornings, he would put off in his boat, and, if the wind did not serve, would pull all the way to Peter Port, a good fourteen miles there and back, for the purpose of meeting his friend, and looked on it as a high privilege.

When, at times, he took me with him, I, too, looked on it as a mighty privilege; for Peter Port, even on a Sabbath morning, was, to a boy whose life was spent within the shadow of the Autelets, so to speak, a great and bustling city, full of people and houses and mysteries, and of course of wickedness, all of which excited my liveliest imaginings.

In the evening we would pull back, or run before the west wind if it served, and my grandfather would thoughtfully con over the gains of the day as another might tell the profits of his trading. Master Claude Gray was a man of parts, well read, an Englishman, and it was doubtless from him that my grandfather drew some of that love of books which distinguished him above any man I ever knew on Sercq, not excepting even the Seigneur, or the Sénéchal, or the Schoolmaster, or the Parson.

His library consisted of five books which he valued beyond anything he possessed, chiefly on account of what was in them and what he got out of them; to some extent also, in the case of three of them, for what they represented to him.

The first was a very large Bible bound in massive leather-covered boards, a present from Master Claude Gray to his friend, and brother in Christ, Philip Carré, and so stated in a very fine round hand on the front page. It contained a number of large pictures drawn on wood which, under strict injunctions as to carefulness and clean hands and no wet fingers, I was occasionally allowed to look at on a winter's Sabbath evening, and which always sent me to bed in a melancholy frame of mind, yet drew me to their inspection with a most curious fascination when the next chance offered.

Another was Mr. John Bunyan's "Pilgrim's Progress," also with woodcuts of a somewhat terrifying aspect, yet not devoid of lively fillips to the imagination.

Then there was a truly awful volume, "Fox's Book of Martyrs," with pictures which wrought so upon me that I used to wake up in the night shrieking with terror, and my mother forbade any further study of it; though Krok, when he came to be able to read, would hang over it by the hour, spelling out all the dreadful stories with his big forefinger and noting every smallest detail of the pictured tortures.

These two my grandfather had bought in Peter Port at a sale, together with a copy of Jean de la Fontaine's "Fables Choisies" in French, with delightful pictures of all the talking beasts.

And — crowning glory from the purely literary point of view — a massive volume of Plays by William Shakespeare, and to this was attached a history and an inscription of which my grandfather, in his quiet way, was not a little proud.

When the *Valentine*, East Indiaman, went ashore on Brecqhou in the great autumn gale, the year before I was born, — that was before the Le Marchants set themselves down there, — my grandfather was among the first to put out to the rescue of the crew and passengers. He got across to Brecqhou at risk of his life, and, from his knowledge of that ragged coast and its currents, managed to float a line down to the sinking ship by means of which every man got safe ashore. There was among them a rich merchant of London, a Mr. Peter Mulholland, and he would have done much for the man who had saved all their lives.

"I have done naught more than my duty," said my grandfather, and would accept nothing.

But Mr. Mulholland stopped with him for some days, while such of the cargo as had floated was being gathered from the shores — and, truth to tell, from

the houses — of Sercq, that is to say some portion of
it, for some went down with the ship and in some of
the houses there are silken hangings to this day.   And
the rich Englishman came to know what manner of
man my grandfather was and his tastes, and some time
after he had gone there came one day a great parcel
by the Guernsey cutter, addressed to my grandfather,
and in it was that splendid book of Shakespeare's
plays which, after his Bible, became his greatest delight.   An inscription, too, which he read religiously
every time he opened the book, though he must have
known every curl of every letter by heart.

It was a wonderful book, even to look at.   When
I grew learned enough to read it aloud to him and my
mother and Krok of a winter's night, I came by degrees, though not by any means at first, to understand
what a very wonderful book it was.

When one's reading is limited to five books it is
well that they should be good books.   Every one of
those books I read through aloud from beginning to
end, not once but many times, except indeed the long
lists of names in the Bible, which my grandfather said
were of no profit to us, and some other portions which
he said were beyond me, and which I therefore made
a point of reading to myself, but got little benefit from.

But to these books, and to the habit of reading them
aloud which impressed them greatly on my memory,
and to my own observation of men and things and
places through the eyes which these books helped to
open, and to the wise words of my grandfather, and

the quiet faithful teaching of my mother, and to all that old Krok taught me without ever speaking one word — I know that I owe everything, and that is why it was necessary to tell you so much about them.

If the telling has wearied you, I am sorry. For myself, I like to think back upon it all, and to trace the beginnings of some things of which I have seen the endings, and of some which are not ended yet, thank God! — and to find, in all that lies between, the signs of a power that is beyond any power of man's, and is, indeed, and rightly I think, beyond even the power of any man's full understanding.

CHAPTER VI

AND Carette —

I recall her in those days in a thousand different circumstances, and always like the sunlight or the lightning, gleaming, sparkling, flashing. For she could be as steadily radiant as the one and as unexpectedly fickle as the other, and I do not know that I liked her any the less on that account, though truly it made her none too easy to deal with at times. Her quick changes and childish vagaries kept one at all events very much alive and in a state of constant expectation. And whenever I think of her I thank God for Jeanne Falla, and all that that wisest and sharpest and tenderest of women was able to do for her.

For, you see, Carette was peculiarly circumstanced, and might have gone to waste but for her aunt Jeanne.

Her mother died when she was six years old, after four years' life on Brecqhou, and Carette was left to be utterly spoiled by her father and six big brothers, wild and reckless men all of them, but all, I am sure, with tender spots in their hearts for the lovely child who seemed so out of place among them, though for anyone outside they had little thought or care.

My own thoughts delight to linger back among these

46

earlier scenes before the more trying times came. If you will let me, I will try to picture Carette to you as I see her in my mind's eye, and I can see her as she was then as clearly as though it were yesterday.

I see a girl of ten, of slight, graceful figure, and of so active a nature that if you found her quite still you feared at once that something was wrong with her.

Her face was very charming, browned richly with the kiss of sun and wind, and without a freckle, yet not so brown as to hide the rich colour of her feelings, which swept across her face as quickly as the cloud-shadows across the sparkling face of the sea.

Her eyes were large and dark — all alight with the joy of life; sparkling with fun and mischief; blazing forked lightnings at some offence, fancied as often as not; big with entreaty that none could refuse; more rarely — in those days — deep with sober thought; but always — shining, sparkling, blazing, entreating — the most wonderful and fascinating eyes in the world to the boy at her side, on whom they shone and sparkled and blazed and entreated, and moulded always to her imperious little will.

A sturdy boy of twelve, short if anything for his age at that time, though later he grew to full Sercq height and something over; but strong and healthy, with a pair of keen blue eyes, and nothing whatever distinctive about his brown face, unless it was a touch of the inflexible honesty which had been diligently instilled into him from the time he was three years old. Perhaps also some little indication of the stubborn determination which must surely have come from his grandfather, and which some people called obstinacy.

Anyway the girl trusted him implicitly, ruled him imperiously, quarrelled with him at times but never beyond reason, and always quickly made it up again, and in so delightful a fashion that one remembered the quarrel no more but only the making-up, — beamed upon him then more graciously than before, and looked to him for certain help in every time of need.

Inseparables these two, except when the Gouliot waters were in an evil humour and rendered the passage impossible, for her home was on Brecqhou and his was on Sercq. Fortunately for their friendship, Aunt Jeanne Falla lived on Sercq also, and Carette was as often to be found at Beaumanoir as at her father's house on Brecqhou, and it was to her father's liking that it should be so. For he and the boys were often all away for days at a time, and on such occasions, as they started, they would drop Carette on the rough shore of Havre Gosselin, or set her hands and feet in the iron rings that scaled the bald face of the rock, and up she would go like a goat, and away to the welcome of the house that was her second and better home. What Carette would have been without Aunt Jeanne I cannot imagine; and so — all thanks to the sweet, sharp soul who took her mother's place.

See these two, then, as they lay in the sweet short herbage of Tintageu or Moie de Mouton, chins on fist, crisp light hair close up alongside floating brown curls, caps or hats scorned impediments to rapid motion, bare heels kicking up emotionally behind, as they surveyed their little world, and watched the distant ships, and dreamed dreams and saw visions.

Very clear in my memory is one such day, by reason of the fact that it was the beginning of a new and highly satisfactory state of matters between the boy and the girl.

Carette, you understand, was practically prisoner on Brecqhou except at such times as the higher powers, for good reasons of their own, put her ashore on Sercq. And, often as this happened, there were still many times when she would have been there but could not.

She had startled her companion more than once by wild threats of swimming the Gouliot, which is a foolhardy feat even for a man, for the dark passage is rarely free from coiling undercurrents which play with a man as though he were no more than a piece of seaweed, and try even a strong swimmer's nerve and strength. And when she spoke so, the boy took her sharply to task, and drew most horrible pictures of her dead white body tumbling about among the Autelets, or being left stranded in the rock pools by Port du Moulin, nibbled by crabs and lobsters and pecked by hungry gulls, or, maybe, lugged into a sea-cave by a giant devil-fish and ripped into pieces by his pitiless hooked beak.

At all of which the silvery little voice would say, "Pooh!" but all the same the slim little figure would shiver in the hot sunshine inside its short blue linsey-woolsey frock, and the dark eyes would grow larger

·than ever at the prospect, especially at the ripping by the giant pieuvre in which they both believed devoutly, and eventually she would promise not to throw her young life away.

"But all the same, Phil, I do feel like trying it when I want to come over and they won't let me."

And — "Don't be a silly," the boy would say.   "If you go and get yourself drowned, in any stupid way like that, Carette, I'll never speak to you again as long as I live."

They were lying so one day on the altar rock behind Tintageu, the boy gazing dreamily into the vast void past the distant Casquets, where, somewhere beyond and beyond, lay England, the land of many wonders, — England, where the mighty folks had lived of whom he had read in his grandfather's great book of plays, — and strange, wild notions he had got of the land and the people; England, where they used to burn men and women at the stake, and pinch them with hot irons, and sting them to death with bees, and break them in pieces on wheels — a process he did not quite understand, though it seemed satisfactorily horrible; England, which was always at war with France, and was constantly winning great fights upon the sea; England, of whom they were proud to be a part, though — somewhat confusingly to twelve years old — their own ordinary speech was French — a wonderful place that England, bigger even than Guernsey, his grandfather said, and so it must be true.   And sometime, maybe, he would sail across the sea and see it all for himself, and the great city of London which was bigger even than Peter Port, though that indeed seemed almost past belief and the boy had his doubts.

He told Carette of England and London at times, and drew so wildly on his imagination — yet came so very far from the reality — that Carette flatly denied the possibilities of such things, and looked upon him as a romancer of parts, though she put it more briefly.

She herself lay facing west, gazing longingly at Herm and Jethou, with the long line of Guernsey behind. Guernsey bounded her aspirations. Sometime she was to go with Aunt Jeanne to Guernsey, and then she would be level with Phil, and be able to take him down when he boasted too wildly of its wonderful streets and houses and shops.

Suddenly she stiffened, as a cat does at distant sight of a mouse, gazed hard, sat up, jumped to her feet and began to dance excitedly as was her way.

"Phil! Phil!" and the boy's eyes were on the object at which her dancing finger pointed vaguely.

"A boat!" said he, jumping with excitement also, for the boat Carette had sighted was evidently astray, and, moreover, it was, as they could easily see, even at that distance, no island boat, but a stranger, a waif, and so lawful prey and treasure-trove if they could secure it.

"Oh, Phil! Get it! I want it! It's just what I've been wanting all my life!"

It was a mere yellow cockleshell of a thing, almost round, and progressing, with wind and tide, equally

well bow or stern foremost, its holding capacity a man
and a half maybe, or say two children.

It came joggling slowly along, like a floating patch
of sunlight, among the sun-glints, and every joggle
brought it nearer to the grip of the current that was
swirling south through the Gouliot. Once caught in
the foaming race, ten chances to one it would be smashed
like an eggshell on some black outreaching fang of the
rocks.

The boy took in all the chances at a glance and sped
off across the narrow neck to the mainland, tore along
the cliff round Pegane and Port à la Jument, then away
past the head of Saut de Juan, and down the cliff side
to where the black shelves overhang the backwater of
the Gouliot.

He shed his guernsey during the safe passage between
Jument and Saut de Juan. The rest of his clothing,
one garment all told, he thoughtfully dropped at the
top of the cliff before he took to the shelves. The girl
gathered his things as she ran, and danced excitedly
with them in her arms as she saw his white body launch
out from the lowest shelf far away below her, and go
wrestling through the water like a tiny white frog.

They had travelled quicker than the careless boat,
and he was well out among the first writhings of the
Race before it came bobbing merrily towards him.
She saw his white arm flash up over the yellow side
and he hung there panting. Then slowly he worked
round to the fat stern, and hauled himself cautiously
on board, and stood and waved a cheerful hand to her.

Then she saw him pick up a small piece of board from the flooring of the boat and try to paddle back into the slack water. And she saw, too, that it was too late. The Race had got hold of the cockleshell and a piece of board would never make it let go. Oars might, but there were no oars.

She danced wildly, saw him give up that attempt and paddle boldly out, instead, into the middle of the coiling waters, saw him turn the cockleshell's blunt nose straight for the Pass, and stand watchfully amidships with his board poised to keep her to a true course if that might be.

The passage of the Race is no easy matter even with oars and strong men's hands upon them. A cockleshell and a board were but feeble things and the girl knew it, and, dancing wildly all the time because she could not stand still, looked each second to see the tiny craft flung aside and cracked on the jagged rocks.

But, with a great raking pull here, and a mighty sweep there, kneeling now, and now standing with one foot braced against the side for leverage, the boy managed in some marvellous way to keep his cockleshell in midstream. The girl watched them go rocking down the dark way, and then sped off across the headland towards Havre Gosselin. She got there just in time to see a boat with two strong rowers plunging out into the Race past Pierre au Norman, and knew that the boy was safe, and then she slipped and tumbled down the zigzag to meet them when they came in. The boy would want his clothes, and she wanted to see her boat. For of course it would be hers, and now she would be able to come across from Brecqhou whenever she wished.

The matter was not settled quite so easily as that, however.

She was dancing eagerly among the big round stones on the shore of Havre Gosselin, when the boat came in, with the cockleshell in tow and the small boy sitting in it, with his chin on his knees and shaking still with excitement and chills.

"All the same, mon gars, it was foolishness, for you might have been drowned," said the older man of the two, as they drew in to the shore, and the other man nodded agreement.

" I — w-w-wanted it for C-C-Carette," chittered the boy.

"Yes, yes, we know.　But — And then there is M. le Seigneur, you understand."

"But, Monsieur Parré," cried the small girl remonstratively, "it would never have come in if Phil had not gone for it.　It would have got smashed in the Gouliot or gone right past and been lost.　And, besides, I do so want it."

"All the same, little one, the Seigneur's rights must be respected.　You'd better go and tell him about it and ask him —"

" I will, mon Gyu!" and she was off up the zigzag before he had finished.

And it would have been a very different man from Peter le Pelley who could refuse the beguilement of

Carette's wistful dark eyes, when her heart was set on her own way, as it generally was.

The Seigneur, indeed, had no special liking for the Le Marchants, who had sat themselves down in his island of Brecqhou without so much as a by-your-leave or thank you. Still, the island was of little use to him, and to oust them would have been to incur the ill-will of men notorious for the payment of scores in kind, so he suffered them without opposition.

Carette told us afterwards that the Seigneur stroked her hair, when she had told all her story and proffered her request, assuring him at the same time that the little boat would be of no use to him whatever, as it could not possibly hold him.

"And what do you want with it, little one?" he asked.

"To come over from Brecqhou whenever I want, M. le Seigneur, if you please."

"My faith, I think you will be better on Sercq than on Brecqhou. But you will be getting drowned yourself in the Gouliot, and that would be a sad pity," said the Seigneur.

"But I can swim, M. le Seigneur, and I will be very, very careful."

"Well, well! You can have the boat, child. But if any ill comes of it, remember, I shall feel myself to blame. So be careful for my sake also."

And so the yellow cockleshell became Carette's golden bridge, and thereafter her comings and goings knew no bounds but her own wilful will and the states of the tides and the weather.

Krok's ideas in the matter of seigneurial rights of flotsam and jetsam were by no means as strict as his master's, especially where Carette was concerned. In his mute, dog-like way he worshipped Carette. In case of need, he would, I believe, have given his left hand in her service; and the right, I think he would have kept for himself and me. He procured from somewhere a great beam of ship's timber, and with infinite labour fixed it securely in a crevice of the rocks, high up by the Galé de Jacob, with one end projecting over the shelving rocks below. Then, with rope and pulley from the same ample storehouse, he showed Carette how she could, with her own unaided strength, hitch on her cockleshell and haul it up the cliffside out of reach of the hungriest wave. He made her a pair of tiny sculls too, and thenceforth she was free of the seas, and she flitted to and fro, and up and down that rugged western coast, till it was all an open book to her. But so venturesome was she, and so utterly heedless of danger, that we all went in fear for her, and she laughed all our fears to scorn.

CHAPTER VII

HOW I SHOWED ONE THE WAY TO THE BOUTIQUES

ANOTHER scene stands out very sharply in my recollection of the boy and girl of those early days, from
the fact that it gave our island folk a saying which
lasted a generation, and whenever I heard the saying
it brought the whole matter back to me.

"Show him the way to the Boutiques," became, in
those days, equivalent to "mislead him — trick him —
deceive him" — and this was how it came about.

I can see the boy creeping slowly along the south
side of Brecqhou in a boat which was big enough to
make him look very small. It was the smaller of the
two boats belonging to the farm, but it was heavily
laden with vraic. There had been two days of storm,
the port at Brecqhou was full of the floating seaweed,
and the fields at Belfontaine hungered for it. Philip
Carré and Krok and the small boy had been busy
with it since the early morning, and many boat loads
had been carried to Port à la Jument as long as the
flood served for the passage of the Gouliot, and since
then, into Havre Gosselin for further transport when
the tide turned.

The weather was close and heavy still, sulky looking, as though it contemplated another outbreak before

settling to its usual humour. There was no sun, and now and again drifts of ghostly haze trailed over the long sullen waves.

But the small boy knew every rock on the shore of Brecqhou, and the more deadly ones that lay in the tideway outside, just below the surface, and whuffed and growled at him as he passed. His course shaped itself like that of bird or fish, without apparent observation.

The boat was heavy, but his bare brown arms worked the single oar over the stern like tireless little machines, and his body swung rhythmically from side to side to add its weight to his impulse.

He kept well out round Pente-à-Fouille with its jagged teeth and circles of sweltering foam. The tide was rushing south through the Gouliot Pass like a millrace. It drove a bold furrow into the comparatively calm waters beyond, a furrow which leaped and writhed and spat like a tortured snake with the agonies of the narrow passage. And presently it sank into twisting coils, all spattered and marbled with foam, and came weltering up from conflict with the rocks below, and then hurried on to further torment along the teeth of Little Sark.

At the first lick of the race on his boat's nose, the small boy drew in his oar without ever looking round, dropped it into the rowlock, fitted the other oar, and bent his sturdy back to the fight.

The twisting waters carried him away in a long swirling slant. He pulled steadily on and paid no heed,

and in due course was spat out on the other side of the
race into the smooth water under lee of Longue Pointe.
Then he turned his boat's nose to the north and pulled
through the slack in the direction of Havre Gosselin.

He was edging slowly round Pierre au Norman,
where a whip of the current caught him for a moment,
when a merry shout carried his chin to his shoulder
in time to see, out of the corner of his eye, a small white
body flash from a black ledge above the surf into the
coiling waters beyond.   He stood up facing the bows
and held the boat, till a brown head bobbed up among
the writhing coils.   Then a slim white arm with a
little brown hand swept the long hair away from a pair
of dancing eyes, and the swimmer came slipping through
the water like a seal.

But suddenly, some stronger coil of the waters below
caught the glancing white limbs.   They sprawled awry
from their stroke, a startled look dimmed the dancing
eyes with a strain of fear.

" Phil ? "

And in a moment the boy in the boat had drawn in
his oars, and kicked off his shoes, and was ploughing
sturdily through the belching coils.

" You're all right, Carette," he cried, as he drove
up alongside, and the swimmer grasped hurriedly at
his extended arm.   " We've done stiffer bits than this.
Now — rest a minute! — All right? — Come on then
for the boat.   Here you are! — Hang on till I get in!"

He drew himself up slowly, and hung for a moment
while the water poured out of his clothes.   Then,

with a heave and a wild kick in the air, he was aboard,
and turned to assist his companion. He grasped the
little brown hands and braced his foot against the gun-
wale. "Now!" and she came up over the side like
a lovely white elf and sank panting among the golden
brown coils of vraic.

"It was silly of you to jump in there, you know,"
said the boy over his shoulder, as he sat down to his
oars and headed for Pierre au Norman again. "The
race is too strong for you. I've told you so before."

"You do it yourself," she panted.

"I'm a boy and I'm stronger than you."

"I can swim as fast as you."

"But I can last longer and the race is too strong for
me sometimes."

"B'en! I knew you'd pick me up."

"Well, don't you ever do it when I'm not here, or
some day the black snake will get you and you'll never
come up again."

He was pulling steadily now through the back water
of Havre Gosselin; — past the iron clamps let into the
face of the rock, up and down which the fishermen
climbed like flies; — past the moored boats; — avoid-
ing hidden rocks by the instinct of constant usage, till
his boat slid up among the weed-cushioned boulders
of the shore, and he drew in his oars and laid them
methodically along the thwarts.

The small girl jumped out and wallowed in the
warm lip of the tide, and finally squatted in it with
her brown hands clasped round her pink-white knees

— unabashed, unashamed, absolutely innocent of any possible necessity for either — as lovely a picture as all those coasts could show.

Her long hair, dark with the water, hung in wet rats' tails on her slim white shoulders, which were just flushed with the nip of the sea. The clear drops sparkled on her pretty brown face like pearls and diamonds, and seemed loth to fall. Her little pink toes curled up out of the creamy wash to look at her.

"Where are your things?" asked the boy.

"In the cave yonder."

"Go and get dressed," he said, looking down at her with as little thought of unseemliness as she herself.

"Not at all. I'm quite warm."

"Well, I'm going to dry my things," and he began to wriggle out of his knitted blue guernsey. "Also," he said, following up a previous train of thought, "let me tell you there are devil-fish about here. One came up with one of our pots yesterday."

"Pooh! I killed one with a stick this morning. They're only baby ones; comme ça," and she measured about two inches between her little pink palms.

"This one was so big," and he indicated a yard or so between the flapping sleeves of the guernsey in which his head was still involved.

"I don't believe you, Phil Carré," she said with wide eyes. "You're just trying to frighten me."

"All right! Just you wait till one catches hold of your leg when you're out swimming all by yourself.

If I'd known you'd be so silly I'd never have taught you."

"You didn't teach me. You only dared me in and showed me how."

"Well, then! And if I hadn't you'd never have learnt."

"Maybe I would. Someone else would have taught me."

"Who then?"

And to that she had no answer. For if the good God intends a man to drown it is going against His will to try to thwart him by learning to swim, — such, at all events, was the very prevalent belief in those parts, and is so to this day.

As soon as the boy was free of his clothes, he spread them neatly to the sun on a big boulder, and with a whoop went skipping over the stones into the water, till he fell full length with a splash and began swimming vigorously seawards. The small girl sat watching him for a minute and then skipped in after him, and the cormorants ceased their diving and the seagulls their wheelings and mewings, and all gathered agitatedly on a rock at the further side of the bay, and wondered what such shouts and laughter might portend.

But suddenly the boy broke off short in his sporting, and paddled noiselessly, with his face straining seawards.

"What is it then, Phil? Has the big pieuvre got hold of your leg?" cried the girl, as she splashed up towards him.

He raised a dripping hand to silence her, and while the dark eyes were still widening with surprise, a dull boom came rolling along the wind over the cliffs of Brecqhou.

"A gun," said the boy, and turned and headed swiftly for the shore.

"Wait for me, Phil!" cried the girl, as she skipped over the stones like a sunbeam and disappeared into the black mouth of the cave.

"Quick then!" as he wrestled with his half-dried clothes, still sticky with the sea water.

He was fixing the iron bar, which served as anchor for his boat, under a big boulder, when she joined him, still buttoning her skirt, and they sped together up the hazardous path which led up to La Frégondée. He gave her a helping hand now and again over difficult bits, but they had no breath for words. They reached the top panting like hounds, but the boy turned at once through the fields to the left and never stopped till he dropped spent on the short turf of the headland by Saut de Juan.

"Ah!" he gasped, and sighed with vast enjoyment, and the girl stared wide-eyed.

Down Great Russel, between them and Herm, two great ships were driving furiously, with every sail at fullest stretch and the white waves boiling under their bows. Further out, beyond the bristle of reefs and islets which stretch in a menacing line to the north of Herm, another stately vessel was manœuvring in advance of —

"One — two — three — four — five — six," counted the boy, "and each one as big as herself."

Every now and again came the sullen boom of her guns and answering booms from her pursuers.

"Six to one!" breathed the boy, quivering like a pointer. "And she's terrible near the rocks. Bon Gyu! but she'll be on them! She'll be on them sure," and he jumped up and danced in his excitement. "You can't get her through there! — Ay-ee!" and he funnelled his hands to shout a warning across three miles of sea in the teeth of a westerly breeze.

"Silly!" said the girl from the turf where she sat with her hands round her knees. "They can't hear you!"

"Oh guyable! Oh bon Gyu!" and he stood stiff and stark as the great ship narrowed as she turned toward them suddenly, and came threading her way through the bristling rocks, in a way that passed belief and set the hair in the nape of the boy's neck crawling with apprehension.

"Platte Boue!" he gasped, as she came safely past that danger. "Grand Amfroque!" and he began to dance.

"Founiais!" and she came out into Great Russel with a glorious sweep, shook herself proudly to the other track, and went foaming past the Equêtelées and the Grands Bouillons, swept round the south of Jethou, and began short tacking for Peter Port in wake of her consorts.

Since the guns, the drama out there had unfolded

itself in silence, and silence was unnatural when such goings-on were toward. The small boy danced and waved his arms and cheered frantically. The ships beyond the reefs were streaming away discomfited to the northeast, in the direction of La Hague.

The small girl nursed her knees, and watched the ships with only partial understanding of it all in her looks.

"Why are you so crazy about it?" she asked.

"Because we've won, you silly!"

"Of course! We're English. But all the same we ran away."

"We're English," — and there was a touch of the true insular pride in her voice, but they spoke in French, and not very good French at that, and scarce a word of English had one of them at that time.

"Pooh! Three little corvettes from two men-o'-war and four big frigates! And let me tell you there's not many men could have brought that ship through those rocks like that. I wonder who it is. A Guernsey man for sure!" [1]

His war dance came to a sudden stop with the fall of a heavy hand on his shoulder, and he jerked round in surprise. It was a stout, heavily-built man in blue cloth jacket and trousers, and a cap such as no island man ever wore in his life, and a sharp ratty face such as no island man would have cared to wear.

[1] A very similar story is told of Sir James Soumarez in the *Crescent* off Vazin Bay in Guernsey. His pilot was Jean Breton, who received a large gold medal for the feat.

"Now, little corbin, what is it you are dancing at?" he asked, in a tongue that was neither English nor French nor Norman, but an uncouth mixture of all three, and in a tone which was meant to imply joviality but carried no conviction to the boy's mind.

But the boy had weighed him up in a moment and with one glance, and he was too busy thinking to speak.

"Come, then! Art dumb?" and he shook the boy roughly.

"Mon dou donc, yes, that is it!" said Carette, dancing round them with apprehension for her companion. "He's dumb."

"He was shouting loud enough a minute ago," and he pinched the boy's ear smartly between his big thumb and finger.

"It's only sometimes," said Carette, lamely. "You let him go and maybe he'll speak."

"See, my lad," said the burly one, letting go the boy's ear, but keeping a grip on his shoulder. "I'm not going to harm you. All I want to know is whether you've seen any sizable ships hanging about here lately. — You know what I mean!"

The small boy knew perfectly what he meant, and his lip curled at thought of being mistaken for the kind of boy who would open his mouth to a preventive man. He shook his head, however.

"Not, eh? Well, you know the neighbourhood anyway. Take me to the Boutiques."

"The Boutiques?" cried Carette.

"Ah! The Boutiques. You know where the Boutiques are, I can see."

They both knew the Boutiques. It would be a very small child on Sercq who did not know that much. The small boy knew too, that both the Boutiques and the Gouliot caves had nooks and niches in their higher ranges, boarded off and secured with stout padlocked doors, where goods were stored for transfer to the cutters and chasse-marées as occasion offered, just as they were in the great warehouses of the Guernsey merchants. He had vague ideas that so long as the goods were on dry land the preventive men could not touch them, but of that he was not perfectly certain. These troublesome customs' officers were constantly having new powers conferred on them. He had overheard the men discussing them many a time, and the very fact of this man trying to find the Boutiques was in itself suspicious. But the man was a stranger. That was evident from his uncouth talk and foolish ways, and the small boy's mind was made up in a moment.

Carette was watching anxiously, with a wild idea in her mind that if she flung herself at the preventive man's feet and held them tightly, the boy might wriggle away and escape.

But the boy had a brighter scheme than that. He turned and led the way inland, and dropped a wink to Carette as he did so, and her anxious little brain jumped to the fact that the stranger was to be misled.

Her sharpened faculties perceived that the best way

to second his efforts was to pretend a vehement objection to his action and so lend colour to it.

"Don't you do it, Phil!" she cried, dancing round them. "Don't you do it, or I'll never speak to you again as long as I live."

Phil marched steadily on with the heavy hand gripping his shoulder.

"Sensible boy!" said the preventive man.

As every one knows, the Boutiques lie hid among the northern cliffs by the Eperquerie. But once lose sight of the sea, amid the tangle of wooded lanes which traverse the island, and without the guidance of the sun, it needs a certain amount of familiarity with the district to know exactly where one will come out.

The small boy stolidly led the way past Beaumanoir, and Carette wailed like a lost soul alongside. Jeanne Falla looked out as they passed and called out to know what was happening.

"This wicked man is making Phil show him the way to the Boutiques," cried Carette, and the wicked man chuckled, and so did Jeanne Falla.

They passed the cottages at La Vauroque. The women and children crowded the doors.

"What is it, then, Carette?" they cried. "Where is he taking him?"

"He is making him show him the way to the Boutiques," cried Carette, crumpling her pretty face into hideous grimaces by way of explanation.

"Oh, my good!" cried the women, and the procession passed on along the road that led past Dos d'Ane.

The steamy haze lay thicker here. The wind drove it past in slow coils, but its skirts seemed to cling to the heather and bracken as though reluctant to loose its hold on the island.

They passed down a rough rock path with ragged, yellow sides, and stood suddenly looking out, as it seemed, on death.

In front and all around — a fathomless void of mist, which curled slowly past in thin, white whorls. The only solid thing — the raw yellow path on which they stood. It stretched precariously out into the void and seemed to rest on nothing. From somewhere down below came the hoarse, low growl of sea on rock. Otherwise the stillness of death. — The Coupée!

Sorely trying to stranger nerves at best of times was that wonderful narrow bone of a neck which joins Little Sercq to Sercq — six hundred feet long, three hundred feet high, four feet wide at its widest at that time, and in places less, and with nothing between the crumbling edges of the path and the growling death below but ragged falls of rock, almost sheer on the one side and little better on the other. On a clear day the unaccustomed eye swam with the welter of the surf below on both sides at once; the unaccustomed brain reeled at thought of so precarious a passage; and the unaccustomed body, unless tenanted by a fool, or possessed of nerves beyond the ordinary or of no nerves at all, turned as a rule at the sight and thanked God for the feel of solid rock behind, or else went humbly down on hands and knees and so crossed in safety with lowered crest.

To the eyes of the rat-faced man the path seemed but a wavering line in the wavering mist. His hand gripped the boy's shoulder, grateful for something solid to hang on to. And gripped it the harder when Carette skipped past them and disappeared along that knife edge of a dancing path.

"Come on!" said the boy, — the first words he had spoken.

But the preventive man's eyes were still fixed in horror on the place where the girl had vanished.

"Come on!" said the boy again, and shook himself free, and went along the path.

"Aren't you coming?" he asked, — a shadow in the mist.

But the preventive man was feeling cautiously backwards for solid rock.

"Then I can't show you the Boutiques," said the boy, and passed out of sight into the mist.

CHAPTER VIII

ARE the later days ever quite as full of the brightness and joy of life as the earlier ones? Wider, and deeper, and fuller both of joys and sorrows they are, but the higher lights hold also the darker shadows, and experience teaches, as Jeanne Falla used to say, — "N'y a pas de rue sans but." — Neither lights nor shadows last, and the only thing one may count upon with absolute certainty is the certainty of change.

But in the earlier days one's horizon is limited, and so long as it is clear and bright one does not trouble about possible storms — wherein, I take it, the spirit of childhood is wiser than the spirit of the grown, until the latter learn that wisdom which men like my grandfather call faith, and so draw near again to the trustful simplicity of the earlier days.

Altogether bright and very clear are my recollections of those days when Carette and I, and Krok whenever he could manage it, roamed about that western coast of our little island, till we knew every rock and stone, and every nook and cranny of the beetling cliffs, and were on such friendly terms with the very gulls and cormorants that we knew many of them by sight, and were on visiting terms so to speak, though perhaps

71

never very acceptable visitors, among their homes and families.

Krok knew it all like a book, only better; for actual books were of late acquaintance with him, and these other things he had studied, in his way, for half his life.

In the hardest working life there are always off times, and Krok's Sundays, outside the simple necessities of farm life, had always been his own. His one enjoyment had been to scramble and poke and peer — without knowledge, indeed, or even understanding, save such as came of absorbed watchfulness, but still with the most perfect satisfaction — among the hidden things of nature which lay in pools, and under stones, and away in dark caves where none but he had been.

And all these things he introduced us to with very great enjoyment, revealing to us at a stroke, as it were, the wonders which had taken him years to find out for himself.

With him we lay gazing into the wonderful rock gardens under the Autelets when the tide was out; — watching the phosphorescent seaweeds flame in the darker pools; seeking out the haunts where the sea anemones lay in thousands, waving their long, pale arms hungrily for food and closing them hopefully on anything that offered, even on one's fingers which they presently rejected as unsatisfying.

He would silently point out to us the beauties of the sea, ferns and flowers, and the curious ways and habits of the tiny creeping things and fishes, and we three would lie by the hour, flat on the rocks, chin in fist, watching the comedies and tragedies and the strange chancy life of the pools. And they were absorbing enough to keep even Carette quiet, although her veins seemed filled with quicksilver and her life went on springs.

And at times he would take us up the cliffs, to points of vantage from which we could look down into the sea-birds' nests and watch them tending their young.

And — greatest wonder of all, and only when we had solemnly promised, finger on lip, never to disclose the matter under any conditions to anyone whatsoever — he led us right into the granite cliffs themselves, sometimes through dark mouths that gaped on the shore, sometimes by narrow clefts half-way up, some-times down strange, rough chimneys from the heights above.

Hand in hand we would creep, stumbling and slip-ping, clinging tightly to one another for protection against ghosts, spirits, and fairies, in all of which we half believed in spite of all wiser teaching, and never daring to speak above a whisper for fear of we knew not what, but always in mortal terror of losing Krok, and so being left to wander till we died, or fell into some dark pool and were drowned, or, more horribly still, were caught by the tide and driven back step by step into far dark corners till the end came.

I can hear, now as I write, the uncouth croak from which Krok got his name, but which to us, in those awesome places, was sweeter than music. And I can

hear the beating of his stick on the rocks to guide us
in the dark, — one blow to tell us where he was; two,
to look out for difficulties; three, water. But at times
he would bring with him a torch made of tar and grease
and rope, and then we would go in greater comfort and
wax almost bold at times, though never without scared
glances over our shoulders at the black mouths which
gaped hungrily for us at every turn and corner.

We were, I believe, the very first — of our time at
all events — to penetrate into some of the caves which
have since become a wonder to many, and if we did
not understand how very wonderful they really were,
they were to us treasure-houses of delight and a never
failing enjoyment.

Some of the higher caves were used as secret store-
houses for goods which a far-away government —
with which our people had little to do and which did
not greatly concern them, — chose to embargo in
various ways. And it was in the secret shipment of
these to various ports in England and France that the
special trade of the islands largely consisted. So absolutely free of all restrictions had our people always
been, indeed so specially privileged in this way above
all other lands, that it took many years to bring them
under what they looked upon as the yoke. And some
of them never could, or would, understand why it
should be considered unlawful for them to do what their
fathers had always done without let or hindrance.
Whatever the outside world might say, they saw no
wrong, except on the part of those who tried to stop

them, and whom therefore they set themselves to cir-
cumvent by every means in their power, and were
mightily successful therein. Moreover, the island
spirit resented somewhat this interference in their
affairs by what was, after all, a conquered people.
For the privileges of the islands were granted them
originally by the sovereigns of their own race who captured England from the Saxon Kings. We of the
islands never have been conquered. At Hastings we
were on the winning side, and we have been a race
to ourselves ever since, though loyal always to that
great nation which sprang like a giant out of the loins
of the struggle.

Foremost among the free-traders were Carette's
father and brothers on Brecqhou, whereby, as I have
said, Carette spent much of her time on Sercq with
her Aunt Jeanne Falla, which was all for her good and
much to her and my enjoyment.

When, by rights of flotsam and jetsam and gift and
trover, she became the proud possessor of her little
yellow boat, the day rarely passed without her flitting
across to spend part of it at Beaumanoir or Belfontaine, unless the weather bottled her up on Brecqhou.

One time, however, is very clear in my memory
when two whole days passed, and fine days too, without any sign of her, and Aunt Jeanne Falla knew nothing more of her than I did.

My grandfather was out fishing in our smaller boat,
and Krok was bringing home vraic in the larger, but
it was not lack of a boat that could keep me from news

of Carette. I scrambled down the rocks by Saut de Juan, strapped my guernsey and trousers on to my head with my belt, and swam across through the slack of the tide without much difficulty.

As I drew in to the Galé de Jacob I saw the yellow cockle-shell hanging from its beam, and, between fear and wonder as to what could have taken Carette, I scrambled in among the boulders and clambered quickly up the back stairs into Brecqhou.

The Le Marchants discouraged visitors, and I had never been ashore there except on the outer rocks after vraic. Carette never talked much about her home affairs, and except that the house was built of wood I knew very little about it. When I reached the top and stood on Belème cliff, the sight of Sercq as I had never seen it before filled me with a very great delight. From Bec du Nez at one end to Moie de Bretagne at the other every cleft and chasm in the long line of cliffs was bared to my sight. Some stood naked, shoulder high; and some were clothed with softest green to their knees. Here were long green slides almost to the water's edge; and here grim heaps of black rock flung together and awry in wildest confusion.

Up above was the work of man, the greenery of fields and trees, soft and beautiful in the sunshine, but these reached only to the cliff edge. Wherever the land had fallen away, the wind and the sea had worked their will, and the scarred and bitten rocks bore witness to it. The black tumbled masses of the Gouliot were right before me, and in the gloomy channel between, the tide, through which I had come, writhed and rolled like a wounded snake, even at the slack.

I had seen Sercq from the outside many times before, but only from water level, which limits one's view, though the towering cliffs are always wondrous fine, and more striking perhaps from below than from above. But Brecqhou always cut the view on one side or the other, whereas now, for the first time, I saw the whole western side of the island at a glance, and, boy as I was, it impressed me deeply and made me swell with ·pride. For, you see, thanks to my grandfather and my mother and Krok, my eyes were opening, even then, to the wonders and beauties among which I lived.

I turned at last and tramped through the heather and ferns and the breast-high golden-rod, tumbling among the rabbit holes with which the ground was riddled, towards the house which stood in a hollow in the centre of the island. And I stared hard at it, for I had never seen the like before.

It was not like our Sercq houses, granite-built, thick-walled, low in the sides and high in the roof. It stood facing Sercq, that is with its back to the south and west, and the far end of it seemed to start out of the ground and come sloping up to the front, till, above the door-way, it was perhaps ten feet high. As a matter of fact cunning advantage had been taken of a dip in the ground, and the house, built against the inside of the hollow and sloping very gradually upwards, left nothing for the wild winter gales from the south west to lay

hold of. The wildest wind that ever blew leaped off
the edge of the hollow and went shrieking up the black
sky, but never struck down at the squat gray house
below. It was a good-sized house, wide-spread and
all on one floor, and though it was only built of wood it
looked very strong and lasting, and to my thinking
very comfortable. Coming towards it from the front,
it looked as though a great ship had run head on into
the hollow and sunk partly into the ground, leaving
her stern high and dry. For the front was in fact
built up of fragments of an East Indiaman, and the
windows were her bulging stern windows, carved and
ornamented, though now all weathered to an ashen gray,
and on each side of the doorway ran a stout carved
wooden railing which had come from a ship's poop.

When I had done staring at all this I went rather
doubtfully to the door, with my eyes playing about all
round, for the Le Marchants, as I have said, did not
favour visitors and I was not sure of my welcome.

There seemed no one about, however, and at last I
summoned courage to knock gently on the door, which
was of thick heavy wood of a kind quite new to me,
and had once been polished.

"Hello, then! Who's there?" said a voice inside.

I waited, but no one came. It was no good talking
through a door, so I lifted the latch doubtfully and
put in my head.

It was a large wide room, larger than Jeanne Falla's
kitchen at Beaumanoir, and though there was no fern-
bed—and it was the first living-room I had seen without

one — there was a look of great warmth and comfort about it. There was a fire of driftwood smouldering in a wide clay chimney-place and a sweet warm
smell of wood smoke in the air. There were a number
of wooden chairs, and a table, and several black great
oaken chests curiously carved, and a great rack hanging from the roof, on which I saw hams, and guns, and
tarpaulin hats, and oars, and coils of rope. The far
end of the room was dark to one coming in out of the
sunshine, but, in some way, and I can hardly tell how,
it seemed to me that when the winter gales screamed
over Brecqhou that would be a very comfortable room
to live in.

I could still see no one, till the voice cried out at
sight of me:

"Now who in the name of Satan are you, and what
do you want here?" And then, in a ship's bunk at
the far end of the room, I saw a face lifted up and scowling at me.

It was the face of a young man, and but for the black
scowl on it, and a white cloth tied round above the
scowl, it might have been good looking, for all the Le
Marchants were that.

"I'm Phil Carré," I faltered. "I've come to look
for Carette."

And at that, Carette's voice came, like a silver pipe,
from some hidden place:

"Phil, mon p'tit, is that you? I'm here, but you
mustn't come in. I'm in bed. I've got measles.
Father's gone across to see Aunt Jeanne about it."

"I was afraid you'd got drowned, or hurt, or something," I said. "If it's only measles — "

"Just that — only measles, and it doesn't hurt the least bit."

"How long will it be before you're better?"

"Oh, days and days, they say."

"Oh! — And have you got it too?" I asked of the man in the bunk.

And he looked at me for a minute and then laughed, and said, "Yes, I've got it too. Don't you come near me," for I had come into the room at sound of Carette's voice, and he looked very much nicer when he laughed.

"Oh — Hilaire!" cried the unseen Carette. "What a great big — "

"Ta-ta!" laughed her brother. "Little yellow heels should keep out of sight," — which was not meant in rudeness, but only, according to an island saying, that little people should not express opinions on matters which don't concern them.

Before he could say more, the door behind me swung open and a surprised voice cried:

"Diantre! What is this? And who are you, mon gars?" and I was facing Carette's father, Jean Le Marchant, of whose doings I had heard many a wild story on Sercq.

He was a very striking-looking man, tall and straight, and well-built. His face was keen as a hawk's, and tanned and seamed and very much alive. His eyes were very sharp and dark, under shaggy white eyebrows. They seemed to go through me like a knife, and made me wish I had not come. His hair was quite white, and was cut so short that it bristled all over and added much to his fierce wide-awake look, as though he scented dangers all round and was ready to tackle them with a firm hand. He had a long white moustache, and no other hair on his face.

While I was still staring at him, Carette's voice came from its hiding-place:

"It is Phil Carré come to look for me, father. He is my good friend. You will give him welcome."

"Ah-ha! Mademoiselle commands"; and the keen face softened somewhat and broke into a smile, which was still somewhat grim. "Monsieur Phil Carré, I greet you! I can hardly say you are welcome as I do not care for visitors. But since you came to get news of the little one I promise not to kill and eat you, as you seem to expect."

"Merci, Monsieur!" I faltered. For, from all accounts, he was quite capable of the first, though the second had not actually suggested itself to me.

"How did you come? I did not see any boat."

"By the Galé de Jacob. I swam across."

"Ma foi! Swam across! You have courage, mon gars," and I saw that I had risen in his estimation.

"He swims like a fish, and he has no fear," chirped Carette from her hiding-place.

"All the same, bon dieu, the Gouliot is no pond," and he looked through me again. "How old are you, mon gars?"

"Thirteen next year."

"And what are you going to make of yourself when you grow up?"

"I don't know."

"For boys of spirit there are always openings," he said, and I knew very well what he meant, and shook my head.

"Ah, so! You are not free-traders at Belfontaine," he laughed. At which I shook my head again, feeling a trifle ashamed of our uncommon virtue, which could not, I thought, commend itself to so notorious a defier of preventive law.

"All the same he is a fine man, your grandfather, and a seaman beyond most. You will follow the sea? — or are you for the farming?"

"The sea sure, but it will be in the trading, I expect."

"It is larger than the farming, but not very large after all."

"When will I be able to see Carette, M'sieur?"

"Not for ten days or so. As soon as she is well enough I shall carry her over to Mistress Falla's. Then you can see her."

"Thank you, M'sieur. I think I will go now."

"Going back same way?"

"Yes, sir."

"I'll see you off. Sure you can manage it?"

"Oh, yes. Good-bye, Carette!" as he moved towards the door.

"Good-bye, Phil! I'll be at Aunt Jeanne's just as soon as I can," piped Carette, out of the darkness of her inner room.

And John Le Marchant led me back across the island to the Galé de Jacob, and stood watching me from Belème till I scrambled in among the rocks at the foot of Saut de Juan.

That was the first time I visited Carette's home and met her father, though her brothers I had seen at times on Sercq, viewing them from a distance with no little awe on account of the many strange stories told about them. They were not in the habit of mixing much with the island men, however. They kept their own counsel and their own ways, and this aloofness did not make for good comradeship when they did come across.

It was years before I set foot on Brecqhou again.

These brief glimpses of those bright, early days I have set down that you might know us as we were. For myself I delight to recall them, but if I were to tell you one quarter of all our doings and sayings when we were boy and girl together, with but one will — and that Carette's — it would make a volume passing bounds.

And it is possible that my recollection of these things is coloured somewhat with the knowledge and feeling of the later times, for a man may no more fully enter again into the thoughts of his childhood than he may enter full grown into his childhood's clothes. I have told them, however, just as they are present in my own mind, and they are at all events true.

CHAPTER IX

TEN years make little change in the aspect of Sercq, nor ten times ten for that matter, though the learned men tell us that the sea and wind and weather take daily toll of the little land and are slowly and surely wearing it away. It has not changed much in my time, however, and I have no doubt it will still stand firm for those who are to follow.

But ten years in the life of a boy and girl, — ten years which about double in number those that have gone, and increase experiences tenfold, — these indeed bring mighty changes.

In those ten years I grew from boy to man, and Carette Le Marchant grew into a gracious and beautiful woman, and — we grew a little apart.

That was inevitable, I suppose, and in the natural course of things, for even two saplings planted side by side will, as they grow into trees, be wider apart at the top than they are down below. And perhaps it is right, for if they grew too close together both would suffer. Growth needs space for full expansion if it is not to be lop-sided. And boy and girl days cannot last forever.

Those ten years taught me much — almost all that I ever learned, until the bitterer experiences of life brought it all to the test, and sifted out the chaff, and left me knowledge of the grain.

And once again I would say that to my mother, Rachel Carré, and to my grandfather and Krok, and to William Shakespeare and John Bunyan and to my grandfather's great Bible, I owe in the first place all that I know. All those books he made me read very thoroughly, and parts of them over and over again till I knew them almost by heart. And at the time I cannot say that this was much to my liking, but later, when I came to understand better what I read, no urging was needed, for they were our only books, except Fox's Martyrs in which I never found any very great enjoyment, though Krok revelled in it. And I suppose that a man might pass through life, and bear himself well in it, and never feel lonely, with those books for his companions.

I should not, however, omit mention of M. Rousselot, the schoolmaster, who took a liking to me because of the diligence which was at first none of my own, but only the outward showing of my mother's and grand-father's strict oversight. But, as liking begets liking, I came to diligence for M. Rousselot's sake also, and finally for the sake of learning itself. And also I learned no little from Mistress Jeanne Falla, who had the wisest head and the sharpest tongue and the kindest heart in all Sercq.

But I was never a bookworm, though the love of knowledge and the special love of those books I have named is with me yet.

"Whatever you come to be, Phil, though it be only a farmer-fisherman, you will be all the better man and the happier for knowing all you can," my grandfather would say to me, when we grew into close fellowship with my growing years. "It is not what a man is in position, but what he is in himself that makes for his happiness. And I think" he would add thoughtfully, "that the more a man understands of life and the more he thinks upon it, — in fact, the more he has inside himself, the less he cares for the smaller things outside." And I believe he was right.

He taught me all he knew concerning the farm and the land and the crops, and taught me not by rule of thumb, but showed me the why and wherefore of things, and opened the eyes of my understanding to notice the little things of nature as well as the great, which many people, I have found, pass all through their lives without ever seeing at all.

The same with the fishing. He and Krok gave me all they had to give, and, without vainglory, but simply as grateful testimony to their goodness, I think that at two-and-twenty I knew as much as any of my age in Sercq, and more than most. I knew, too, that there were things I did not know, and did not care to know, and for that, and all the higher things, I have to thank my dear mother and my grandfather.

But growth in its very nature requires a widening sphere. Contentment comes of experience and satisfaction, and youth, to arrive at that, must needs have the experience, but craves it as a rule for itself alone.

Sercq is but a dot on the map, and not indeed that on most, and outside it lay all the great world teeming with wonders which could only be seen by seeking them.

Up to the time I was sixteen, and Carette fourteen, we were comrades of the sea and shore and cliffs, and very great friends. Then Aunt Jeanne Falla insisted on her being sent to school in Peter Port, — a grievous blow to us both, for which we lived to thank her. For Carette, clever as she was by nature, and wonderfully sharp at picking things up, had no inducements at home towards anything beyond bodily growth, except, indeed, when she was at Beaumanoir with Aunt Jeanne, and those times were spasmodic and were countered by her returns to the free and easy life on Brecqhou. And Aunt Jeanne loved her dearly, and knew what was best for her, and so she insisted, and Carette went weeping to Peter Port to the Miss Mauger's school in George Road.

Her going made a great gap in my life, and the outer things began to call on me. My ideas respecting them were dim and distorted enough, as I afterwards found, but their call was all the more insistent for that. Lying flat on Tintageu, chin on fist, I would watch the white-sailed ships pushing eagerly to that wonderful outer world and long to be on them. There were great ships carrying wine and brandy to the West Indies, where the people were all black, and the most wonderful plants grew, and the palm trees. And to Canada and Newfoundland, where the great icebergs

came down through the mist. And some carrying fish
to the Mediterranean, whose shores were all alive with
wonders, to say nothing of the chances of seeing some
fighting on the way, for England was at war with France
and Spain and rumours of mighty doings reached us
at times. And some taking tea and tobacco to Ham-
burg and Emden, where the people were all uncouth
foreigners, who spoke neither French nor English and
so must offer mighty change from Sercq.

Then there were multitudes of smaller vessels, sloops
and chasse-marées, bound on shorter and still more
profitable, if more dangerous voyages. Wherever they
were going, on whatsoever errand bent, it was into the
great, outside world, and they all cried, "Come!"

Those shorter flights to the nearer shores had a
special appeal of their own, and the stories one heard
among one's fellows — of the wild midnight runs into
Cornish creeks and Devon and Dorset coves, of en-
counters now and again with the revenue men, of
exhilarating flights and narrow escapes from government cutters — these but added zest to the traffic in
one's imagination which, in actual fact, might possibly
have been found wanting.

The moral aspects of the free-trade business did not
trouble me in the slightest in those days. It was the old
established and natural trade of the islands, for which
they had evidently been set just where they were with
that special end in view. We looked upon it as very
much akin to the running of cargoes in to blockaded
ports — a large profit for a large risk and no ill-feeling,

though, indeed, at times, human nature would out, and attempts at the enforcement of laws, in the making of which we had no hand, would result in collisions, and occasionally in the shedding of blood. Incidents of that kind were, of course, to be regretted, and were certainly not sought for by our island men, though doubtless at times the wilder spirits would seek reprisal for the thwarting of their plans. But when even one of the great men in England, who made these laws against free-trading, could tell his fellow-lawmakers that the mind of man never could conceive of it as at all equalling in turpitude those acts which are breaches of clear moral virtue — how should it be expected that the parties chiefly interested should take a stricter view of the matter?

In course of time my longing for the wider life found expression, first in looks and at last in words, which indeed were not needed, for my mother had seen and understood long before I spoke.

And when my words found vent she was ready for them, and I learned how firmly set upon her way may be a woman whom one has always looked upon as gentlest of the gentle and retiring beyond most.

"Not that, Phil, not that. Anything but that. I would sooner see you in your grave than a free-trader," — which seemed to me an extreme view to take of the matter, but I know now that she had her reasons and that they were all sufficient for her.

My grandfather set his face against it also, though, indeed, my mother's strong feeling would have been enough for me. He, however, being a man, understood better, perhaps, what was in me, for he had been that way himself, and he set himself to further my craving.

The only other openings were in the legitimate trading to foreign parts, or service on a King's ship, or on a privateer, which latter business had come to be of very great importance in the islands. And between those three there could not be any question which my mother and grandfather would favour. For the perils of the sea are considerable in themselves, and are never absent from any mother heart in the islands. But add to them the harshness of the King's service, and the possibilities of sudden death at the hands of the King's enemies, and there was no doubt as to which way the mother heart would incline.

For myself, so hungry was I for wider doings, I would have put my neck under the yoke sooner than not go at all, and when they saw that spread my wings I must, they consented to my shipping on one of the Guernsey traders to foreign parts, and my heart was lighter than it had been for many a day.

I was eighteen, tall and strong, and, thanks to my grandfather and Krok, a capable seaman, so far as the limited opportunities of our little island permitted, and the rest would come easily, for all their teaching had given me a capacity to learn.

That first parting from home and my mother and grandfather and Krok was a terrible wrench, full as I was of the wonderful world I was going out to see. I had never been away from them before, and the sight of my mother's woeful attempts at cheerfulness came near to breaking me down and remained with me for many a day. In my eagerness for the wider life I had forgotten the hole my going must make in hers. And yet I do not think she would have had me stay, for she was as wise as she was gentle, and she ever set other people's wishes before her own. She had borne a man-child, and the inevitable island penalty of parting with him she bore without a murmur, though the look on her face told its own tale at times.

"Change of pasture is good for young calves," was Jeanne Falla's characteristic comment when they were discussing the matter one evening. And when my mother, in a moment of weakness, urged the likelihood, if not the absolute certainty, of my never returning alive, Aunt Jeanne's trenchant retort — "Go where you can, die where you must," put an end to the discussion and helped me to my wishes.

My grandfather procured me a berth as seaman on the barque *Hirondelle* of Peter Port, Nicolle master, and in her I made three voyages — to the West Indies, then on to Gaspé in the St. Lawrence, and thence to the Mediterranean. That was our usual round, and what with contrary winds, and detentions in various ports, and the necessity of waiting and dodging the enemy's cruisers and privateers, the voyages were long ones and not lacking in incident.

My story, however, is not concerned with them, except incidentally, and I will refer to them as little as possible.

My grandfather went across with me to Peter Port the first time. He had known George Nicolle many years and felt me safe in his hands, and his confidence was well placed. The *Hirondelle* was a comfortable ship and I never heard a real word of complaint aboard of her. Growling and grumbling there was occasionally, of course, or some of the older hands would never have been happy, but it amounted to nothing and there was no real ground for it.

She was still only loading when we boarded her, and it was three days later before we cast off and headed up Little Russel for the open sea.

CHAPTER X

THAT first night in Peter Port, when my grandfather had wrung my hand for the last time, looking at me with prayers in his eyes, and bidding me do my duty and keep clean, and had put off for home in his boat, and work was over for the day and I my own master, I decided on making a call which was much in my heart, and to which I had been looking forward for days past.

I cleaned myself up, and made myself as smart as possible, and set off for the Miss Mauger's school in George Road.

It was not until I saw the house that doubts began to trouble me as to the fitness of my intention. It was a much larger house than any I had ever been in, and there was a straightness and primness about it which somehow did not suggest any very warm welcome to a young sailorman, whose pride in his first appointment and in the spreading of his wings for his first flight underwent sudden shrinkage.

It took me a good half-hour's tramping to and fro, past the house and back again, eyeing it carefully each time as though I was trying to discover the best way to break into it, to screw my courage up to the point. There were two windows on each side of the door and two rows of five above, fourteen in all, and every window had its little curtains rigged up exactly alike to a hair's-breadth. If any one of them had been an inch awry I should have known it and would have felt less of an intruder.

I had not seen Carette for over six months, and the last time she was home most of my time, when we met, had been spent in discovering and puzzling over the changes that had come over her. These ran chiefly towards a sobriety of behaviour which was not natural to her, and which seemed to me assumed for my special benefit and tantalisation, and I was expecting every minute to see the sober cloak cast aside and the laughing Carette of earlier days dance out into the sunshine of our old camaraderie.

Aunt Jeanne Falla's twinkling eyes furthered the hope. But it was not realised. Carette unbent, indeed, and we were good friends as ever, but there was always about her that new cloak of staidness and lady-like polish which became her prettily enough indeed, but which I could very well have done without. For, you see, in all our doings hitherto, she had always looked up to me as leader, even when she twirled my boyish strength about her finger and made me do her will. And now, though I was bigger and stronger than ever, she had, in some ways, gone beyond me. She was, in fact, seeing the world, such as it was in Guernsey in those days, and it made me feel more than ever how small a place Sercq was, and more than ever determined to see the world also.

I warped myself up to Miss Mauger's green front door at last and gave a valiant rap of the knocker, and hung on to it by sheer force of will to keep myself from running away when I had done it. And when a maid in a prim white cap opened the door, I had lost my tongue, and stood staring at her till she smiled encouragingly as though she thought I might have come to ask her out for a walk.

" I've come to see Carette — Ma'm'zelle Le Marchant I mean," I stammered, very red and awkward.

" If you'll come in I'll tell Miss Mauger," she smiled, and I stepped inside and was shown into one of the front rooms with the very straight curtains. The room inside was very stiff and straight also. It occurred to me that if all the other rooms were like it Carette must have found them a very great change from Brecq-hou. Perhaps it was living among these things that had such an effect upon her that she could not shake it off when she came home for the holidays. The stiff, straight chairs offered me no invitation to be seated, and I stood waiting in the middle of the room. Then the door opened and a little elderly lady came in, and saluted me very formally with a curtsey bow which rather upset me, for no one had ever done such a thing to me before. It made me feel awkward and ill at ease.

Miss Mauger seemed to me very like her drawing-room, straight and precise and stiff. Her face reminded me somewhat of Aunt Jeanne Falla's, but lacked the kindly twinkle of the eyes which redeemed Aunt Jeanne's

shrewdest and sharpest speeches. She had little flat
rows of gray curls, tight to her head, on each side of
her face, for all the world like little ormer shells sticking to a stone.

"Monsieur Le Marchant?" she asked.

"No, Madame — Ma'm'zelle. I am Phil Carré."

"Oh! — You are not then one of Mademoiselle
Le Marchant's brothers?"

"No, Ma'm'zelle."

"Oh!"

"We have always been friends since we were children," I explained stumblingly, for her bright little
eyes were fixed on me, through her gold-rimmed spectacles, like little gimlets, and made me feel as if I was
doing something quite wrong in being there.

"Ah!" which seemed to imply that she had sus-
pected something of the kind, and it was a good thing
for Carette that she was safely removed from such
companionship in the future.

"And I am going off on my first voyage to the West
Indies —"

"Ah!" in a tone that seemed to say that as far as
she and her house were concerned, it was to be hoped
I would stop there.

"And I thought I would like to see Carette again
before I went —"

"Ah! — And may I ask if you have sought permission from Mademoiselle Le Marchant's relatives
before making this call?"

"Permission? — To see Carette? No, Madame —

Ma'm'zelle. I never dreamed of such a thing. Permission to see Carette! Ma fé!"

"Ah!" — ("What a strangely innocent young man!
— or is it impudent boldness?" That was what was
going on in her mind, I think, as she bored at me with
the little gimlets. But she said —) "We make it an
inflexible rule not to allow our young ladies to see any
but their own relations, except, of course, with the
special permission of their relatives or guardians."

"If I had known I would have got a letter from
Aunt Jeanne Falla, but such a thing never entered
into my head for a moment."

"You know Madame Le Marchant — Miss Jeanne
Falla that was?"

"Know Aunt Jeanne? — Well, I should — I mean,
yes, Madame, — I mean Ma'm'zelle. She has known
me from the day I was born."

"Ah! — And you think she would have accorded
you permission to see Mademoiselle?"

"Why, of course she would. She would never
dream of me being in Peter Port without calling to see
Carette."

She looked me through and through again, and said
at last:

"If you will excuse me for a moment I will consult
with my sisters. It is a matter which concerns them
also, and I should wish them to share the responsibility," and she dropped me another frigid little salute
and backed out of the door.

And I felt very sorry for Carette, and did not wonder

so much now at the little stiffnesses of manner I had
noticed in her the last time we met.

And presently the door opened, and the little lady
stole in again with the same little formal greeting, and,
after looking at me till I felt cold about the neck, said,
— "You wish to see Mademoiselle Le Marchant?"
And then I noticed that the little ormer shell curls
about this little lady's face were not all gray, but mixed
gray and brown, and that this little face was, if anything, still more frigidly ungracious than the last, a
regular little martinet of a face, and I knew that it
must be another of the Miss Maugers.

"Yes, Ma'm'zelle, with your permission."

"My sister states that you are acquainted with
Madame Le Marchant, of Beaumanoir, whom we used
to know intimately — "

"I have known Aunt Jeanne from the day I was
born," I said, perhaps a trifle vehemently, for the
absurdity of all these precautions between myself and
Carette began to ruffle me. In fact, I began to feel
almost as though there must be some grounds for their
doubts about me which I had never hitherto recognised
in myself, and it made me more decided than ever to
have my own way in the matter.

"My grandfather is Philip Carré of Belfontaine," I
said, with a touch of the ruffle in my voice, "and he is
a great friend of Mr. Claude Gray — "

"The Quaker," she said, with a pinch of the thin
little lips.

And then the door opened, and, with the usual

curtsey, still another Miss Mauger joined us, and her little ormer shells were all brown, and she wore no spectacles, and the corners of her mouth were on a level with the centre and looked as if they might on occasion even go up instead of down. She looked at me half mistrustfully, like a bird which doubts one's intentions towards its bit of plunder, and then, just like the bird, seemed to gauge my innocence of evil, and bent and whispered into her sister's gray and brown ormer shells.

"My sister informs me that Mademoiselle Le Marchant has been apprised of your visit and has expressed a desire to see you, and so — "

"Under the circumstances," said the other.

"Under the circumstances, we will make an exception from our invariable rule and permit this interview."

"On the understanding — " began the other.

"On the understanding that it is not to form a precedent — "

"And also," said the younger sister hastily, "that one of us is present."

"Certainly, that one of us is present," said the elder.

"By all means," I said, "and I am very much obliged to you. I really do not mean to eat Carette nor even to run away with her."

"We should certainly prevent any attempt of the kind," said the elder sister severely.

They whispered together for a moment, then she shook out her prim skirts, and dropped me a curtsey, and went away to fetch Carette.

"You see we have to be very strict in such matters," said the younger Miss Mauger, settling herself very gracefully on a chair so that her skirts disposed themselves in nice straight lines. "With forty young ladies under one's charge, one cannot be too careful."

"I am quite sure you are very careful of them, Ma'm'zelle," I said, at which she actually smiled a very little bird-like smile. "I will tell Aunt Jeanne how very careful you are next time I see her, and she will laugh and say, 'Young maids and young calves thrive best under the eyes of their mistress.'"

"I do not know much about calves" — and then the door opened and Carette came in.

She ran up to me with both hands outstretched.

"Oh, Phil, I was so afraid I was not to see you. And you are going away? How big you're getting! How long will you be away?"

This was very delightful, for I had been fearing that the little touch of stiffness, which I had experienced the last time I saw her, and which I now quite understood, might have grown out of knowledge.

"We are going first to the West Indies and then on to Canada. It may be a long time before I'm back, and I did want to see you once more before I went. I began to fear I was not going to."

"Oh, we're very strict here, you know, and we have rules. Oh, heaps of rules! But I knew dear Miss Maddy would manage it when she knew how I wanted to see you," and she ran up to Miss Maddy and kissed the little brown ormer shells over her ears, and Miss

Maddy patted them hastily lest the tiny kiss should have set them awry.

"And how did you leave them all in Sercq? And when did you see Aunt Jeanne last? And who's taking care of my boat? And —"

"Wait!" I laughed, "or I shall forget some of them. I saw Aunt Jeanne this morning just before I left. She thought we sailed at once. She would have sent you her love and maybe some gâche if she had known—"

"Ah, ma fé! How I wish she had known!" sighed Carette longingly, for Aunt Jeanne Falla's gâche had a name all over Sercq.

"And everybody is well except old Père Guérin, and he is cutting a new tooth, they say, and it makes him sour in the temper."

"Why, he's over ninety!" exclaimed Carette.

"Ninety-two next January. That's why he's so annoyed about it. And your boat is safe in the top nook of Port du Moulin, all covered over with sailcloth and gorse. Krok and I did it, and he will soak it for ten days before you come home, and have it all ready for you."

"The dear old Krok!"

"Oh, we have taken very great care of it, I assure you. But maybe you will be too grown up to care for it by the time you get back."

"Perhaps!" And oddly enough — though indeed it may have been only my own thought, and without reasonable foundation — thereupon there seemed to fall between us a slight veil of distance. So that, though we talked of Sercq and of our friends there, it seemed to me that we were not quite as we had been, and I could not for the life of me tell why, nor, indeed, for certain if it were so or not.

When I was leaving, however, Carette put both her hands in mine and gave me Godspeed as heartily as I could wish, and I made my best bow to Miss Maddy and went back to the *Hirondelle* well pleased at having seen Carette' and at her hearty greeting and farewell, but with a little wonder and doubt at my heart as to what the final effect of all this schooling might be.

CHAPTER XI

As I said, I am not going to waste time telling you of my three long voyages, beyond what is absolutely necessary. These lie for the most part like level plains in my memory, though not without their out-jutting points. But the heights and depths lay beyond.

Very clear to me, however, is the fact that it was ever-growing thought of Carette, more even, I am bound to confess, than thought of my mother and grandfather, that kept me clear of pitfalls which were not lacking to the unwary in those days as in these. Thought of Carette, too, that braced me to the quiet facing of odds on more than one occasion.

Our second voyage was distinguished by a whole day's fierce fighting with a French privateer off the Caicos Islands while proceeding peacefully on our way from the newly acquired island of Trinidad to the St. Lawrence. It was my first experience of fighting, and a hot one at that. Between killed and wounded we lost five men, but the Frenchman left ten dead on our deck the first time he boarded, and eight the second, and after that did not try again. But he dogged us all the rest of that day and did his best to cripple us, until a fortunate shot from a carronade which Master Nicolle

ran out astern nipped his foremast and set us free. I got
a cut from a cutlass in the left arm, but it healed readily
and Captain Nicolle was pleased to compliment me
on my behaviour. But, to tell the truth, I was so
angry at the Frenchman's insolent interference with
us, that I thought of nothing at the time but taking it
out of him with hearty thrust and blow whenever
chance offered.

On our third voyage the *Hirondelle* went ashore in
a gale off Cape Hatteras, and Captain Nicolle and half
our crew were drowned. The rest of us scrambled
ashore sans everything, but were well treated, and as
soon as we could travel were forwarded to New York
and in time found a ship to take us to London.

So, that, on the whole, I had seen a fair amount of
life, and death, and the larger world outside, and felt
my years almost doubled from what they were when I
used to lie on Tintageu and watch the white-sailed
ships pressing out to the great beyond.

But the things that stand out now most clearly in my
memory are the home-comings and the partings and
all they meant to me, but more especially the home-
comings — the eager looking forward from the moment
our bows pointed homewards; the joy of seeing my
mother and grandfather and dear old Krok and George
Hamon — Uncle George by adoption, failing that
closer relationship which Providence had denied him
— sympathetic listener to all our childish troubles and
kindly rescuer from endless scrapes; the biting intensity
of longing to meet Carette again, and to find out how

things were with her and how things were between
us, a longing that taught me the meaning of heartache.

For this was how matters stood between us — at
least as I saw them.   Each time I came home I managed, in one way or another, to get a sight, at all events,
of Carette, though in some cases little more.   Twice
I stormed the maiden fortress in George Road, and ran
the gauntlet of the Miss Maugers with less discomfiture
than on the first occasion, through Miss Maddy's sympathy and my added weight of years and experience.
And once Carette was making holiday with Aunt
Jeanne, and Beaumanoir saw more of me than did
Belfontaine.

And my very vivid recollection of all those times
is this — that Carette grew more beautiful each time
I saw her, both in mind and body; that my feeling
for her grew in me beyond all other growth, though
the years were building me solidly; and that a fear
sprang up in me at last that she was perhaps going to
grow out of my reach, as she certainly was growing
out of my understanding.

Each time we met, her greeting was of the warmest
and had in it the recollection of those earlier days.
That, I said to myself, was the real Carette.

And then there would gradually come upon us that
thin veil of distance, as though the years, and the
growth, and the experiences of life were setting us a
little apart.   And that, I said, was the Miss Maugers.

For my part I would have had Carette as satisfied
with my sole companionship as in the days when we

romped bare-legged among the pools and rocks, and
woke the basking gulls and cormorants with our shouts,
and dared the twisting currents with unfettered limbs
and no thought of wrong. These things in all their
fulness of delight were, of course, no longer possible
to us. But the joyous spirit of them I would fain have
retained, and I found it slipping elusively away.

We were, in fact, and inevitably, putting away the
things of our childhood and becoming man and woman,
with all the wider and deeper feelings incident thereto.
The changes were inevitable and — Carette grew in
some ways more quickly than I did. So that, whereas
I had always been undisputed leader in all things,
even when it was the accomplishing of her wishes,
now I found myself looking up to her as something
above me, possibly beyond me, something certainly
to strive after with all that was in me, and without which
everything else would be nothing.

Perhaps I had been inclined to take things somewhat
for granted. Jeanne Falla did not fail, in due course,
to tell me so, and she was a very shrewd woman and
understood her kind better than any man that ever
was born. Now, taking things for granted is always,
and under any circumstances, but most especially
where the unknown is in question, a most unwise
thing to do. And what can equal for unfathomable-
ness the workings of a woman's heart?

I had never given a thought to any other girl than
Carette, unless by way of unfavourable comparison.
It is true I had never came across any girl so well

worth thinking about. The merry dark eyes with
their deepening depths; the sweet wide mouth that
flashed so readily into laughter, and set one thinking
of the glad little waves and little white shells on Herm
beach; the mane of dark brown hair — she wore it
primly braided at the Miss Maugers' — in which gleams
of sunshine seemed to have become entangled and
never been able to find their way out — these went
with me through the soft seductions of the Antilles,
and the more experienced beguilements of the Mediterranean, and armed me sufficiently against them all; —
these also that filled with rosy light many a long hour
that for my comrades was dark and tedious, and kept
my heart high and strong when the times were hard
and bitter.

I had wondered at times, but always pleasurably,
at the very unusual amount of education Carette was
getting, for it was unusual at that time and under the
circumstances, so far as I understood them. But I
rejoiced at it, remembering my grandfather's saying
in my own case; and even when the results of it seemed
to drop little veils between us, I am certain I never
wished things otherwise so far as Carette was concerned,
though perhaps for my own sake I might.

Jean Le Marchant of Brecqhou had prospered in
his business, I knew. His six stalwart sons had been
too busy contributing to that prosperity to acquire
any great book-learning. They were all excellent
sailors, bold free-traders, and somewhat overbearing
to their fellows. It was only slowly that the idea came

to me that the blood that was in them might be of a
different shade and kind from that which flowed so
temperately in our cool Sercq veins.

It was much thinking of Carette and her ever-growing beauty and accomplishments which brought me
to that. Truly there was no girl in all Sercq like her.
nor in Guernsey I would wager, and her father and
brothers also were very different from the other island
men. As likely as not they were French, come over to
escape the troubles. That would account for many
things, and the idea, once in my mind, took firm root
there. Sometime, when opportunity offered, I would
ask Jeanne Falla. She would certainly know all about
her own husband's family. Whether she would tell
me was quite another matter.

Up to now, you see, Carette, as Carette, had sufficed,
but now Carette was growing out of herself and her
surroundings, and it was the why and wherefore of
this that my thoughts went in search of. For if Carette
grew out of her surroundings she might grow beyond
me, and it behooved me to see to it, for she had grown
to be a part of my life, and life without her would be
a poor thing indeed.

And all these things I used to turn over and over
in my heart during the sultry night watches in the West
Indies, when the heat lightnings gleamed incessantly
all round the horizon, and it was too hot to sleep even
when off duty; and during the grimmer watches round
about Newfoundland, with the fog as thick as wool
inside and outside one, and the smell of the floating

bergs in the air; and most of all when we were
plunging homeward as fast as we could make it,
and the call of Carette drew my heart faster than
my body till my body fairly ached for sight and sound
of her.

CHAPTER XII

HOW AUNT JEANNE GAVE A PARTY

IT was on my return from my fourth voyage — in the brig *Sarnia* — that things began to happen.

The voyage had been a disastrous one all through. We had bad weather right across to the Indies, and had to patch up there as best we could. It was when we were slowly making our way north that a hurricane, such as those seas know, caught us among the Bahamas and brought us to a sudden end.

The ship had been badly strained already on the voyage out, and the repairs had been none too well done. Our masts went like carrots and we were rolling helplessly in the grip of the storm, pumping doggedly but without hope against seams that gaped like a sieve, when the Providence that rules even hurricanes flung us high on a sandy coast and left us there to help ourselves.

Of our blind wanderings in that gruesome land of swamps and sand, which, when we at last escaped from it, we learned was Florida, I must not write here. It was months before such of us as were left crawled through into civilisation, and it is not too much to say that every day of the time after we parted from the wreck we carried our lives in our hands. It was six-

110

teen months almost to a day before I set foot once
more on Peter Port quay. For beggars cannot be
choosers, and for the very clothes we stood in we were
indebted to the kind hearts who took pity on us in the
American States. We had had to wait at every point
till means for forwarding us could be found, and we
were welcomed in Peter Port as men returned from the
dead. Within two hours I was scrambling up through
the ferns and gorse above Port à la Jument to the welcome that awaited me at home.

I peeped through the window before going in, and
saw the table laid for supper and my mother busy at
the hearth. She turned when I entered, supposing
it was my grandfather and Krok, and then with a cry
she was on my neck.

Ah, how good it was to feel her there, and to find
her unbroken by all the terrible waiting! She had
hoped and hoped, and refused to give up hoping long
after the others had done so. She told me, between
smiles and tears, that each time I went she had felt
that she had probably seen me for the last time. "But,"
she said quietly, "I left you in the good God's hands,
and I believed that however it was with you it would
be well."

Then my grandfather and Krok came in, and my
grandfather said very fervently, "Now God be praised!"
and wrung my right hand as if he could never wring
it enough, while Krok wrung the other, with eyes that
stood out of his head like marbles and yet were full of
tears.

During supper I told them shortly what had befallen us, and I had so much to tell, and they so much to hear, that we none of us supped over well, yet none of us had probably ever enjoyed a supper like it.

Then in turn I was hungry for news, and began asking about this one and that, intending so to come presently to Carette without baring my heart. But my dear mother, guessing perhaps what was in me, gave me full measure.

"Jeanne Falla has a party to-night, my boy, and Carette is stopping with her. You should go down and give them a surprise."

"I will go," I said, and jumped up at once to see if, among the things I had left behind when I went away, I could find enough to rig myself out suitably to the occasion.

My mother had a new blue guernsey just finished for me, a wonderful guernsey, when you think of it. She had, I think, gone on working at it, after the others had given me up, just to show her trust in Providence, and her dear eyes shone when she saw me in it. Loans from my grandfather, whose full stature I had now attained, and whose contribution was of importance, and from Krok, who would have given me one of his eyes if I had needed it, filled all my requirements, and I set off for Beaumanoir about nine o'clock as glad a man as any in Sercq that night. And oh, the sweetness of the night and all things in it. The solemn pulse of the great sea in Saut de Juan; the voices of many waters in the Gouliot Pass; the great dusky cushions of gorse studded with blooms that looked white under the moon; the mingling in the soft salt air of the scent of hedge roses and honeysuckle, of dewy, trodden grass and the sweet breath of cows — ay, even the smell of the pigsties was good that night, and mightily refreshing after the dank everglades of Florida.

Aunt Jeanne's hospitable door stood wide. She kept open house that night, for the old observances were dear to her ever-young heart. I walked right into her kitchen, and she met me with a cry of amazement and delight, and every wrinkle in the weather-browned face creased into a smile.

"Why, Phil, mon gars! Is it possible?" she cried. "You are welcome as one from the dead. Though, ma fé, I hoped all along, as your mother did. And, my good! what a big fellow it is! And not bad-looking, either! I used to think you'd grow up square. You were the squarest boy I ever saw. But foreign parts have drawn you out like a ship's mast."

She was draggiug me by the hand all the time, and now halted me in front of the great square fern-bed in the corner between the window and the hearth, and stood looking up into my face with the air of an artist awaiting approval of her latest masterpiece. A dear old face, sharp-featured, clever, all alive with the brightness of that which was in her, and with two bright dark eyes sparkling like a robin's under the black silk sunbonnet which gossips said she wore day and night.

I knew she looked just all that, but no eyes or thought had I for Aunt Jeanne or anyone else just then.

For here in front of me was the great green fern-bed, green no longer, but transformed into a radiant shrine of flowers. Nine feet long it was, and not much less in width, and its solid oaken sides rose some two feet from the floor. It was heaped indeed with the bronze-green fronds and russet-gold stalks of fresh-cut bracken, but this was only the ordinary work-a-day foundation and was almost hidden beneath a coverlet of roses — roses of every hue from damask-red to saffron-yellow and purest white, heaped and strewn in richest profusion and filling the room with perfume. From somewhere in the roof above, long sprays of creeping geranium and half-opened honeysuckle and branches of tree fuchsia hung down to the sides of the couch and formed a canopy, the most beautiful one could imagine. For the flowers of the honeysuckle looked like tiny baby-fingers reaching down for something below, and the red and purple fuchsias looked like a rain of falling stars. And beneath it sat the Queen of the Revels dressed all in white, her unbound hair rippling about her like a dark sunset cloud, till it lost itself among the creamy, many-coloured petals below, — Carette, the loveliest flower of all.

She had shaken her hair over her face to veil her modesty at the very outspoken admiration of some of the earlier comers, but I caught the sparkle of her dark eyes as she looked up at me through the silken mesh, and the sweet, slim figure set the flowery canopy shaking with its restrained eagerness. And my heart jumped within me at the lovely sight.

Disregardful of custom, I was stooping to speak to her, when Aunt Jeanne dragged me away with a gratified laugh, and a quick "Nenni, nenni! She may not speak till the time comes, or dear knows what will happen to us! Come away, mon gars, and tell me where you have been, and what you have been doing "; and she sat me down in a corner at the far end of the big dresser, and herself beside me so that I should not get away, and made me talk, but I could not take my eyes for a moment off the slim white figure on the radiant bed of roses.

A most delightful place at all times was that great kitchen at Beaumanoir, with its huge fireplace like a smaller room opening off the larger, and put to many other uses besides simply that of cooking; — its black oak presses and dressers and shelves all aglow with much polishing, and bright with crockery and pewter; its great hanging-rack under the ceiling, laden with hams and sides of bacon and a hundred and one odds and ends of household use; and the great table in the corner weighted now with piles of currant cake— Aunt Jeanne's gâche had a name in Sercq — and more substantial faring still.

There were about a score of young men and girls there, with a sprinkling of older folk, and every minute brought fresh arrivals to add to the talk and laughter. Each newcomer on entering paid homage to the silent figure on the green-bed, and gave me boisterous welcome home as they came to receive a word of greeting from the mistress of the house.

Everyone knew everyone else most intimately. Scarce one but was related to half the people in the room. And all were in the gayest of spirits, for there, in a far corner, old Nicholas Grut every now and again gave the strings of his fiddle an impatient twang, as an intimation that all this was sheer waste of time, and that the only proper business in life was dancing. And presently they would begin, and they would dance until the sun rose, and then — well, the new day had its own rites and ceremonies, and eyes were bright and pulses leaping, and hearts were all aflutter with hopes and fears of what the day might bring.

"And who is this, Jeanne Falla?" I asked, as one came in whom I had never seen before — a young man, dark and well-looking, and very handsomely dressed compared with the rest of us. And he stood so long before the green-bed, gazing at Carette, that there sprang up in me a sudden desire to take him by the neck and drag him away, or, better still, to hurl him through the open door into outer darkness.

"Tiens!" said Aunt Jeanne softly. "It is the young Torode—"

"Torode? I do not know him. Who is he?"

"C'est ça. It is since you left. His father has settled himself on Herm. He is a great man in these parts nowadays. They do say" —

"They do say —?" I asked, as she stopped short.

"Bon dou! They say many strange things about

M. Torode. But you know how folks talk," she murmured.

"And what kind of things do they say, Aunt Jeanne?"

"Oh, all kinds of things. He's making a fine streak of fat —"

"So much the better for him."

"Maybe! But, mon dou, when a man gets along too quickly, the others will talk, you know. They say he has the devil's own luck in all he undertakes. He has three of the fastest chasse-marées in the islands, and they say he's never lost a cargo yet. And they say he has dealings with the devil and Bonaparte and all the big merchants in Havre and Cherbourg. But of late he's gone in for privateering, and the streak's growing a fat one, I can tell you. He's got the finest schooner in these waters, and ma fé, broth and soup are both alike to him, I trow! Oh, yes, he can see through a fog, can Monsieur Torode."

"And what does Peter Port say to it all?"

"Pergui! Peter Port didn't like having its bread taken out of its mouth, — not that its bread contents Monsieur Torode, not by a very long way. Fine doings there are on Herm, they say, when they're all at home there. But he's too big and bold a man to interfere with. He pays for the island, they say, and a good price, too. Some say he's a wealthy emigré turning his talents to account. For myself —" and the black sunbonnet nodded knowingly.

"You don't care for him over much, Aunt Jeanne?" and I felt unreasonably glad that it was so.

"Ma fé, I've never set eyes on the man and never wish to! But such luck is not too natural, you understand. The devil's flour has a way of turning to bran, and what comes with the flood goes out with the ebb sometimes."

"All the same you invite the young one here."

"The door of Beaumanoir is wide to-night, and everyone who chooses to come is welcome. Though I wouldn't say but what some are more welcome than others. — Brecqhou and Herm have dealings together, you understand," she murmured presently. "That is how this youngster finds himself here — Bernel, they call him. The old one is much away and the young one does his business hereabouts. And see the airs he puts on! One would think the island belonged to him, and he hasn't had the grace to come and say how d'ye do to me yet. For myself —"

"For yourself, Aunt Jeanne?"

"Eh b'en!" with a twinkle. "One likes one's own calves best, oui gia!" and I felt like kissing the little old brown hand.

Young Torode had joined the others and was laughing and joking with the girls, though it seemed to me that the men received him somewhat coldly. Then some remark among them directed his attention to Jeanne Falla and myself in the corner behind the dresser, and he came over at once.

"Pardon, Mistress Falla!" he said. — I think I have said before that Aunt Jeanne was more generally called by her maiden name of Falla than by her married one of Le Marchant, and she preferred it so. — "I was wondering where you were. You have given us a most charming surprise," — with a nod towards the flower-decked green-bed. "But why is the goddess condemned to silence?"

"Because it's the rule. And, ma fé, it is good for a girl's tongue to be tied at times." Then, in answer to the inquiring looks he was casting at me, she said, "This is Phil Carré of Belfontaine, whom some folks thought dead. But I never did, and he's come back to show I was right. This is M. Bernel Torode of Herm, Phil, mon gars."

And young Torode and I looked into one another's eyes and knew that we were not to be friends. What he saw amiss in me I do not know, but to me there was about him something over-masterful which roused in me a keen desire to master it, or thwart it.

"You are but just home, then, M. Carré?" he asked.

"This evening."

"From —?"

"From Florida last by way of New York."

"Ah! Many ships about?"

"Not many but our own."

"There will be no bones left to pick soon," he laughed. "And the appetite grows. And what with the preventive men and their new powers it will soon be difficult to pick up an honest living."

"From all accounts M. Torode manages it one way or another," I said.

"All the same it gets more difficult. It's a case of too many pots and not enough lobsters."

And then Jeanne Falla, who had gone across to the others, suddenly clapped her hands, and Nicholas Grut's hungry bow dashed into a quickstep that set feet dancing in spite of themselves.

And Carette sprang up from her seat and stepped out of her bower, and her face, radiant at her release, had in it all the loveliness of all the flowers from among which she came. The roses clung to her white gown as though loth to let her go and strewed the ground, as she passed, and no man's heart but must have jumped the quicker at sight of her coming towards him with welcome in her eyes and hands.

She came straight across to us, and the other girls watched eagerly to see which of us she would speak to first — for Midsummer Eve is as full of signs and omens as Aunt Jeanne's gâche of currents.

She gave a hand to each of us, the left to me and the right to young Torode, and the left is nearer the heart, said I to myself.

"Phil, mon cher," she cried joyously. "It is good to see you alive and home again. And some foolish ones said you were gone for good! And you are bigger and browner than ever" — and she held me off at arm's length for inspection. "And when did you arrive?"

"I reached home just in time for supper."

"Ah, how glad your mother would be! She and Aunt Jeanne and I were the only ones who hoped still, I do believe."

"May I beg the first dance, Mademoiselle?" broke in young Torode, for the couples were whirling past us and he had waited impatiently while we talked.

"I must go and tie up my hair first. It looks like a tangle of vraic," she laughed, and slipped away by the sides of the room and disappeared through the doorway. And young Torode immediately took up his post there to claim his dance as soon as she returned.

I was vexed with myself for giving him first chance. But truly my thoughts had not been on the dancing but only on Carette herself, and I would have been content to look at her and listen to her all the evening without a thought of anything more.

Young Torode's visible intention of keeping to himself as much of her company as possible put me on my mettle, however, and when he dropped her into a seat after that dance, I immediately claimed the next.

I could dance as well, I think, as any man in Sercq, at that time, but I felt myself but a clumsy sailorman after watching young Torode. For his easy grace and confidence put us all into the shade and did not, I am afraid, tend to goodwill and fellowship on our part.

The other men I noticed had but little to say to him or he to them. He danced now and then with one or other of the girls, and they seemed to regard it more as an honourable experience than as matter of great enjoyment. And the man with whose special belle-amie he was dancing would sit and eye the pair gloomily the while, and remain silent and sulky for a time afterwards.

But, except for such little matters as that, we had a right merry time of it. Aunt Jeanne saw to that as energetically as though the hospitality of Beaumanoir had had doubts cast upon it, a thing that never could have happened. But Aunt Jeanne was energetic in all things, and this was her own special yearly feast. And, ma fé, one may surely do what one likes with one's own, and though one cannot recover one's youth one can at all events live young again with those who are young.

The lively spirits of the younger folk worked so upon their elders, that Uncle Henry Vaudin, who was seventy if he was a day, actually caught hold of Aunt Jeanne, as she was flitting to and fro, and tried to dance her into the whirling circle. But the result was only many collisions and much laughter, as the youngsters nearly galloped over them, and Aunt Jeanne and her partner stood in the centre laughing, till that dance was over.

Then she immediately challenged him to the hat dance, as being less trying to the legs and requiring more brain, and calling on Carette to make their third, they danced between three caps laid on the floor, in a way that earned a storm of applause.

Then two of the men danced the broom dance — each holding one end of the broom and passing it neatly under their arms, and over their heads, and under their legs, as they danced in quick step to the music.

And, in the intervals of such hard work, we ate — cold meats, cunningly cooked and of excellent quality, because Aunt Jeanne had bred them herself; and the best made bread and the sweetest butter in Sercq, and heaps of spicy gâche, all of Aunt Jeanne's own making. And we drank cider of Aunt Jeanne's own pressing, and equal to anything you could get in Guernsey. And now and again the men-folk smoked in the door-way, and if the very excellent tobacco she provided for them was not of her own growing, it was only because she had not so far undertaken its cultivation, and because tobacco could be got very cheap when you knew how to get it.

And then we danced again till the walls spun round quicker than ourselves, and even Uncle Nico's seasoned arms began to feel the strain. And still — "Faster! Faster!" cried the men, and the girls would not be beaten. And the ropes of flowers above the green-bed swung as though in a summer gale, and the roses leaped out and joined in the dance, till the smell of them, as they were trampled by the flying feet, filled all the room.

Then, while we lay spent and panting, the men mopping themselves with their kerchiefs, and the girls fanning themselves with theirs, Aunt Jeanne, who had had time to recover from her unwonted exertions with Uncle Henry Vaudin, recited some of the old-time poems of which she managed to carry a string in her head, in addition to all the other odds and ends which it contained.

She gave us "L' R'tou du Terre-Neuvi oprès san Prumi Viage" —

> "Mais en es-tu bain seu, ma fille?
> Not' Jean est-i don bain r'v'nu?
> Tu dis qué nou l'a veu en ville,
> I m'étonn' qu'i n'sait déjà v'nu" —

eighteen long verses, full of tender little touches, telling
of the hysterical upsetting in the mother's heart at the
safe return of her boy from the perils of the sea.

And to me, who had just seen it all in my own mother's
heart, it struck right home, and came near to making
me foolish in the matter of wet eyes. And besides,
Aunt Jeanne would keep looking at me, as she reeled
it off in her sharp little voice, which was softer than I
had ever heard it before, and that made Carette and
all the other girls look at me also, till I was glad when
she was done, I was getting so uncomfortable.

Then, when at last the poor sailor-boy in the story
was so full that he could not take another bite — not
even a bite of pancake on which his mother in her
upsetting had sprinkled salt instead of sugar — that
poem came to an end, and by way of a change Aunt
Jeanne plunged headlong into —

> "Ma Tante est une mênagère
> Coum je cré qu'i gn'y'en à pouit" —

hitting off in another twenty long verses the strong
and weak points of an old and very managing Auntie,
not unlike herself in her good points, and very unlike
her in her bad ones. And we joyfully pointed them all
back at the managing Auntie in front of us, good and
bad points alike, and laughed ourselves almost black
in the face at the most telling strokes; all except young
Torode, who laughed, indeed, but not heartily like the

rest, — rather as though he thought us an uncommonly childish set of people for our ages. And so we were that night, and enjoyed ourselves mightily.

Then young Torode sang, " Jean Grain d'orge," in a fine, big voice, and Carette sang " Nico v'nait m'faire l'amour," in a very sweet one, and I was sorely troubled that I had never learned to sing.

Then to dancing again, and it was only then, as I leaned against the door-post watching Carette go round and round with young Torode, in a way that I could not help but feel was smoother and neater than when my arm was round her, that a chance word between two girls sitting near me startled me into the knowledge that I had been guilty of another foolishness, and had overlooked another most important matter that night. You see, I had been in a flutter ever since I reached home, and one cannot think of everything.

" Oh, Father Guille has promised him his horse and so — " said the girl, between giggles and whispers, and it hit me like a stone to think how stupid I had been. And after a moment's thought I slipped away and ran quickly down the lane to La Vauroque, calling myself all manner of names through my teeth, and thumped lustily on George Hamon's door.

He was in bed and fast asleep, and it took much thumping before I heard a sleepy growl in the upper room, and at last the window rattled open and Uncle George's towsled head came out with a rough —

" Eh, b'en, below there? What's afire? Can't you let a man — "

"It's me, Uncle George — Phil Carré. I'm sorry—"

"Phil!— Bon dou! Phil come back alive!" in a tone of very great surprise. And then very sternly — "Tiens donc, you down there! You're not a ghost, are you?"

"Not a bit of a ghost, Uncle George. I got home this evening. I'm up at Jeanne Falla's party at Beaumanoir, and I've only just remembered that I haven't got a horse for to-morrow."

"Aw then — a horse for to-morrow! Yes — of course!" and he began to gurgle inside, though bits of it would come out — "A horse! Of course you want a horse! And who —?"

"Can you let me have Black Boy — if you've got him yet?"

"I'll come down, mon gars. Wait you one minute," and very soon the door opened and he dragged me in, gripping my hand as if it were a rudder in a gale, so that it ached for an hour after.

"And you're all safe and sound, mon gars! —"

"As safe and sound as Sercq, Uncle George. Can you let me have Black Boy?"

"Pergui! But it's a happy woman your mother will be this night. She never would give you up, Phil. It's just wonderful —"

"'Tis, sure! Can you spare me Black Boy?"

"Aw, now, my dear, but I'm sorry! You see, I'd no idea of you coming, and the young Torode came along this very afternoon, and begged me to lend him Black Boy, and I promised, not knowing — But there's Gray Robin. You can have him. He's a bit heavy, maybe, but he's safe as a cart, and Black Boy's got more than a bit of the devil in him still. Will you be crossing the Coupée?"

"I suppose so."

"Well, take my advice and get down and lead over. It's more than a bit crumbly in places. I've made young Torode promise not to ride Black Boy across."

"All right! When can I have Gray Robin?"

"Now, if you like."

"I'll be back at four. May I have some of your roses, Uncle George?"

"All of them, if you like, mon gars. Bon dou, but I'm glad to see you home again!"

"I'd like a few to trim Robin up with."

"I'll see to it. It's good to see you back, Phil. Your mother didn't say much, but she was sore at heart, I know, though she did put a bold face on it."

"I know. — You don't mind my running away now, Uncle George. You see —"

"Aw, I know! Gallop away back, my boy. And — say, Phil, mon gars — don't let that young cub from Herm get ahead of you. He's been making fine play while you've been away." And I waved my hand and sped back to the merry-making.

CHAPTER XIII

HOW WE RODE GRAY ROBIN

IT was close upon the dawn before Jeanne Falla's party broke up, and as I jogged soberly down the lane from La Vauroque on Gray Robin, I met the jovial ones all streaming homewards.

A moment before, the quiet gray lane, with its fern-covered banks and hedges of roses and honeysuckle all asleep and drenched with dew, was all in keeping with my spirits which were gray also, partly with the weariness of such unaccustomed merriment, and still more at thought of my various stupidities.

They all gathered round me and broke out into fresh laughter.

"Ma fé, Phil, but you're going to make a day of it! We wondered where you'd got to."

"Bon dou donc, you're in your pontificals, mou gars!"

"Is it a bank of roses you're riding then?" and Gray Robin hotched uncomfortably though still half asleep.

"The early bird gets the nicest worm. Keep ahead of the Frenchman, Phil, and good luck to you!"

"Good luck to you all!" and their laughing voices died away along the lanes, and I woke up Gray Robin and went on to Beaumanoir.

I hitched the bridle over the gatepost, and lighted
my pipe, and strolled to and fro with my hands deep
in the pockets of my grandfather's best blue pilot-
cloth jacket, for there was a chill in the air as though
the night must die outright before the new day came.

Now sunrise is small novelty to a sailorman. But
there is a mighty difference between watching it across
the welter of tumbling waves from the sloppy deck of
a ship, and watching it from the top of the knoll outside Beaumanoir, with Carette fast asleep behind the
white curtains of the gray stone house there.

Little matter that it might be hours before she came,
— since Jeanne Falla knew that rest was as necessary
to a girl as food, if she was to keep her health and good
looks. I could wait all day for Carette if needs be,
and Gray Robin was already fast asleep on three legs
with the fourth crooked comfortably beneath him.

I can live that morning over again, though the years
have passed.

. . . All the west was dark and dim. The sea was
the colour of lead. Brecqhou was a long black shadow.
Herm and Jethou were darker spots on the dimness
beyond, and Guernsey was not to be seen. The sky
up above me was thin and vague. But away in the
east over France, behind long banks of soft dark cloud,
it was thinner and rarer still, and seemed to throb with
a little pulse of life. And behind the white curtains
in the gray stone house, Carette lay sleeping.

— At midnight the girls had melted lead in an
iron spoon, and dropped it into buckets of water, amid

bubbles of laughter, to see what the occupations of
their future husbands would be. They fished out the
results with eager faces, and twisted them to suit their
hopes. Carette's piece came out a something which
Jeanne Falla at once pronounced an anchor, but which
young Torode said was a sword, and made it so by a
skilful touch of the finger.

. . . The air had been very still as though asleep,
like all things else except the sea. And the sea still
lay like lead out there, but I began to catch the gleam
of white teeth along the sides of Brecqhou, and down
below in Havre Gosselin I could hear the long waves
growling among the rocks. And now there came a
stir in the air like the waking breaths of a sleeper.
The shadows behind Herm and Jethou thickened and
darkened. The little throb of life behind the banks of
cloud in the east quickened and grew. The sky there
looked thin and bright and empty, as if it had been
swept bare and cleansed for that which was to come.
Up above me soft little gray clouds showed suddenly,
all touched with pink on their eastern sides, while the
sky behind them warmed with a faint dun glow. A
cock in the Beaumanoir yard woke suddenly and crowed
and the challenge was answered from La Vauroque.
Jeanne Falla's pigs grunted sleepily at the disturbance.
The pigeons rumbled in their cote, and the birds began
to twitter in the trees about the house. And behind
the white curtains there, Carette lay sleeping.

— I had asked her, the first chance that offered,
after I got back from seeing George Hamon. We were

spinning round in a double quickstep which tried even Uncle Nico's seasoned arm.

"Carette," I whispered into the little pink shell of an ear, so near my lips that it was hard to keep from kissing it — "Will you ride with me to-morrow?" and my heart went faster than my feet and set me tumbling over them. For Midsummer Day is Riding Day in Sercq, and he who asks a maid to share his horse that day is understood to desire her company on a longer journey still, and her consent to the one is generally taken to mean that she agrees to the other as well. So my little question held a mighty meaning, and no wonder my heart went quicker than my feet and set me stumbling over them as I waited for her answer.

"Not to-morrow, Phil," she whispered, and my heart stood still. Then it went on its way like a wave out of the west, when she murmured, "It's to-day we ride, not to-morrow," meaning that we had danced the night out.

"Then you will, Carette? You will?"

"You're late in the day, you know," she said, teasing still, as maids will when they know a man's heart is under their feet.

"But I only got home this evening —"

"Monsieur Torode asked me hours ago."

"But you haven't promised him, Carette?" and I felt as though all my life depended on her answer.

"I said I'd see. But —"

"Then you'll come with me, Carette," and I felt like kissing her there before them all.

"I'll tell you what I'll do, Phil. I'll go with one of you and come back with the other."

"But — Carette! —"

"You should not have left it so late, you see."

And with that I had to be content, though it was not at all to my mind, since I had looked for more.

. . . The eastern sky was filled to overflowing with pure thin light. The edges of the long dark banks of cloud that lay in front of it were rimmed with crimson fire. And from every quarter where the shadows lay gray clouds streamed up to greet the sun. They crept up the heavens, slow and gray and heavy, but as they climbed they lightened. They changed from gray to white. Their fronts were touched with the crimson fire. They spread wide wings and set me thinking of angels worshipping, and all the waiting clouds below threw out long streamers towards the day, like soft white arms in prayer. And behind the white curtains there, Carette lay sleeping.

— Gray Robin fell suddenly off one leg on to the other in his sleep, and woke with a discontented snuffle. Down in Havre Gosselin the seagulls were calling — "Miawk, miawk, miawk, miawk, miawk, — mink, mink, mink, mink, — kawk, kawk, kawk, kawk — keo, keo, keo, keo, keo."

— The sky up above was thin and blue. The soft white clouds were like a mackerel's back, and every scale was rimmed with red gold. The east was all a-throb. The long bands of cloud were silver above and glowing gold below. The sun rose in a silence that seemed to me wonderful. If all the world had broken out into the song that filled my heart it would have seemed but right. Every cloud in all the sky seemed to bow in homage before him.

I had seen many and many a sunrise, but never before one like this. For there, behind the curtains, Carette lay sleeping. And I was waiting for her. And it was Riding Day, and she was going to ride with me on Gray Robin.

And gay beyond his wont or knowledge was Gray Robin that day, though I think, myself, he had his own suspicions of it even in his dreams. For when he got fully awake, and took to looking at himself, and found out by degrees how very fine he was, he felt shy and awkward, and shook himself so vigorously that bits of his finery fell off. For, you see, Uncle George, knowing what was right and proper under the circumstances, and throwing himself in the matter because it was for me, had brought all his skill into play. He had fished out a length of old net from his stores, and turned it to great account. He had draped it in folds over Gray Robin's broad flanks, and brought it round his chest, and wherever the threads would hold a stem he had stuck in red and white and yellow roses, and had tied bunches of them at his ears and along his bridle, so that the steady old horse looked like an ancient charger in his armour.

And as I watched him examining into all these things I could see his wonder grow, and he asked himself what in the name of Hay his friends and acquaintances would think of it all when they saw him, and he snuffled with disgust.

It was close upon six o'clock when Gray Robin pricked up his ears at sound of hoofs in the lane between the high hedges, and young Torode rode up on Black Boy. He drew rein sharply at sight of me and a curse jerked out of him. And at the sight of Gray Robin in his gay trappings, Black Boy danced on his hind legs and pretended to be frightened out of his wits.

Torode brought him to reason with a violent hand and flung himself off with a black face.

"How then, Carré?" he broke out. "Mademoiselle promised to ride with me to-day."

"And with me also. So she said she would ride half the day with each of us."

"But, nom-de-dieu, what is the good of that? There is no sense in it."

"It is her wish."

He flogged a gorse bush angrily with a switch he had cut for Black Boy's benefit, and looked more than half inclined to fling himself back on to his horse and ride away, which would have been quite to my taste. Black Boy watched him viciously, with white gleams in his eyes, and winced at sound of the switch.

But before Torode had made up his mind, Jeanne Falla's sharp voice called from the gate: "Now then, you two, the coffee's getting cold. Come in and eat while you have the chance."

Coffee never tastes so good as just after morning watch, and I turned in at once, while young Torode

proceeded to make sure that Black Boy should not
make off while he was inside.

Aunt Jeanne's brown old face creased up into something like a very large wink as we went up the path,
and she said softly, "First pig in trough gets first bite.
You'll enjoy a cup of coffee at all events, mon gars.
Seems to me there are two Black Boys out there,
n'es c' pas?"

And if such coffee as Jeanne Falla made, with milk
warm from the cow, could have been curdled by sour
looks, young Torode had surely not found his cup to
his liking.

His ill-humour was not simply ill-concealed, it was
barely kept within bounds, and was, to say the least
of it, but poor return for Aunt Jeanne's double hospitality. But Aunt Jeanne, far from resenting it,
seemed actually to enjoy the sight, and as a matter
of fact, I believe she was hoping eagerly that Carette
would come down in time to partake of it also.

She chatted gaily about her party and plumed herself on its success.

"We did it all our own selves, the little one and I.
Nothing like washing your own shirt if you want it
well done," brimmed she.

"It couldn't have been better, Aunt Jeanne. And
as for the gâche — it was simply delicious."

"Crais b'en! If there's one thing I can do, it's
make gâche. And it's not all finished yet," and she
went to the press, and brought out a cake like a cart-
wheel, and cut it into spokes.

"There are not many things you can't do, it seems to me, Aunt Jeanne," I said. "That cider was uncommonly good too."

"Ma fé, when you've learned to make cider for the Guernsey men you can make it for most folks, I trow. . . . It's a tired man you'll be to-night, Phil, mon gars. We were just turning in, the little one and I, when we heard a horse snuffle outside, and nothing would satisfy her but she must up and peep out of the window, and she said, "Why, there's Phil Carré standing on the knoll. Mon Gyu, what does he want there at this time of day?" And I said, "Come away into bed, child, and don't catch your death of cold. You're half asleep and dreaming. There's no one out there." "Yes, there is," said she, "and it's Phil Carré. I know his shape." But I was sleepy and I said, "Well, he'll keep till morning anyway, and if you don't get some sleep you'll look like a boiled owl, and there'll be no riding for you, miss, Phil Carré or no Phil Carré." — all of which was gall and wormwood to young Torode, as Jeanne Falla quite well knew and intended.

And presently Carette came down, looking like a half-opened rose after a stormy night, and with just as much energy in her as might be expected in a girl who had danced miles of quick-step but a few hours before, and at a pace which Uncle Nico's arm had not forgotten yet.

There was to me something almost sacred in the look of her with the maiden sleep still in her eyes, which set her apart from us and above us, and I could have

sat and looked at her for a long time and required no
more.

She was all in white again, and Aunt Jeanne, when
she had given her coffee and a slice of gâche, and had
coaxed her to eat, slipped out into the garden, and came
back presently with an apron-full of red roses all wet
with dew, and proceeded to pin them round her hat, and
on her shoulder, and at her breast, and in her waistband.

"V'la!" said the dear old soul, standing off and
eying her handiwork with her head on one side like
a robin. "There's not another in the island will come
within a mile of you, ma garche!" and it was easy to
see the love that lay deep in the sharp old eyes.

We had hardly spoken a word since Carette came
down, beyond wishing her good-day, and she herself
seemed in no humour for talk. And for myself, I
know I felt very common clay beside her, and I would,
as I have said, been well content to simply sit and
watch her.

Aunt Jeanne continued to talk of the party, a subject that would not fail her for many a week to come,
for those sharp eyes of hers saw more than most people's
and she never forgot what they told her.

It was only when Carette had finished her pretence
of eating, and it was time to be starting, that young
Torode asked politely, — "With whom do you ride
first, Mademoiselle, — since we are two?"

And Carette said sweetly, "Since Phil was here first
I will ride first with him, Monsieur, and afterwards
with you."

"Do you cross the Coupée?" asked Aunt Jeanne anxiously.

"But, of course!" said Torode. "That is where the fun comes in."

"Bon Gyu, but that kind of fun does not please me! Some of you will find yourselves at the bottom some day, and that will end the riding in Sercq."

"It's safe enough if you have a firm hand — that is, if you know how to ride at all," — a shot aimed at me, but which failed to wound.

"I don't like it," said Aunt Jeanne again, with a foreboding shake of the head and a meaning look at me.

"Well, we won't be the first to cross," I said, to satisfy her. "We'll see how the others get on, and no harm shall come to Carette, I promise you."

Gray Robin was dozing again, but I woke him up with a poke, and climbed up onto his broad back with as little damage to his rose-armour as I could manage, and Aunt Jeanne carried out a chair so that Carette could get up behind me without disarranging herself.

And a happy man was I when the soft arms clasped me firmly round the waist, although I knew well enough that it was the correct thing for them to do, and that there was nothing more in it than a strong desire on the rider's part not to fall off. But for that troublesome young Torode, and all that was implied in the fact that Carette's arms would be round him on the homeward journey, I would have been the happiest man in Sercq that day. As it was, it was in my mind to make the most of my half of it.

Young Torode sprang on Black Boy with a leap that put our more cautious methods very much into the shade, and also stirred up all Black Boy's never-too-well-concealed evil temper. A horse of spirit ever objects to the double burden of man and man's master, and, through thigh and heel and hand, he can tell in the most wonderful fashion if the devil's aboard as well.

We left them settling their little differences and jogged away down the lane, and the last we saw of Aunt Jeanne she was leaning over the gate looking hopefully at the fight before her. But presently we heard the quick beat of hoofs behind, and they went past us with a rush — Black Boy's chin drawn tight to his chest which was splashed with white foam flecks, his neck like a bow, and the wicked white of his port eye glaring back at us like a danger signal.

"Monsieur Torode has got his hands full, I think," I said.

"And Monsieur Black Boy carries more than he likes."

"I'm glad you're not on board there, Carette."

"I think I am too — just now," she laughed quietly.

We took the north road at La Vauroque, where we came on George Hamon gazing gloomily after Black Boy and his rider, who were flying along the road to Colinette, and judging from his face there was a curse on his lips as he turned to us, which was very unusual with him. He brightened, however, when he saw us.

"B'en! That's all right," he said very heartily.

"Gray Robin is a proud horse this day, Ma'm'zelle, with the prettiest maid in the island on his back — and the best man," he added meaningly. "I'm just hoping that crazy Frenchman will bring my Black Boy back all safe and sound. He's got more than a bit of the devil in him at times — the horse, I mean. The other too, may be. And he's more used to harness than the saddle. However — luck to you!"

He waved his hand and we jogged on past the Cemetery, and so by La Rondellerie and La Moinerie, where the holy Maglorius once lived — as you may see by the ruins of his house and the cells of his disciples —to Belfontaine, where my mother came out with full eyes to give us greeting.

And to prevent any mistake which might put Carette to confusion, I did my clumsy best to make a joke of the matter.

"Your stupid was nearly too late, mother, and so Carette rides out with me and back with Monsieur Torode."

"Under the circumstances it was very good of Carette to give you a share, mon gars."

"Oh, I'm grateful. One's sheaf is never quite as one would have it, and one takes the good that comes."

"How glad you must have been to see him back, Mrs. Carré," said Carette. "You never gave him up, I know."

"No, I never gave him up," said my mother quietly.

"I think he ought to have stopped with you all day

to-day," said Carette. "I feel as if I was stealing him."

"Only borrowing!" smiled my mother. "It is good to be young, and the young have their rights as well as the old. Good luck to you and a fine ride!" and I shook up Gray Robin and we went on.

"Be very careful if you cross the Coupée, Phil," she called after us. "There was a fall there the other day, your grandfather was saying, and the path has not been mended yet."

I waved my hand and we went on. From a distant field, where they were busy with their hay, my grand-father and Krok saw us passing along the road, and straightened up and shaded their eyes with their hands, and then waved us heaps of good luck, and we jogged on along the road to the Eperquerie.

CHAPTER XIV

It was a day of days — a perfect Midsummer Day. The sky was blue without a cloud, the blaze of the gorse was dimming, but the ferns and foxgloves swung in the breeze, the hedgerows laughed with wild roses and honeysuckle, and the air was full of life and sweetness and the songs of larks and the homely humming of bees. And here was I come back from the Florida swamps and all the perils of the seas, jogging quietly along on that moving nosegay Gray Robin, with the arms of the fairest maid in all Sercq round my waist, and the brim of her hat tickling my neck, and her face so close to my shoulder that it was hard work not to turn and kiss it.

My mind was set to make the most of my good fortune, but the thought of young Torode, and of Carette riding back with him, kept coming upon me like an east wind on a sunny day, and I found myself more tongue-tied than ever I had been with her before, even of late years.

Did she care for this man? Had his good looks, which I could not deny, cast dust in her eyes? Could she be blind to his black humours, which, to me, were more visible even than his good looks?

From what Aunt Jeanne had said he was by way of being very well off. And perhaps the results of the Miss Maugers teachings would incline a girl to consider such things. I thought they probably would. I know they made me feel shy and awkward before her, though I told myself furiously that all that was only a matter of outside polish, and that inside I was worthy of her as any, and loved her as none other could. But the outside she could see, and the inside she could not, and I could not yet tell her, though I could not but think she must know.

And then, what had I to offer her in place of Torode's solid advantages? Just myself, and all my heart, and two strong arms. They were good things, and no one in the world could love her as I did. But to a girl brought up as she had been of late would they be enough? And would these things satisfy her father, who had always been much of a mystery to us all, and who might have his own views as to her future, as the education he had given her seemed to indicate.

I had plenty to think about as we jogged along on Gray Robin, and Carette was thoughtful too.

Now and again, indeed, the clinging arms would give me a convulsive hug which set my blood jumping, but that was only when Gray Robin stumbled, and it meant nothing more than a fear of falling overboard on her part and I could not build on it.

We chatted, by snatches, of the party and of things that had happened in my absence. But of the sweet whispers and little confidences which should set all riders on Riding Day above all the rest of the world, there were none between us, and at times we fell to silence and a touch of constraint.

On Eperquerie Common I got down, and led Gray Robin cautiously over the long green slopes among the cushions of gorse and the waist-high ferns, and down the rocky way to the knoll above the landing-place. And as we sat on the soft turf among the empty shells, looking out over the long line of weather-bitten headlands and tumbled rocks, with the blue sea cream-ing at their feet, I suppose I must have heaved a sigh, for Carette laughed and said:

"Ma fé, but you are lively to-day, Phil."

"I'm sorry," I said. "I was thinking of the old times when we used to scramble about here as merry as the rock pipits. They were very happy days, Carette."

"Yes," she nodded, "they were happy days. But we've grown since then."

"One can't help growing, but I don't know that it makes one any happier."

"Tell me all you did out there," she said, and I lay in the sunshine and told her of our shipwreck, and of the Florida swamps, and of the great city of London, through which I had come on my way home. And then, somehow, our talk was of the terrible doings in France, not so very many years before, of which she had never heard much and I only of late. It was probably the blue line of coast on the horizon which set us to that, and perhaps something of a desire on my part to show her that, if she had been learning things at the Miss Maugers, I also had been learning in the greater world outside.

It was very different from the talk that usually passes between riders on Riding Day. For every horse that day is supposed to carry three, though one of them nestles so close between the others that only bits of him may be seen at times in their eyes and faces.

But it was all no use. With young Torode in my mind, and Jean Le Marchant's probable intentions respecting Carette, and Carette's own wonderful growth which seemed to put us on different levels, and the smallness of my own prospects, — I could not bring myself to venture any loverly talk, though my heart was full of loving thoughts and growing intention.

I had been telling her of the doings in Paris, and in Nantes and elsewhere, and she had been dreadfully interested in it all, when suddenly she jumped up with a sharp —

"Phil, you are horrid to-day. I believe you have been telling me all these things just because Monsieur Torode is a Frenchman."

"Torode? — Pardie, I had forgotten Torode for the moment! He is too young to have had any hand in those doings, anyway."

"All the same he is a Frenchman, and it was Frenchmen who did them."

"And you think I was hitting at him behind his back! It is not behind his back I will hit him if needs be, and the time comes. But I had no thought of him,

Carette. These are things I heard but lately, and I thought they might be of interest to you. Did you ever know me strike a foul blow, Carette?" I asked hotly.

"No, never! I was wrong, Phil. Let us ride again and forget the heads tumbling into the baskets and those horrid women knitting and singing."

So we climbed the rocky way, and then I got Gray Robin alongside a rock, and we mounted without much loss and went our way down the lanes in somewhat better case. For I was still somewhat warm at her thinking so ill of me, and she, perceiving it, did her best to make me forget it all.

And now we began to meet other merry riders, and their outspoken but mistaken congratulations testified plainly to the island feeling in favour of island maids mating with island men, and perhaps made Carette regret her Solomon-like decision of the night before. It made me feel somewhat foolish also, at thought of what they would say when they saw her riding back with young Torode.

A cleverer man would no doubt have turned it all to account, but I could not. All I could do was to carry it off as coolly as possible to save Carette annoyance, and to affect a lightness and joviality which were really not in me.

And some of these meetings were full of surprise for Carette, but mostly they only confirmed her expectations. For girls have sharp eyes in such matters, and generally know how things are going, and I have no doubt she and Aunt Jeanne talked them over together. And there was not much went on in Sercq without Aunt Jeanne knowing all about it.

And so it would be —

"Who is this then? Elie Guérin and — ma fé — Judith Drillot! Now, that's odd, for I always thought — "

"Perhaps they're only pretending," I murmured, and Carette kicked her little heels into Gray Robin's ribs so hard that she nearly fell off at his astonished jump.

"B' jou, Judi! B' jou, Elie! Good luck to you!" she cried, as they drew rein alongside, their faces radiant with smiles both for themselves and for us.

"Now, mon Gyu, but I am glad to see you again, Phil Carré, and to see you two together!" said Elie, with the overflowing heartiness of a fully satisfied man.

"Oh, we're only just taking a ride to see how other folks are getting on," I said. "Carette exchanges me for Monsieur Torode later on. You see I only got home last night, and he had asked her already."

"Mon Gyu!" gasped Judi, and we waved our hands and rode on, leaving them gaping.

Then it would be —

"Mon Gyu! *That's* all right! Here are Charles Hamon and Nancy Godfray come together at last. And high time, too! They've been beating about the bush till we're all tired of watching them. B' jou, Nancy! B' jou, Charles! All joy to you!"

There were many such meetings, for we could see the

riders' heads bobbing in every lane. And twice we met young Torode, galloping at speed, and showing to great advantage on Black Boy, whose ruffled black coat was streaked with sweat and splashed with foam, and who was evidently not enjoying himself at all.

"I'm getting the devil out of him so that he'll be all quiet for the afternoon," cried Torode, as he sped past us one time. And Gray Robin tried to look after his mate, and jogged comfortably along thanking his stars that, if he did feel somewhat of a fool, he had decent, quiet folk on his back, and was not as badly off as some he knew that day.

So we came along the horse-tracks, down by Pointe Robert and crossed the head of the Harbour Road, past Derrible, and heard the sea growling at the bottom of the Creux, and then over Hog's Back into Dixcart Valley, and so, about noon, into the road over the Common which lay to the Coupée.

Most of our friends were already there, — some on this side waiting to cross, the more venturesome sitting in the heather and bracken on the further side, with jokes and laughter and ironical invitations to the laggards to take their courage in their hands and come over.

There was quite a mob in the roadway on the Common, the girls sitting on their horses, most of the men on foot.

"How is the path?" I asked, as I got down for a look.

"I've seen it better and I've seen it worse," said

Charles Vaudin. "But, all the same, you know, —
on horseback — " and he shook his dead doubtfully.

"When it's only your own feet you have to look
after it's right enough," said Elie Guérin. "But when
it's a horse's, and they're four feet apart, it's a different
kind of game. I'm going to lead over, let those others
say what they will. Will you walk, Judi, or will you
ride? I can lead the old boy all right."

"I can trust you, mon gars," said the girl, and kept
her seat while Elie led the horse slowly and cautiously
over the narrow way with possible death in very foot
of it. And all the rest watched anxiously.

The path was at this time about four feet wide in
most places, crumbly and weatherworn here and there,
but safe enough for ordinary foot traffic. But even so,
— without a rail on either side, with the blue sea foaming and chafing among the rocks three hundred feet
below, and horribly visible on both sides at once, — the
twisted path when you were on it felt no more than a
swinging thread.

It was not every head that could stand it, and small
blame to those that could not.

Here and there, in the three hundred feet stretch,
great rock pinnacles stood out from the precipitous
depths and overshadowed the path, and encouraged
the wayfarer by offering him posts of vantage to be
attained one by one. But they were far apart, and at
best it was an awesome place even on foot, while with a
horse the dangers were as plain as the path itself.

Still it was a point of honour to cross the Coupée on

Riding Day, and some even compassed it cautiously without dismounting, and took much credit to themselves, though others might call it by other names.

Some of the girls preferred to take no risks, and got down and walked wisely and safely amid the laughter and good-humoured banter of the elect across the gulf. Most, however, showed their confidence in their swains, and at the same time trebled their anxieties, by keeping their seats and allowing their horses to be led across.

Young Torode came galloping across the Common while Gray Robin and Carette and I were still waiting our turn. He reined in Black Boy with a firm hand, and the ruffled black sides worked like bellows, and the angry black head jerked restively, and the quick-glancing eyes looked troubled and vicious.

Torode laughed derisively as Elie Guérin set out with cautious step to lead his old horse over, with Judith Drillot clutching the saddle firmly and wearing a face that showed plainly that it was only a stern sense of duty to Elie that kept her up aloft.

"Ma foi!" laughed Torode. "He would do it better in a boat. It's well seen that Monsieur Guérin was not born to the saddle. Has no one ridden across yet?"

"But, yes, — Helier Godfray rode over all right. All the same —" said one, with a shrug and shake of the head.

"It's as easy as any other road if you've got a steady head and a firm hand," said Torode.

I HELD HIM FIRMLY BY THE HEAD AND SOOTHED HIM WITH
ENCOURAGING WORDS

"Will you ride, Carette, or walk?" I asked. "I shall lead Gray Robin."

She looked down into my eyes for one moment, and I looked up into hers. She did not like the Coupée, I knew, but she would not put me to shame.

"I will ride," she said.

"You're never going to lead across, Carré?" cried Torode. "And with a horse like a Dutch galliot! Man alive! let me take him over for you! — Shall I?" and he bustled forward, looking eagerly up at Carette.

"Stand back!" I said brusquely. "You'll have quite enough to do to take yourself across, I should say," and we were off.

"I'll bring you back on Black Boy," cried Torode consolingly to Carette.

Gray Robin's mild eyes glanced apprehensively into the depths as we went slowly over, and his ears and nostrils twitched to and fro at the growl of the surf down below on either side. I held him firmly by the head and soothed him with encouraging words. The old horse snuffled between gratitude and disgust, and Carette clung tightly up above, and vowed that she would not cross on Black Boy whatever Torode might say.

She was devoutly thankful, I could see, when Gray Robin stepped safely on to the spreading bulk of Little Sercq. I lifted her down and loosed the old horse's bit and set him free for a crop among the sweet, short grasses of the hillside, while we sat down with the rest to watch the others come over.

Caution was the order of the day. Most of the girls kept their seats and braved the passage in token of confidence in their convoys. Some risked all but accident by meekly footing it, and accepted the ironical congratulations on the other side as best they might.

Young Torode had waited his turn with impatience. He and Black Boy were on such terms that the latter would have made a bolt for home if the grasp on his bridle had relaxed for one moment. Again and again his restlessness had suffered angry check which served only to increase it. Neither horse nor rider was in any state for so critical a passage as the one before them. There was no community of feeling between them, except of dislike, and the backbone of a common enterprise is mutual trust and good feeling.

To do him that much justice, Torode must have known that under the circumstances he was taking unusual risk. But he had confidence in his own skill and mastery, and no power on earth would have deterred him from the attempt.

He leaped on Black Boy, turned him from the gulf and rode him up the Common. Then he turned again and came down at a hard gallop, and reaped his reward in the startled cries and anxious eyes of the onlookers. The safe sitters in the heather on the further side sprang up to watch, and held their breath.

"The fool!" slipped through more clenched teeth than mine.

The stones from Black Boy's heels went rattling

down into the depths on either side. The first pinnacles were gained in safety. Just beyond them the
path twisted to the right. Black Boy's stride had
carried him too near the left-hand pillar. An angry
jerk of the reins emphasised his mistake. He resented
it, as he had resented much in his treatment that
morning already. His head came round furiously, his
heels slipped in the crumbling gravel, he kicked out
wildly for safer holding, and in a moment he was
over.

At the first feel of insecurity behind, Torode slipped
deftly out of the saddle. He still held the reins and
endeavoured to drag the poor beast up. But Black
Boy's heels were kicking frantically, now on thin air,
now for a second against an impossible slope of rock
which offered no foothold. For a moment he hung
by his forelegs curved in rigid agony, his nostrils wide
and red, his eyes full of frantic appeal, his ears flat to
his head, his poor face pitiful in its desperation. Torode shouted to him, dragged at the reins — released
them just in time.

Those who saw it never forgot that last look on
Black Boy's face, never lost the rending horror of his
scream as his forelegs gave and he sank out of sight,
never forgot the hideous sound of his fall as he rolled
down the cliff to the rocks below.

The girls hid their faces and sank sobbing into the
heather. The men cursed Torode volubly, and regretted that he had not gone with Black Boy.

And it was none but black looks that greeted him,

when, after standing a moment, he came on across the
Coupée and joined the rest.

"It is a misfortune," he said brusquely, as he came
among us.

"It is sheer murder and brutality," said Charles
Vaudin roughly.

"Guyabble! It's you that ought to be down there,
not yon poor brute!" said Guérin.

"Tuts, then! A horse! I'll make him good to
Hamon."

"And, unless I'm mistaken, you promised him not
to ride the Coupée," I said angrily, for I knew how
George Hamon would feel about Black Boy.

"Diable! I believe I did, but I forgot all about it
in seeing you others crawling across. Will you lend
me your horse to ride back, Carré? Mademoiselle
rides home with me."

"Mademoiselle does not, and I won't lend you a
hair of him."

"That was the understanding. Mademoiselle promised."

"Well, she will break her promise, — with better
reason than you had. I shall see her safely home."

"Right, Phil! Stick to that!" said the others, and
Torode looking round felt himself in a very small
minority, and turned sulkily and walked back across
the Coupée.

The pleasure of the day was broken. Black Boy's
face and scream and fall were with us still, and presently we all went cautiously back across the narrow

way. And no girl rode, but each one shuddered as she passed the spot where the loose edge of the cliff was scored with two deep grooves, and we others, looking down, saw a tumbled black mass lying in the white surf among the rocks.

CHAPTER XV

GEORGE HAMON was sorely put out at the loss of his horse and by so cruel a death. In his anger he laid on young Torode a punishment hard to bear.

For when the young man offered to pay for Black Boy, Uncle George gave him the sharpest edge of his tongue in rough Norman French, and turned him out of his house, and would take nothing from him.

"You pledged me your word and you broke it," said he, "and you think to redeem it with money. Get out of this and never speak to me again! We are honest men in Sercq, and you — you French scum, you don't know what honour means." And Torode was forced to go with the unpayable debt about his neck, and the certain knowledge that all Sercq thought with his angry creditor and ill of himself. And to such a man that was bitterness itself.

During the ten days that followed Riding Day, my mind was very busy settling, as it supposed, the future, — mine and Carette's. For, whether she desired me in hers or not, I had no doubts whatever as to what I wanted myself. My only doubts were as to the possibilities of winning such a prize.

The effect of the Miss Maugers' teaching on Carette

156

herself had been to lift her above her old companions, and indeed above her apparent station in life, though on that point my ideas had no solid standing ground. For, as I have said, the Le Marchants of Brecqhou were more or less of mysteries to us all, and there had been such upsettings just across the water there, such upraisings and downcastings, that a man's present state was no indication of what he might have been. The surer sign was in the man himself, and much pondering of the matter led me to think that Jean Le Marchant might well be something more than simply the successful smuggler he seemed, and that Carette's dainty lady ways might well be the result of natural growth and not simply of the Miss Maugers' polishing.

I would not have had it otherwise. I wanted the very best for her; and if she were by birth a lady, let the lady in her out to the full. Far better that the best that was in her should out and shine, than be battened under hatches and kept out of sight. Better for herself, if it was her nature; and better for the rest of us who could look up and admire. For myself, I would sooner look up than down, and none knew as I did — unless it were Jeanne Falla — how sweet and generous a nature lay behind the graces that set her above us. For none had known her as I had, during all those years of the camaraderie of the coast.

But, while I wished her every good, I could not close my eyes to several things, since they pressed me hard. That, for instance, we were no longer boy and girl together. And that, whereas Carette used to look up

to me, now the looking up was very much the other
way. What her feelings might be towards me, as I
say, I could not be sure; for, little as I knew of girls, I
had picked up enough scraps of knowledge to be quite
sure in my own mind that they were strangely unaccountable creatures, and that you could not judge either
them or a good many other things entirely by outside
appearances. And again, it was borne in upon me
very strongly, and as never before, that, where two
start fairly level, if one goes ahead, the other must
exert himself or be left behind. Carette was going
ahead in marvellous fashion. I felt myself in danger
of being left behind, and that set my brain to very
active working.

I had a better education, in the truest sense of the
word, than most of my fellows, thanks to my mother
and grandfather and Krok and M. Rousselot, the
schoolmaster. That gave me the use of my brains.
I had in addition a good sound body, and I had travelled and seen something of the world. Of worldly
possessions I had just the small savings of my pay and
nothing more, and common sense told me that if I
wanted to win Carette Le Marchant, I must be up and
doing, and must turn myself to more profitable account.

I do not think there was in me any mercenary motive
in this matter. I am quite sure that in so thinking of
things I attributed none to Carette. It seemed to me
that if a man wanted a wife, he ought to be able to
keep her, and I considered the girl who married a man
of precarious livelihood — as I saw some of them do

— very much of a fool. I have since come to know, however, that that is only one way of looking at it, and that to some women the whole-hearted love of a true man counts for very much more than anything else he can bring her.

For money, simply as money, I had no craving whatever. For the wife it might help me to, and the security and comfort it might bring to her, I desired it ardently, and my thoughts were much exercised as to how to arrive at it in sufficiency. I found myself at one of the great crossroads of life, where, I suppose, most men find themselves at one time or another. I knew that much — to me perhaps everything — must depend on how I chose now, and I spent much time wandering in lonely places, and lying among the gorse cushions or in the short grass of the headlands, thinking of Carette and trying to see my way to her.

There were open to us all, in those days, four ways of life — more, maybe, if one had gone seeking them, but these four right to our hands.

I could ship again in the trading line, — and sometime, a very long way ahead, I might come to the command of a ship, if I escaped the perils of the sea till that time came. But I could not see Carette very clearly in that line of life.

I could join a King's ship, and go fight the Frenchmen and all the others who were sometimes on our side and sometimes against us. But I could not see Carette at all in that line of life.

I could settle down to the quiet farmer-fisherman

life on Sercq, as my grandfather had done with great contentment. But I was not my grandfather, and he was one in a thousand, and he had never had to win Carette.

And, lastly, — I could join my fellows in the smuggling or privateering lines, in which some of them, especially the Guernsey men, were waxing mightily fat and prosperous.

For reasons which I did not understand, but which I do now, since I learned about my father, my mother's face was set dead against the Free Trading. And so I came to great consideration of the privateering business and was drawn to it more and more. The risks were greater, perhaps, even than on the King's ships, since the privateer hunts alone and may fall easy prey to larger force. But the returns were also very much greater, and the life more reasonable, for on the King's ships the discipline was said to be little short of tyranny at times, and hardly to be endured by free men.

When, as the result of long turning over of the matter in my own mind, I had decided that the way to Carette lay through the privateering, I sought confirmation of my idea in several likely quarters before broaching it at home.

"Ah, then, Phil, my boy! Come in and sit down and I'll give you a cup of my cider," was Aunt Jeanne's greeting, when I dropped in at Beaumanoir a few days after the party, not without hope of getting a sight of Carette herself and discussing my new ideas before her.

"No, she's not here," Aunt Jeanne laughed softly, at my quick look round. "She's away back to Brecqhou. Two of them came home hurt from their last trip, and she's gone to take care of them. And now, tell me what you are going to do about it, mon gars," she asked briskly, when I had taken a drink of the cider.

"About what then, Aunt Jeanne?"

"Tuts, boy! Am I going blind? What are an old woman's eyes for if not to watch the goings-on of the young ones? You want our Carette. Of course you do. And you've taken her for granted ever since you were so high. Now here's a word of wisdom for you, mon gars. No girl likes to be taken for granted after she's, say fourteen, — unless, ma fé, she's as ugly as sin. If she's a beauty, as our Carette is, she knows it, and she's not going to drop into any man's mouth like a ripe fig. Mon Gyu, no!" — with a crisp nod.

"It's true, every word of it," I said, knowing quite well that those clever old brown eyes of hers could bore holes in me and read me like a book. "Just you tell me what to do, Aunt Jeanne, and I'll do it as sure as I sit here."

"As sure as you sit there you never will, unless you jump right up and win her, my boy. That young Torode is no fool, though he is hot-headed enough and as full of conceit as he can hold. And, pergui, he knows what he wants."

"And Carette?"

Aunt Jeanne's only answer to that was a shrug.

She was, as I think I have said, a very shrewd person.
I have since had reason to believe that she could, if
she had chosen, have relieved my mind very consider-
ably, but at the moment she thought it was the spur I
needed, and she was not going to lessen the effect of
what she had said. On the contrary, she applied it
again and twisted it round and round.

"He's good-looking, you see. That is — in the
girls' eyes. Men see differently. And he's rich, or
he will be, though, for me, I would not care what
money a man had if the devil had his claw in it, mon
Gyu, no! But there you are, mon gars. There he
is with all that, and here are you with nothing but just
your honest face and your good heart and your two
strong arms. And what I want to know is — what
are you going to do about it?"

"What would you do if you were me, Aunt
Jeanne?"

"Ah, now we talk sense. What would I do? Ma
fé, I would put myself in the way of making something,
so that I'd feel confidence in asking her."

"That's just it. I can't ask her till I'm in some
position to do so. I've been thinking all round it —"

"B'en?"

"I could go trading again —"

"And get drowned, maybe, before you've made
enough to pay for a decent funeral," snorted Aunt
Jeanne, contemptuously.

"I could go on a King's ship —"

"And get bullied to death for nothing a day."

"The free-trading my mother won't hear of."

"Crais b'en!"

"Why I don't know —"

"Never mind why. She has her reasons without doubt."

"So there's nothing for it but the privateering."

"B'en! Why couldn't you say so without boxing the compass, mon gars? Privateering is the biggest chance nowadays. Of course, the risks —"

"That's nothing if it brings me to Carette. Aunt Jeanne —"

"Well, then?"

"I wish you'd tell me something."

"What then?" she asked warily.

"I get a bit afraid sometimes that Carette is not intended for a plain common Sercqman. Has M. Le Marchant views —"

"Shouldn't be a bit surprised, mon gars. I know I would have if she were mine. But, all the same, it is Carette herself will have the final say in the matter, and meanwhile — well, the more she learns the better. Isn't it so?"

"Surely. The more one learns the better, unless —"

"Yes, then?"

"Well, unless it makes one look down on one's friends."

"Do you look down on your mother? And do you look down on me? Yet I'll be bound you think you know a sight more than both of us put together."

"No, I don't. But —"

"And yet you've had more learning than ever came our way."

"Of a kind. But —"

"Exactly, mon gars! And that other is the learning that doesn't come from books. And all your learning and Carette's will only prepare you for these other things. With all your learning you are only babies yet. The harder tasks are all before you."

"And you think I may hope for Carette, Aunt Jeanne?"

"If you win her. But you'll have to stir yourself, mon gars."

"I've sometimes wondered —" I began doubtfully, and stopped, not knowing how she might take my questioning.

"Well, what have you wondered?" and she peered at me with her head on one side like a robin's.

"Well — you see — she is so different from the others over there on Brecqhou."

"Roses grow among thorns."

"Yes, I know, —"

"Very well! . . . All the same, — you are right, mon gars. She is different — and with reason. Her mother was well-born. She was daughter to old Godefroi of St. Heliers, the shipowner. Jean was sailing one of his ships. It was not a good match nor a suitable one. The old man turned them out, and Jean came here with her and his boys and settled on Brecqhou. It is as well you should know, for it may come into the account. Jean would make her into a lady like her mother. For me, I would like to see her an honest man's wife, — that is, if he's able to keep her."

"I'm for the privateering," I said, jumping up as briskly as if I'd only to walk aboard.

"I'll wish you luck and pray for it, my boy."

"That should help. Good-by, Aunt Jeanne!"

My mind was quite made up, but, all the same, I went to George Hamon to ask his advice and help in the matter, as I always had done in all kinds of matters and never failed to get them. I found him strolling among his cabbages with his pipe in his mouth.

"Uncle George, I want your advice," I began, and he smiled knowingly.

"Aw! I know you, mon gars. You've made up your mind about something and you want me to help you get over your mother and grandfather. Isn't that about it? And what is it now?"

"I want to be up and doing and making something—"

"I understand."

"And privateering seems the best thing going. I want to try that. What do you say?"

"Some have done mightily well at it —"

"You see," I said eagerly, "there is only that or the free-trading, or the West Indies again, or a King's ship —"

He nodded understandingly.

"And none of them hold any very big chances — except the free-trading. And there —"

"I know! Your mother won't hear of it. She has her reasons, my boy, and you can leave it at that. . . .

She won't like the privateering either, you know, Phil,"
he said doubtfully, as though he did not care over
much for the job he was being dragged into.

"I'm afraid she won't, Uncle George. That's
why —"

"That's why you come to me," he smiled.

"That's it. You see, I've got to be up and doing,
because —"

"I know," he nodded. "Well, come along, and
let's get it over," and we went across the fields to Belfontaine.

My mother met us at the door, and it was borne in
upon me suddenly that as a girl she must have been
very good-looking. There was more colour than usual
in her face and the quiet eyes shone brightly. I thought
she guessed we had come on some business opposed
to her peace of mind, but I have since known that there
were deeper reasons.

"You are welcome, George Hamon," she said.
"What mischief are you and Phil plotting now?"

"Aw, then! It's a bad character you give me,
Rachel."

"I know he goes to you for advice and he might do
worse. He's been restless since he came home. What
is it?"

"Young blood must have its chance, you know.
And change of pasture is good for young calves, as
Jeanne Falla says."

"Hasn't he had change enough?"

"Where is Philip?"

"Down vraicking with Krok in Saignie. A big drift came in this morning and we want all we can get for the fields."

"Give them a hand, Phil, and then bring your grandfather along. And I'll talk to your mother."

My grandfather and Krok had got most of the seaweed drawn up onto the stones above tide level, and as soon as we had secured the rest they came up to the house with me, wet and hungry. I had told my grandfather simply that George Hamon was there, but said nothing about our business. He greeted him warmly.

"George, my boy, you should come in oftener."

"Ay, ay! If I came as often as I wanted you'd be for turning me out," — with a nod to Krok, who replied with a cheerful smile and went to the fire.

"You know better. Your welcome always waits you. What's in the wind now?"

"Phil wants to go privateering," said my mother. "And George has come to help him."

"Ah, I expected it would come to that," said my grandfather quietly. "It's a risky business, after all, Phil," — to me, sitting on the green bed and feeling rather sheepish.

"I know, grandfather. But there are risks in everything, and —"

"And, to put it plainly, he wants Carette Le Marchant, and he's not the only one, and that seems the quickest way to her," said George Hamon.

My mother's quiet brown eyes gave a little snap and he caught it.

"When a lad's heart is set on a girl there is nothing he won't do for her. I've known a man wait twenty years for a woman —"

She made a quick little gesture with her hand, but he went on stoutly —

"Oh yes, and never gave up hoping all that time, though, mon Gyu, it was little he got for his —"

"And you think it right he should go?" interrupted my mother hastily. And, taken up as I was with my own concerns, I understood of a sudden that there was that between my mother and George Hamon which I had never dreamed of.

"I think he will never settle till he has been. And it's lawful business, and profitable, and your objection to the free-trading doesn't touch it. There is some discipline on a privateer, though it's not as bad as on a King's ship. My advice is — let him go."

"It's only natural, after all," said my grandfather, with a thoughtful nod. "Who's the best man to go with, George?"

"Torode of Herm makes most at it, they say. But —"

"A rough lot, I'm told, and he has to keep a tight hand on them. But I know nothing except from hearsay. I've never come across him yet."

"Jean Le Marchant could tell you more about him than anyone else round here," said Uncle George, looking musingly at me. "They have dealings together in trading matters, I believe. Then, they say, John Ozanne is fitting out a schooner in Peter Port.

He's a good man, but how he'll shape at privateering
I don't know."

"Who's going to command her?" I asked.

"John himself, I'm told."

"Then I'll go across and see Jean Le Marchant,"
I said.

At which prompt discounting of John Ozanne Uncle
George laughed out loud.

"Well, I don't suppose it can do any harm, if it
doesn't do much good. He's at home, I believe.
Someone got hurt on their last run, I heard —"

"Yes, Aunt Jeanne told me, — two of them."

"Maybe you'll not find them in any too good a
humour, but you know how to take care of yourself."

"I'll take care of myself all right."

"Will you stop and have supper with us, George?"
asked my grandfather.

"Yes, I will. It's a treat to sup in company," and
my mother busied herself over the pots at the fire.

I had often wondered why Uncle George had never
married. He was such a good fellow, honest as the
day, and always ready to help anybody in any way.
And yet, ever since his mother died, and that must have
been ten years ago at least, he had lived all alone in his
house at La Vauroque, though he had prospered in
various ways and was reputed well to do. He lived
very simply — made his own coffee of a morning, and
for the rest depended on an old neighbour woman, who
came in each day and cooked his meals and kept the

house clean. Yes, I had often wondered why, and not until this night did I begin to understand.

Long afterwards, when he was telling me of other matters, it did not greatly surprise me to learn that he had waited all these years in hopes of my mother coming round to him at last. And the wall of division that stood between them and stirred him to bitterness at times — not against her, but against what he counted her foolish obstinacy — was the fact that long ago my father had gone down to the sea and never come back, as many and many an island man had done since ever time began. But she had her own rigid notions of right and wrong, narrow perhaps, but of her very self, and she would not marry him, though his affection never wavered even when he felt her foolishness the most.

It was strange, perhaps, that I should jump to sudden understanding of the matter when all my thoughts just then were of my own concerns. But love, I think, if somewhat selfish, is a mighty quickener of the understanding, and, even though all one's thoughts are upon one subject, a fellow-feeling opens one's eyes to the signs elsewhere.

We talked much of the matter of my going, that night over the supper table, or my grandfather and George Hamon did, while my mother and Krok and I listened. And wonderful stories Uncle George told of the profits some folks had made in the privateering — tens of thousands of pounds to the owners in a single fortunate cruise, and hundreds to every seaman.

But my mother warmed to the matter not at all. She sat gazing silently into the fire and thought, maybe, of those who lost, and of those whose shares came only to the last cold plunge into the tumbling graveyard of the sea. While as for me, in my own mind I saw visions of stirring deeds, and wealth and fame, and Carette seemed nearer to me than ever she had been since she went to Peter Port.

CHAPTER XVI

THE next morning found me running in under La Givaude for the landing-place on Brecqhou, where my boat could lie safely in spite of the rising tide.

I was in the best of spirits, for low spirits come of having nothing to do, or not knowing what to do or how to do it. My next step was settled, lead where it might. I was going privateering, and now I was going to see Carette, and I intended to let her know that I was going and why, so that there should be no mistake about it while I was away.

I scrambled gaily up to the path that leads into the island, and everything was shining bright like the inside of an ormer shell — the sea as blue as the sky, except close under the headlands where it was clear soft green; the waves further out flashed in the sunlight and showed their white teeth wherever they met the rocks; and the rocks were yellow and brown and black, and all fringed with tawny seaweed, and here beside me the golden-rod flamed yellow and orange, and the dark green bracken swung lazily in the breeze.

And then, of a sudden, a shot rang out, and a bullet flew past my head, and cut my whistling short.

"What fool's that?" I shouted at the smoke that

floated out from behind a lump of rock in front, and a young man got up lazily from behind it and stood looking at me as he rammed home another charge.

"You'll be hurting someone if you don't take care," I said.

"I do when I care to. That was only a hint. Who are you and what do you want here?"

"I'm Phil Carré of Belfontaine. I want to see Monsieur Le Marchant — and Ma'm'zelle Carette."

"Oh, you do, do you? And what do you want with them?"

"I'll tell them when I see them. Do you always wish your friends good-morning with a musket on Brecqhou?"

"Our friends don't come till they're asked."

"Then you don't have many visitors, I should say."

"All we want," was the curt reply.

He was a tall, well-built fellow, some years older than myself, good-looking, as all the Le Marchants were, defiant of face and careless in manner. He looked, in fact, as though it would not have troubled him in the least if his bullet had gone through my head.

He had finished loading his gun and stood blocking the way, with no intention of letting me pass. And how long we might have stood there I do not know, when I saw another head bobbing along among the golden-rod, and another of the brothers came up and stood beside him.

"What is it then, Martin? Who is he?" he asked, staring at me.

"Says he's Phil Carré of Belfontaine, but —"

And the other dark face broke into a smile. "Tiens, I remember. You came across once before —"

"Yes. You had the measles."

"And what brings you this time, Phil Carré?"

"I want to speak with Monsieur Le Marchant."

"And to see Carette, I think you said, Monsieur Phil Carré," said the other.

"Certainly."

"Come along then," said Helier, the newcomer. "There is no harm in Phil Carré. You have not by any chance gone into the preventive service, Monsieur Carré?" he laughed.

"Not quite. I'm off to the privateering. It's that I want to speak to your father about."

"How then?" he asked with interest, as we walked along towards the great wooden house in the hollow. "How does it concern him?"

"Torode of Herm is the cleverest privateer round here, they say. I thought to try with him, and your father knows more about him than anyone else."

"Ah! Torode of Herm! Yes, he is a clever man is Torode. But he won't take you, mon gars. He picks his own and there is not an island man among them."

The first thing I saw when I entered the house was Carette busy at one of the bunks in the dimness at the far end of the room. She looked round and then straightened up in surprise.

"Why, Phil! What are you doing here? One

moment" — and I saw that she was tying a bandage round the arm of the man in the bunk. His eyes caught the light from the windows and gleamed savagely at me under his rumpled black hair. A similar face looked out from an adjoining bunk. When she had finished she came quickly across to me.

"Measles again?" I said, remembering my former visit.

"Yes, measles," she said, with the colour in her face and questions in her eyes.

"I came to see your father, and if I was in luck, yourself also, Carette."

"He is sleeping," she said, with a glance towards a side room. "He was anxious about these two, and he would take the night watch. They are feverish, you see."

"I will wait."

"He won't be long. He never takes much sleep. What do you want to —" and then some sudden thought sent a flush of colour into her face and a quick inquiry into her eyes, and she stopped short and stood looking at me.

"It's this, Carette —" and then the door of the side room opened quietly and Jean Le Marchant came out, looking at us with much surprise.

He was very little changed since I had seen him last. It was the same keen handsome face, with its long white moustache and cold dark eyes, somewhat tired at the moment with their night duties.

"And this is — ?" he asked suavely, as I bowed.

"It is Phil Carré of Belfontaine, father," said Carette quickly. "He has come to see you."

"Very kind of Monsieur Carré. It is not after my health you came to inquire, Monsieur?"

"No, sir. It is this. I have decided to go privateering, and I want to go with the best man. I am told Torode of Herm is the best, and that you can tell me more about him than anyone else."

"Ah — Torode! Yes, he is a very clever man is Torode — a clever man, and very successful. And privateering is undoubtedly the game nowadays. Honest free-trading isn't in it compared with the privateering, though even that isn't what it was, they say. Like everything else, it is overdone, and many mouths make scant faring. And so you want to go out with Torode?" he asked musingly.

"That is my idea. You see, Monsieur, I have spent nearly four years in the trading to the Indies, and I am about as well off as when I started — except in experience. Now I want to make something — all I can, and as quickly as I can. And," I said, plunging headlong at my chief object in coming, "my reasons stand there," and I pointed to Carette, who jumped at the suddenness of it, and coloured finely, and bit her lip, and sped away on some household duty which she had not thought of till that moment.

Monsieur Le Marchant smiled, and the two young men laughed out.

"Ma foi!" said the old man. "You are frank, mon gars."

"It is best so. I wanted you to know, and I wanted Carette to know, though I think she has known it always. I have never thought of any but Carette, and as soon as I am able I will ask her to marry me."

"Whether I have other views for her or not," said her father.

"No other could possibly love Carette as I do" — at which he smiled briefly and the others grinned — "I have only one wish in life, and that is to care for her and make her happy."

"That is for the future, so we need not talk about it now. If you make a fortune at the privateering — who knows?"

"And what can you tell me of Torode, Monsieur? Is he the best man to go out with?"

"He has been more successful than most without doubt," and the keen cold eyes rested musingly on me, while he seemed to be turning deep thoughts in his mind. "Yes. Why not try him? And after your first voyage come across again and we will talk it over. Martin" — to the man who had given me good-morning with his musket — "you are too long away from your post. Allez!"

"There was nothing in sight till Monsieur Carré came round the corner," said Martin, and went off to his lookout.

"These new preventive men with their constant new regulations are an annoyance," said the old man quietly. "Some of them will be getting hurt one of these days. It is a pity the government can't leave

honest traders alone.   They worry you also on Sercq,
I suppose."

"I hear of them.   But we have nothing to do with
the trading at Belfontaine, so they don't trouble us."

"Ah, no, I remember.   Well, come across again
after your first voyage and tell us how you get on,
Monsieur Carré."

Helier sauntered back with me towards the landing-
place.   Carette had disappeared.   I wondered if my
plain speaking had offended her, but I was glad she
had heard.

I pulled out of the little bay and ran up my lug and
sped straight across to Herm.   Every rock was known
to me, even though it showed only in a ring of widening
circles or a flattening of the dancing waves into a straining coil, for we had been in the habit of fishing and
vraicking here regularly until Torode took possession.
And many was the time I had hung over the side of
the rocking boat and sought in the depths for the tops of
the great rock-pillars which once held up the bridge
that joined Brecqhou to Herm and Jethou.   But now
the fishing and vraicking were stopped, for Torode
liked visitors as little as did Jean Le Marchant.

And as I went I thought of Carette and how she
looked when I spoke about her to her father.   And
one minute I thought I had seen in her a brief look
which was not entirely discontent, and the next minute
I was in doubt.   Perhaps it was a gleam of anger and
annoyance.   I could not tell, for the chief thing I had
seen in her face was undoubtedly a vast confusion at

the publicity of my declaration.   In my mind also was
the contradiction of Helier Le Marchant's assertion
that Torode would take no island man into his crew,
and his father's advice to go and try him.   I was inclined to think that Helier would prove right, for, even
with my four years' experience of men and things, I
saw that Monsieur Le Marchant was beyond my
understanding.

My boat swirled into the narrow way between Herm
and Jethou, where the water came up lunging and
thrusting like great black jelly-fish.   I dropped my
sail and took the oars, and stood with my face to the
bows and pulled cautiously among the traps and snares
that lay thick on every side and still more dangerously
out of sight.   So I crept round the south of Herm and
drew into the little roadstead on the west.

And the first thing I saw, and saw no other for a
while, was the handsomest ship I had ever set eyes on.
A long low black schooner, with a narrow beading of
white at deck level, and masts that tapered off into fishing rods.   She was pierced for six guns a side, and a
great tarpaulin cover on the forecastle and another
astern hinted at something heavier there.   Her lines and
finish were so graceful that I felt sure she was French
built, for English builders ever consider strength
before beauty.   A very fast boat, I judged, but how
she would behave in dirty weather I was not so
sure.   Anyway a craft to make a sailor's heart hungry
to see her loosed and free of the seas.   She sat the
water like a gull, so lightly that one half expected a

sudden unfolding of wings and a soaring flight into the blue.

I was still gazing with all my eyes, and drifting slowly in, when a sharp hail brought me round facing a man who leaned with his arms on a wall of rock and looked over and down at me.

"Hello, there!"

"Hello!" I replied, and saw that it was young Torode himself.

From my position I could see little except the rising ground in the middle of the island, but I got the impression, chiefly no doubt from what I had heard, and from the thin curls of smoke that rose in a line behind him, that there was quite a number of houses there. In fact, the place had all the look of a fortified post.

"Tiens! It is Monsieur Carré, is it not? And what may Monsieur Carré want here?" His tone was somewhat masterful, if not insolent. I felt an inclination to resent it, but bethought me in time that such could be no help to my plans, and that, moreover, nothing was to be gained by concealment.

"I came to see your father. Is he to be seen?"

"So? What about?"

"I want to join his ship there for the privateering. She's a beauty."

"Oh-ho! Tired of honest trading?"

"I didn't know privateering had become dishonest."

"But different from what you've been accustomed to, isn't it?"

"Bit more profitable anyway, so they say. Are you open for any hands?"

But Torode had turned and was in conversation with someone inside the rampart. I heard my own name mentioned, and presently he disappeared and his place was taken by an older man whom I knew instinctively for the great Torode himself.

A massive black head, and a grim dark face, with a week's growth of bristling black hair about it, and a dark moustache, — a strong, lowering face, and a pair of keen black eyes that bored holes in one; that was Torode of Herm as I first set eyes on him.

He stared at me so long and fixedly, as if he had never seen anything like me before, that at last, out of sheer discomfort, I had to speak.

"Monsieur Torode?" I asked, and after another staring pause, he said gruffly:

"B'en! I am Torode. What is it you want?"

"A berth on your ship there."

"And why? Who are you then?"

"Your son knows me. My name is Carré, — Phil Carré. I come from Sercq."

"Where there?"

"Belfontaine."

"Does your father live there?"

"He's dead these twenty years. I live with my mother and my grandfather."

He seemed to be turning this over in his mind, and presently he asked:

"And they want you to go privateering?"

"I don't say they want me to. It's I want to go. They are willing — at all events they don't object."

"And why do you go against their wishes?"

"Well, it's this way, Monsieur Torode. I've been four voyages to the West and there's no great things in it. I want to be doing something more for myself."

"Why don't you try the free-trading?"

"Ah, there! We have never taken to the free-trading, but I don't know why."

"Afraid, maybe."

"No, it's not that. There's more risk privateering."

"Well, then?"

"My folks don't like it. That's all I know."

"But they'll let you go privateering."

"Yes," I said, with a shrug at my own lack of under-standing on that point. "Privateering's honest busi-ness after all."

"And free-trading isn't! You'll never make a privateer, mon gars. You're too much in leading-strings."

"I don't know," I said, somewhat ruffled. " I have seen some service. We fought a Frenchman in the West Indies and I've been twice wrecked."

"So! Well, we're full up, and business is bad or we wouldn't be lying here."

"And you won't give me a trial?"

"No!"

"And that's the last word?"

"That's the last word."

"Then I'll wish you good-day, Monsieur. I must

try elsewhere," and I dropped into my seat and pulled away down the little roadstead.

Monsieur Torode was still leaning over the wall, and watching me fixedly, when I turned the corner of the outer ridge of rocks and crept away through the mazy channels towards Peter Port. When I got farther out and could get an occasional glimpse of the rampart, he was still leaning on it, and still staring out at me just as I had left him.

CHAPTER XVII

THERE was no difficulty in finding John Ozanne.
I made out his burly figure and red-whiskered face
on the harbour wall before I had passed Castle Cornet,
and heard his big voice good-humouredly roaring to
the men at work in the rigging of a large schooner that
lay alongside.

He greeted me with great good-will.

"Why, surely, Phil," he said very heartily, in reply
to my request. "It's not your grandfather's boy I
would be refusing, and it's a small boat that won't
take in one more. What does the old man say to
your going?"

"He's willing or I wouldn't be here."

"That's all right then. What do you think of her?"

We were standing on the harbour wall, looking down
on the schooner on which the riggers were busy renew-
ing her standing gear.

"A good staunch boat, I should say. What can
you get out of her?"

"Ten easy with these new spars, and she can come
up as close as any boat I've ever seen — except maybe
yon black snake of Torode's," — with a jerk of the
head towards Herm. "Seen her?"

"Yes, I've seen her. How's she in bad weather?"

"Wet, I should say. We can stand a heap more than she can."

"When do you expect to get off?"

"Inside a week. Come along and have a drink. It's dry work watching these fellows."

So we went along to the café just behind us, and it was while we were sitting there, sipping our cider, and I was telling him of my last voyage and after-journeyings, that a man came in and slapped down on the table in front of us a printed bill which, as it turned out afterwards, concerned us both more nearly than we knew.

"Ah!" said John Ozanne, "I'd heard of that. If we happen across him we'll pick up that £5000 or we'll know the reason why."

It was a notice sent out by one John Julius Angerstein, of Lloyds in the city of London, on behalf of the merchants and shipowners there, offering a reward of £5000 for the capture, or proof of the destruction, of a French privateer which had for some time past been making great play with British shipping in the Channel and Bay of Biscay. She was described as a schooner of 150 tons or thereabouts, black hull with red streaks, carrying an unusually large crew and unusually heavy metal. She flew a white flag with a red hand on it, her red figure-head was said to represent the same device, and she was known by the name of *La Main Rouge*.

John Ozanne folded the bill methodically and stowed it safely away in his pocket-book.

"It'd be a fortune if we caught him full," he said thoughtfully. "They say he takes no prizes. Just helps himself to what he wants like a highwayman, and then sheers off and looks out for another. Rare pickings he must have had among some of those fat East Indiamen. Here's to our falling in with him!" and we clicked our mugs on that right hopefully.

"What weight do we carry?" I asked, in view of the Frenchman's heavy guns, our own not being yet mounted.

"Four eighteens a side, and one twenty-four forward and one aft. There'll be some chips flying if we meet him, but we'll do our best to close his fist, and stop his grabbing. You're wanting to get back? Come over day after to-morrow and give me a hand. I'll be glad of your help," and I dropped into my boat and pulled out into the wind, and ran up my lug for home.

"So you saw Torode himself, Phil? And what is he like?" asked my grandfather, as I told them the day's doings.

"Big, black, grim-looking fellow. Just what you'd expect. On the whole I'm not sorry I'm going with John Ozanne. He seems pleased to have me too, and that's something."

"I'd much sooner think of you with him," said my mother. "I know nothing of Monsieur Torode, but nobody seems to like him."

George Hamon said much the same thing, and spoke highly of John Ozanne as a cautious seaman, which I well knew him to be.

Jeanne Falla laughed heartily when I told her of my visit to Brecqhou, which I did very fully.

"Mon Gyu, Phil, mon gars, but you're getting on! And you told her to her face before them all that you wanted to marry her? It's as odd a style of wooing as ever I heard."

"Well, you see, I wanted there to be no mistake about it, Aunt Jeanne. If I don't see Carette again before I leave, she will know how the land lies at all events. If she takes to young Torode while I'm away it's because she likes him best."

"And she — Carette — what did she say to it?"

"She didn't say anything."

"Tuts! How did she look, boy? A girl tells more with her face and her eyes than with her tongue, even when they say opposite things."

"I'm not sure how she took it, Aunt Jeanne. How would you have taken it now?"

"Ma fé! It would depend," she laughed, her old face creasing up with merriment. "If it was Monsieur Right I wouldn't have minded maybe, though I might be a bit taken aback at the newest way in courting."

"Well, I thought she looked something like that. And then, afterwards, I wasn't sure she wasn't angry about it. I don't know. I've had so little to do with girls, you see."

"And you'd not know much more, however much you'd had. You're only a boy still, mon gars."

"Well, I'm going to do a man's work, and it's for

Carette I'm going to do it. Put in a good word for me while I'm away, won't you now, Aunt Jeanne? Carette is more to me than anything else in the world."

"Ay, well! We'll see. And you saw Torode himself?"

And I told her all I had to tell about Torode, and John Ozanne, whom she had known as a boy.

"He was always good-hearted was John, but a bit slow and easy-going," said she. "But we'll hope for the best."

"Will Carette be across in the next day or two?"

"I doubt it. Those two who got hurt will need her. If you don't see her you shall leave me a kiss for her," she chirped.

"I'll give you a dozen now," I cried, jumping up, and giving her the full tale right heartily.

"Ma fé, yes! You are getting on, mon gars," she said, as she set the black sun-bonnet straight again. "You tackle Carette that way next time you see her and —"

"Mon Gyu, I wouldn't dare to!" and Aunt Jeanne still found me subject for laughter.

CHAPTER XVIII

I WAS sorely tempted to run across to Brecqhou for one more sight of Carette before I left home, but decided at last to leave matters as they were. Beyond the pleasure of seeing her I could hope to gain little, for she was not the one to show her heart before others, and too rash an endeavour might provoke her to that which was not really in her.

As things were I could cherish the hopes that were in me to the fullest, and one makes better weather with hope than with doubt. Carette knew now all that I could tell her, and Aunt Jeanne would be a tower of strength to me in my absence. I could leave the leaven to work. And I think that if I had not given my mother that last day she would have felt it sorely, and with reason.

The deepest that was in us never found very full vent at Belfontaine, and that, I think, was due very largely to the quiet and kindly, but somewhat rigid, Quakerism of my grandfather. We felt and knew without babbling into words.

So all that day my mother hovered about me with a quiet face and hungry eyes, but never one word that might have darkened my going. She had braced her

heart to it, as the women of those days had to do, and
as all women of all times must whose men go down
to the sea in ships.

And I do not think there was any resentment in her
mind at my feeling for Carette.   For she spoke of her
many times and always in the nicest way, seeing perhaps the pleasure it gave me.   She was a very wise and
thoughtful woman, though not so much given to the
expression of her wisdom as was Jeanne Falla, and I
think she understood that this too was inevitable, and
so she had quietly brought her mind to it.   But after
all, all this is but saying that her tower of quiet strength
was built on hidden foundations of faith, and hope,
and her mother love needed no telling.

Next day my grandfather and Krok made holiday,
in order to carry me over to Peter Port and see the
Swallow for themselves, and my mother's fervent " God
keep you, Phil!" and all the other prayers that I felt
in her arms round my neck, were with me still as we
ran past Brecqhou, and I stood with an arm round the
mast looking eagerly for possible, but unlikely, sight
of Carette.

We were too low down to see the house, which lay
in a hollow.   The white waves were ripping like
comets along the fringe of ragged rocks under the great
granite cliffs, and our boat reeled and plunged under
the strong west wind, and sent the foam flying in sheets
as we tacked against the cross seas.

We were running a short slant past Moie Batarde
before taking a long one for the Grands Bouillons,

when a flutter of white among the wild, black rocks of the point by the Creux à Vaches caught my eye, and surely it was Carette herself, though whether she had known of our passage, or was in the habit of frequenting that place, I could not tell. I took it to myself, however, and waved a hearty greeting, and the last sight I had of her, and could not possibly have had a better, was her hand waving farewells in a way that held much comfort for me many a day to come. I had told my grandfather about Torode's fine schooner, and had enlarged so upon it that he had a wish to see her for himself, and so we were making for the passage between Herm and Jethou, which I had travelled two days before. He knew the way and the traps and pitfalls better even than I did, and ran us in up the wind with a steady hand till the roadstead opened before us. But it was empty. Torode was off after plunder, and we turned and ran for Peter Port. We found John Ozanne as busy as a big bumblebee, but he made time to greet my grandfather very jovially, and showed him all over his little ship with much pride. He was in high spirits and anxious to be off, especially since he had heard of Torode's going.

"He's about as clever as men are made," he said, "and when he goes he goes on business, so it's time for us to be on the move too. We'll make a man of your boy, Philip."

"A privateer?" said my grandfather with a smile.

"Ay, well! I can believe it's not all to your liking, but it's natural after all."

"I'm not complaining."

"I never heard you. But you'd have been better pleased if he hadn't wanted so much."

"Maybe," said my grandfather with his quiet smile, "But as Jeanne Falla says, 'Young calves'—"

"I know, I know," laughed John Ozanne, "She's a famous wise woman is Jeanne Falla, and many a licking she gave me when I was a boy for stealing her apples round there at Cobo."

When my grandfather waved his hand, as they ran out past Castle Cornet, the last link broke between Sercq and myself for many a day. Before I saw any of them again — except the distant sight of the island lying like a great blue whale nuzzling its young, as we passed up Little Russel next morning — many things had happened for the changing of many lives. I had seen much, suffered much, and learned much, and it is of these things I have to tell you.

We cast off next day, amid the cheers and wavings of a great crowd. Half Peter Port stood on the walls of the old harbour. Some had friends and relatives on board, and their shoutings were akin to lusty, veiled prayers for their safe return. Some had eggs in our basket, and in wishing us good speed were not without an eye to the future, and maybe were already counting their possible chickens. We gave them cheer for cheer, and more again for the St. Sampson people. Then, with all our new wings making a gallant show, we swept past Grand Braye, and Ancresse, and turned our nose to the Northwest.

We were all in the best of spirits. The *Swallow* was well found and well armed, and showed a livelier pair of heels than I had looked for, and that, in an Ishmaelitish craft, was a consideration and a comfort. She was roomy, too, and would make better times of bad weather, I thought, than would Torode's beautiful black snake. We were sixty men all told, and every man of us keen for the business we were on, and with sufficient confidence in John Ozanne to make a willing crew, though among us there were not lacking good-humoured jokes anent his well-known, easy-going, happy-go-lucky proclivities. These, however, would make for comfort on board, and for the rest, he was a good seaman and might be expected to do his utmost to justify the choice of his fellow-townsmen, and he was said to have a considerable stake in the matter himself.

We had four mates, all tried Peter Port men, and our only fears were as to possible lack of the enemy's merchant ships in quantity and quality sufficient for our requirements. On the second day out, a slight haze on the sky line shortening our view, the sound of firing came down to us on the wind, and John Ozanne promptly turned the *Swallow's* beak in that direction.

We edged up closer and closer, and when the haze lifted, came on a hot little fight in progress between a big ship and a small one, and crowded the rigging and bulwarks to make it out.

"Little chap's a Britisher, I'll wager you," said old Martin Cohu, the bo's'un.

"A privateer then, and t'other a merchantman."

"Unless it's t'other way on. Anyway the old man will make 'em out soon," and we anxiously eyed John Ozanne working away with his big brass-bound telescope, as we slanted up towards the two ships, first on one tack then on the other.

The larger vessel's rigging we could see was badly mauled, the smaller ship dodged round and round her, and off and on, plugging her as fast as the guns could be loaded and fired.

"That's no merchantman," said Old Martin. "A French Navy ship — a corvette — about fifteen guns a side maybe, and t'other's an English gun-brig; making rare game of her she is, too. Minds me of a dog and a bull."

"Maybe the old man'll take a hand just for practice."

And John Ozanne was quite willing. We were ordered to quarters, and ran in, with our colours up, prepared to take our share. But the commander of the brig had his own ideas on that matter, strong ones too, and he intimated them in the most unmistakable way by a shot across our bows, as a hint to us to mind our own business and leave him to his.

A hoarse laugh and a ringing cheer went up from the *Swallow* at this truly bull-dog spirit, and we drew off and lay-to to watch the result.

The Frenchman was fully three times the size of his plucky little antagonist, but the Englishman as usual had the advantage in seamanship. He had managed to cripple his enemy early in the fight and now had it all his own way. We watched till the Frenchman's

colours came down, then gave the victors another
hearty cheer, and went on our way to seek fighting of
our own.

For three days we never sighted a sail. We had
turned South towards the Bay, and were beginning to
doubt our luck, when, on the fourth day, a stiff, westerly
gale forced us to bare poles.   During the night it waxed
stronger still, and the little *Swallow* proved herself
well.   Next morning a long line of great ships went
gallantly past us over the roaring seas, shepherded by
two stately frigates, — an East Indian convoy homeward bound.   Late that day, the fifth of our cruising,
we raised the topmasts of a large ship and made for
her hopefully.

"A merchantman," said Martin Cohu disgustedly,
"and English or I'm a Dutchman.   One of the convoy
lagged behind.   No pickings for us this time, my lads."

But there was more there than he expected.

There was always the chance of her having been
captured by the French, in which case her capture
would bring some little grist to our mill, and so we
crowded sail for her.   And, as we drew nearer, it was
evident, from the talk among John Ozanne and his
mates, that they could see more through their glasses
than we could with our eyes.

"Guyable!" cried old Martin at last.   "There's
another ship hitched on to her far side.   I can see her
masts.   Now, what's this?   A privateer as like as
not, and we'll have our bite yet, maybe."

And before long we could all make out the thin

masts of a smaller vessel between the flapping canvas of the larger. John Ozanne ordered us to quarters, and got ready for a fight. He gave us a hearty word or two, since every man likes to know what's in the wind.

"There's a schooner behind yonder Indiaman, my lads, and it's as likely as not she's been captured. If so we'll do our best to get her back, for old England's sake, and our own, and just to spite the Frenchman. If the schooner should prove 'The Red Hand,' and that's as like as not, for he's the pluckiest man they have, you know what it means. It'll be hard fighting and no quarter. But he's worth taking. The London merchants have put a price on him, and there'll be that, and himself, and a share in the Indiaman besides, and we'll go back to Peter Port with our pockets lined."

We gave him a cheer and hungered for the fray.

John Ozanne took us round in a wide sweep to open the ships, and every eye and glass was glued to them. As we rounded the Indiaman's great, gilded stern, about a mile away, it did not need John Ozanne's emphatic — "It's him!" to tell us we were in for a tough fight, and that three prizes lay for our taking. We gave John another cheer, tightened our belts, and perhaps — I can speak for one at all events — wondered grimly how it would be with some of us a couple of hours later.

The Frenchman cast off at once and came to meet us, the Red Hand flying at his masthead, the red lump at his bows, the red streak clearly visible just below the open gun-ports.

" Do your duty, lads," said John Ozanne.   " There'll
be tough work for us.   He carries heavy metal.   We'll
close with him at all odds and then the British bull-
dog must see to it."

We gave him another cheer, and then a cloud of
white smoke burst from the Frenchman's fore-deck,
and our topmast and all its hamper came down with a
crash, and our deck rumbled with bitter curses.

" —— him!" said Martin Cohu.   " That's not fair
play.   Dismantling shot or I'm a Dutchman!   It's
only devils and Yankees use shot like that.   —— me,
if we don't hang him if we catch him."

John Ozanne tried him with our long gun forward,
but the shot fell short.   In point of metal the Frenchman beat us, and our best hope was to close with him
as quickly as possible.

But he knew that quite as well as we.   He was well
up to his business, and chose his own distance.   His
next shot swept along our deck, smashing half a dozen
men most horribly, and tied itself round the foot of the
mainmast, wounding it badly.   And then I saw for the
first time that most hideous missile, which the Ameri-
cans had introduced, but which other nations declined
to use, as barbarous and uncivilised.   It was a great,
iron ring round which were looped iron bars between
two and three feet long.   The bars played freely like
keys on a ring, and splayed out in their flight, and did
the most dreadful execution.   Intended originally, I
believe, for use only against hostile spars and rigging,
this rascally freebooter put them to any and every

service, and with his powerful armament and merciless ferocity they went far towards explaining his success.

For myself, and I saw the same in all my shipmates, the first sense of dismayed impotence in the face of those most damnable whirling flails very soon gave place to black fury. For the moment one thing only did I desire, and that was to be within arm's reach of the Frenchman, cutlass in hand. Had he been three times our number I doubt if one of him would have escaped if we had reached him. My heart felt like to burst with its boiling rage, and all one could do was to wait patiently at one's post, and it was the hardest thing I had ever had to do yet.

John Ozanne made us all lie down, save when a change of course was necessary, while he did his utmost to get the weather gauge of the enemy. And he managed it at last by a series of tacks which cost us many men and more spars. Then, throwing prudence to the winds, he drove straight for the Frenchman to board him at any cost. It was our only chance, for his heavier guns would have let him plug us from a distance till every man on board was down.

We gave a wild cheer as we recognised the success of John Ozanne's manœuvring, and every man gripped his steel and ground his teeth for a fight to the death.

But it was not to be. Death was there, but no fight. For, as we plunged straight for the Frenchman, following every twist he made, and eager only for the leap at his throat, our little ship began to roll in a sickly fashion as she had never done before, and men looked into one another's faces with fears in their eyes beyond any all the Frenchman in the world could put there. And the carpenter, who had been on deck with the rest, bursting for the fight, tumbled hastily below and came up in a moment with a face like putty.

"She's going!" he cried, and it was his last word. One of those devilish six feet of whirling bars scattered him and three others into fragments and then shore its way through the bulwarks behind. And the winged *Swallow* began to roll under our feet in the way that makes a seaman's heart grow sick.

The Frenchman never ceased firing on us. No matter. It was only a choice of deaths. Not a man among us would have asked his life from him, even if the chance had been given, and it was not.

My last look at the Frenchman showed him coming straight for us. I saw the great forecastle gun belch its cloud of smoke. The water was spouting up in white jets through our scuppers. It came foaming green and white through our gun ports. Then, in solid green sheets, it leaped up over the bulwarks, and for a moment the long flush deck was a boiling cauldron with a bloody scum, in which twirled and twisted dead men and living, and fragments of the ship and rigging.

When I came up through the roaring green water, I found myself within arm's length of the foretopsail-yard, to which a strip of ragged sail still hung. I hooked my arm over it and looked round for my com-

rades. About a score of heads floated in the belching
bubbles of the sunken ship, but even as I looked the
number lessened, for the island men of those days
were no swimmers. A burly body swung past me.
I grabbed it, dragged it to the spar and hoisted its arm
over it. It was John Ozanne, and presently he recovered sufficiently to get his other arm up and draw
himself chest high to look about him. The light spar
would not support us both, and I let myself sink into
the water, with only a grip on a hanging rope's end to
keep in tow with it.

John Ozanne gazed wildly round for a minute, and
then raised his right arm and volubly cursed the Frenchman who was coming right down on us.

"Oh, you devils! You devils! May —" and then
to my horror, for with the wash of the waves in my
ears I could hear nothing, a small round hole bored
itself suddenly in his broad forehead, just where the
brown and the white met, and he threw up his arms
and dropped back into the water.

I made a grab for him, but he was gone, and even as
I did so the meaning of that hideous little round hole
in his forehead came plain to me. The Frenchman
was shooting at every head he could see.

I dragged the spar over me, and floated under the
strip of sail with no more than my nose showing between it and the wood, and the long, black hull, with
its red streak glistening as though but just new dipped
in blood, swept past me so close that I could have
touched it. Through the opening between my sail

HE DREW HIMSELF CHEST HIGH TO LOOK ABOUT HIM

and the spar I could see grim faces looking over the side, and the flash and smoke of muskets as the poor strugglers beyond were shot down one by one.

I lay there — in fear and trembling, I confess, for against cold-blooded brutality such as this no man's courage may avail — till the last shots had long died away. And when at last I ventured to raise my head and look about me, the Frenchman was stretching away to the Northeast and the Indiaman was pressing to the North and both were far away. The sun sunk like a ball of fire dipped in blood as I watched. The long red trail faded off the waters, and the soft colours out of the sky. The sea was a chill waste of tumbling waves. The sky was a cast-iron shutter. The man-hood went out of me and I sank with a sob on to my frail spar, for of all our company which had sailed so gallantly out of Peter Port five days before, I was the only one left, and the rest had all been done to death in most foul and cruel fashion.

CHAPTER XIX

HOW I FELL INTO THE RED HAND

I MUST have fallen into a stupor as the effect of the terrible strain on mind and body of all I had gone through. For I remember nothing of that first night on the spar, and only came slowly back to sense of sodden pain and hunger when the sun was up. Some sailorly instinct, of which I have no recollection whatever, had taken a turn of the rope under my arms and round the yard, and so kept me from slipping away. But I woke up to agonies of cold — a sodden deadness of the limbs which set me wondering numbly if I had any legs left, — and a gnawing hunger and emptiness. I felt no thirst; perhaps because my body was so soaked with water. In the same dull way the horrors of the previous day came back on me, and I wondered heavily if my dead comrades had not the better lot.

But the bright sun warmed the upper part of me, and I essayed to drag my dead legs out of the water, if perchance they might be warmed back to life also. They came back in time, with horrible pricking pains and cramps which I could only suffer lest I should roll off into the water. And if I had I am not at all sure that I would have struggled further, so weary and broken had the night left me.

All that day I lay on my spar, warmed into meagre life by the sun, and tortured at first with the angry clamour of an empty stomach, for it was full twenty hours since I had eaten, and the wear and tear alone would have needed very full supplies to make good. But in time the bitter hunger gave place to a sick emptiness which I essayed to stay by chewing bits of floating seaweed. And this, and the drying of my body by the sun, brought on a furious thirst, to which the sparkling water that broke against my spar proved a most horrible temptation. So torturing was it in the afternoon that the sodden cold of the night now seemed as nothing in comparison, and to relieve it I dropped my body into the water to soak again.

Not a sail did I see that whole day, but being so low in the water my range was of course very limited. In the times when I could get away for a moment or two from my hunger and thirst, my thoughts ran horribly on the previous day's happenings — those hurtling iron flails against which we were powerless — that little round hole that bored itself in John Ozanne's forehead — that cold-blooded shooting of drowning men — the monstrous brutality of it all! What little blood was in me, and cold as that was, surged up into my head at the recollection and set me swaying on my perch.

And then my thoughts wandered off to the poor souls in Peter Port, hopefully speculating on the luck we were like to have, counting on the return of those whose broken bodies were dredging the bottom below me, — to the shocking completeness of our disasters.

Truly, when it all came back on me like that I felt inclined at times to loose my hold and have done with life. And then the thought of Carette, and my mother, and my grandfather, and Krok, would brace me to further precarious clinging with a warming of the heart, but chiefly the thought of Carette, and the good-bye she had waved to me from the point of Brecqhou.

I might, perhaps, with reason have remembered that what had happened to us was but one of the natural results of warfare — barring of course the murderous treatment of which no British seaman ever would be guilty. But I did not. My thoughts ran wholly on the actual facts, and, as I have said, faintly at times, but to my salvation, on Carette and home.

While the sun shone, and the masses of soft white cloud floated slowly against the blue, hope still held me, if precariously at times. At midday, indeed, the fierce bite of his rays on my bare back — for we had stripped for the fight, and I had on only my breeches and belt — combined with the salting of the previous night and the dazzle of the dancing waves added greatly to my discomfort. I felt like an insect under a burn-ing glass, and suffered much until I had the sense to slice a piece off my sail with my knife and pull it over my raw shoulder bones. But when night fell again, the chill waste of waters washed in on my soul and left me desolate and hopeless, and I hardly hoped to see the dawn.

I remember little of the night, except that it was full of long-drawn agony and seemed as if it would never end. But for the rope under my arms and the loop of the sail, into which sometime during the night I slipped, I must have gone, and been lost.

In the morning the sun again woke what life was left in me. I had been nearly forty-eight hours without food or drink, and strained on the edge of death every moment of that time. It was but the remnant of a man that lay like a rag across the spar, and he looked only for death, and yet by instinct clung to life.

And when my weary eyes lifted themselves to look dully around, there, like a white cloud of hope, came life pressing gloriously towards me — a pyramid of snowy canvas, dazzling in the sunshine, the upper courses of a very large ship.

She was still a great way off, but I could see down to her lower foretop-gallant sail, and to my starting eyes she seemed to grow as I watched her. She was coming my way, and I have little doubt that, in the weakness of the moment and the sudden leap of hope when hope seemed dead, I laughed and cried and behaved like a witless man. I know that I prayed God, as I had never prayed in my life before, that she might keep her course and come close enough for some sharp eye to see me.

Now I could see her fore and main courses, and presently the black dot of her hull, and at last the white curl at her fore-foot, as she came pressing gallantly on, just as though she knew my need and was speeding her best to answer it.

While she was still far away, I raised myself as high

as I could on my spar and waved my rag of sail desperately. I tried to shout, but could not bring out so much as a whisper. I waved and waved. She was coming — coming. She was abreast of me, and showed no sign of having seen me. She was passing — passing. I remember scrambling up on to the spar and waving — waving — waving —

. . . .

I came to myself in the comforting confinement of a bunk. I could touch the side and the roof. They were real and solid. I rubbed my hand on them. There was mighty comfort and assurance of safety in the very feel of them.

I lay between white sheets and there was a pillow under my head. I tried to raise my head to look about me, but it swam like oil in a pitching lamp, and I was glad to drop it on the pillow again. The place was full of creakings, a sound I knew right well.

A door opened. I turned my head on the pillow and saw a stout little man looking at me with much interest.

"Ah, ha!" he said, with a friendly nod. "That's all right. Come back at last, have you? Narrow squeak you made of it. How long had you been on that spar?"

"I remember — a night and a day — and a night — and the beginning of a day," I said, and my voice sounded harsh and odd to me.

"And nothing to eat or drink?"

"I chewed some seaweed, I think."

"Must have been in excellent condition or you'd never have stood it."

"What ship?"

"*Plinlimmon Castle*, East Indiaman, homeward bound. This is sick-bay. You're in my charge. Hungry?"

"No." And I felt surprised at myself for not being.

"I should think not," he laughed. "Been dropping soup and brandy into you every chance we got for twenty-four hours past. Head swimmy?"

"Yes." And I tried to raise it but dropped back on to the pillow.

"Another bit of sleep and you shall tell us all about it." And he went out and I fell asleep again.

I woke next time to my wits, and could sit up in the bunk without my head going round. The little doctor came in presently with another whom I took to be the captain of the Indiaman. He was elderly and jovial looking, face like brown leather, with a fringe of white whisker all round it.

In answer to his questions I told him who I was, and where from, and how I came to be on the spar.

"But, by —!" he swore lustily, when I came to the flying flails and the shooting of the drowning men. "That was sheer bloody murder."

"Murder as cruel as ever was done," I said, and told him further of the round hole that bored itself in John Ozanne's forehead right before my eyes.

"By —!" he said again, and more lustily than ever.

"I hope to God, we don't run across him! Which way did he go, did you say?"

"He went off nor'east, but his prowling ground is hereabouts. What guns do you carry, sir?"

"Ten eighteen-pound carronades."

I shook my head. "He could play with you as he did with us, and you could never hit back."

"—— him!" said the old man, and went out much disturbed.

The cheery little doctor chatted with me for a few minutes, and told me that both they and the Indiaman we saw *Red Hand* looting belonged to the convoy we had seen pass three days before, but, having sprung some of their upper gear in the storm, they had had to put into Lisbon for repairs, and the rest could not wait for the two lame ducks.

"Think he'll come across us?" he asked anxiously.

"I'll pray God he doesn't. For I don't see what you can do if he does."

"I'm inclined to think that the best thing would be to let him take what he wants and go. He let the *Mary Jane* go, you say?"

"She went one way and he the other, when he'd sunk us, and we were told he rarely makes prizes. Just helps himself to the best like a pirate. He's just a pirate, and nothing else."

"Discretion is sometimes the better part of valour," he said musingly. "When you can't fight it's no good pretending you can, and this old hooker can't do more than seven knots, and not often that. We've been last dog all the way round. The frigates used to pepper us till they got tired of it," and he went out and I knew what his advice would be if he should be asked for it.

About mid day I felt so much myself again — until I got on to my feet, when I learned what forty-eight hours' starving on a spar can take out of a man — that I got up and dressed myself, by degrees, in some things I found waiting for me in one of the other bunks.

I hauled myself along a passage till I came to a gangway down which the sweet salt air poured like new life, and the first big breath of it set my head spinning again for a moment.

I was hanging on to the handrail when a man came tumbling down in haste.

"It's you," he cried, at sight of me. "Cap'n wants you," and we went up together, and along the deck to the poop, where the captain stood with his officers and a number of ladies and gentlemen. From the look of them they all seemed disturbed and anxious, and they all turned to look at me as if I could help them.

"Carré," said the Captain, as I climbed the ladder. "Look there! Is that the —— villain?" and pointed over the starboard quarter.

One look was enough for me. I had stared hard enough at that long black hull three days before, while it thrashed us to death with its whirling deviltries. And there was no mistaking the splash of red on his foretopsail.

"It's him, Captain," and the ladies wrung their

hands, while the men looked deadly grim, and the captain took a black turn along the deck and came back and stood in front of them.

"It's not in an Englishman's heart to give in without a fight," he said gruffly. "And I'm not in the habit of asking any man's advice about my own business. But from what this man says that ——— villain over yonder can flay us to pieces at his pleasure and we can't touch him" — and he looked at me.

"That is so," I said.

"If we let him have his way the chances are he'll take all he wants and go. If we fight — My God, how can we fight? We can't reach him. What would *you* do now? You've been through it once with him," he turned suddenly on me.

"I'd give five years of my life to have a grip of his throat —"

"And how'd you get there under these conditions, my man?"

"You can't do a thing, captain. And anything you try will only make it worse. He'll send you one of his damnable cart-wheels aboard and you'll see the effect. You know how far your carronades will carry."

"Get you below all of you," he said to his white-faced passengers. "No need to get yourselves killed. He'll probably go for our spars, but when shots are flying you can't tell what'll happen. Stop you with me!" he said to me, and the poop cleared quickly of all outsiders.

The schooner came on like a racehorse. While yet

a great way off a puff of smoke balled out on his foredeck and disappeared before the report reached us.

"That's blank to tell us to stop. I must have more to justify me than that," said the Captain, and held on.

Another belch of white smoke on the schooner, and in a minute our foremast was sliced through at the cap, and the foretopmast, with its great square sails, and their hamper, was banging on the deck, while the jibs and staysail fell into the sea to leeward, and the big ship fell off her course and nosed round towards the wind.

"—— him! That's dismantling shot and no mistake about it. There's nothing else for it. Haul down that flag!" cried the Captain, and we were captive to *Red Hand*.

"Sink his —— boats as he comes aboard, sir!" said one of the mates in a black fury. "He's only a —— pirate."

"I would if we'd gain anything by it," said the Captain grimly. "But it'd only end in him sinking us. Our pop-guns are out of it," and they stood there, with curses in their throats — it was a cursing age, you must remember — and faces full of gloomy anger, as helpless against the Frenchman's long-range guns as seagulls on a rock.

The schooner came racing on, and rounded to with a beautiful sweep just out of reach of our guns. Practice had made him perfect. He knew his damnable business to the last link in the chain.

We could see his deck black with men, and presently a boat dropped neatly and came bounding towards us.

"Depress your carronades and discharge them," ordered a black-bearded young man in her, in excellent English, as they hooked on. "If one is withdrawn we will blow you out of the water."

The guns were discharged. The schooner gave a coquettish shake and came sweeping down alongside the Indiaman. Some of her crew leaped into our main chains, and lashed the two ships together. Then a mob of rough-looking rascals came swarming up our side, and at their head was one at sight of whom my breath caught in my throat, and I rubbed my eyes in startled amazement lest their forty-eight hours' salting should have set them astray.

But they told true, and a black horror and a cold fear fell upon me. I saw the bloody scum swirling round on the *Swallow's* deck as she sank. I saw the heads of my struggling shipmates disappearing one by one under those felon shots from the schooner. I saw once more that little round hole bore itself in John Ozanne's forehead on the spar. And I knew that there was not room on earth for this man and me. I knew that if he caught sight of me I was a dead man.

For the last time I had seen that grim black face — which was also the first time — he was leaning over the rock wall of Herm, watching me steadfastly as I pulled away from him towards Peter Port, and his face was stamped clear on my memory for all time.

It was Torode of Herm, and in a flash I saw at the bottom of his treachery and my own great peril. No wonder he was so successful and came back full from every cruise, when others brought only tales of empty seas. He lived in security on British soil and played under both flags. By means of a quickly assumed disguise, he robbed British ships as a Frenchman, and French ships as an Englishman. That explained to the full the sinking of the *Swallow* and the extermination of her crew. It was to him a matter of life or death. If one escaped with knowledge of the facts, the devilment must end. And I was that one man.

His keen black eyes swept over us as he came over the side. I shrunk small and prayed God he had not seen me.

He walked up to the Captain and said gruffly: "You are a wise man, monsieur. It is no good fighting against the impossible."

"I know it or I'd have seen you damned before I'd have struck to you," growled the old man sourly.

"Quite so! Now, your papers, if you please, and quick!" and the Captain turned to go for them.

All this I heard mazily, for my head was still whirring with its discovery.

Then — without a sign of warning, like one jerked by sudden instinct, Torode turned, pushed through the double row of men behind whom I had shrunk — and they opened quickly enough at his approach — and raising his great fist struck me to the deck like an ox.

When I came to I was lying in a bunk, bound hand and foot. My head was aching badly, and close above me on deck great traffic was going on between the ship and the schooner, transferring choice pickings of the cargo, I supposed, when my senses got slowly to work again.

But why was I there — and still alive? That was a puzzle beyond me entirely. By all rights, and truly according to my expectation, I should have been a dead man. Why was I here, and unharmed, save for a singing head?

Puzzle as I might I had nothing to go upon and could make nothing of it. But since I was still alive, hope grew in me. For it would have been no more trouble to Torode to kill me — less indeed. And since he had not, it could only be because he had other views.

For a long time the shuffling tread of laden men went on close above my head, for hours, I suppose. The sun was sinking when at last the heel and swing of the schooner told me we were loosed and away.

No shot had been fired, save the first one calling the Indiaman to stop, and the second one that drove the command home. To that extent I had been of service to them, bitter as surrender without a fight had been, for an utterly impossible resistance could only have ended one way and after much loss of life.

Long after it was dark a man came in with a lantern and a big bowl of soup, good soup such as we get in the islands, and half a loaf of bread, and a pannikin of water. He set the things beside me, and untied my hands, and placed the light so that it fell upon me, and stood watching me till I had finished.

From his size I thought it was Torode himself, but he never opened his mouth, nor I mine, except to put food into it. When I had done he tied my hands again and went out.

I slept like a top that night, in spite of it all, and felt better in the morning and not without hope. For, as a rule, civilised men, ruffians though they may be, do not feed those they are going to kill. They kill and have done with it.

The same man brought me coffee and bread and meat, and stood watching me again with his back to the port hole while I ate.

It was, as I had thought, Torode himself, and I would have given all I possessed — which indeed was not overmuch — to know what was passing concerning me in that great black head of his. But I did not ask him, for I should not have expected him to tell me. I just ate and drank every scrap of what he brought me, with as cheerful an air as I could compass, and thanked him politely when I had done.

CHAPTER XX

ON the third day of my confinement, and as near as I could tell about midday, the small round port hole of my cabin was suddenly darkened by a flap of sail let down from above, purposely I judged, and shortly afterwards I found the ship was at rest.

It was after dark when Torode came in, and, without a word, bandaged my eyes tightly, and then called in two of his men, who shouldered me, and carried me up the companion and laid me in a boat. The passage was a short one, about as far I thought as, say, from the anchorage at Herm to the landing-place. Then they shouldered me again, and stumbled up a rocky way and along a passage where their feet echoed hollowly, and finally laid me down and went away. Torode untied my hands and feet and took off the bandage.

By the light of his lantern I saw that I was in a rock room, with rough natural walls, and sweet salt air blowing in from the farther end. There was food and water, and a mattress and blanket. He left me without a word, and locked behind him a grating of stout iron bars which filled all the space between floor and roof. I was long past puzzling over the meaning of it all. I ate my food and lay down and slept.

A shaft of sunlight awoke me and I examined my new prison with care. It was a bit of a natural rock passage, such as I had often seen on Sercq, formed, I have been told, by the decay of some softer material between two masses of rock. It was about eight feet wide, and the roof, some twenty feet above my head, was formed by the falling together of the sides which sloped and narrowed somewhat at the entrance. In length, my room was thirty paces from the iron grating to the opening in the face of the cliff. This opening also was strongly barred with iron. The floor of the passage broke off sharply there, and when I worked out a piece of rock from the side wall, and dropped it through the bars, it seemed to fall straight into the sea, a good hundred feet below. The left-hand wall stopped a foot beyond the iron bars, but at the right hand the rock wall ran on for twenty feet or so, then turned across the front of my window and so obscured the outlook. I hated that rock wall for cutting off my view, but it was almost all I had to look at, and before I said good-bye to it I knew every tendril of every fern that grew on it, and the colours of all the veins that ran through it, and of the close-creeping lichen that clothed it in patches.

By squeezing hard against the bars where they were let into the rock on the right, I found I could just get a glimpse of the free blue sea rolling and tossing outside, and by dint of observation and much careful watching I learned where I was.

For, away out there among the tumbling blue waves,

I could just make out a double-headed rock which the tide never covered, and I recognised it as the Grand Amfroque, one of our steering points in Great Russel.

So, then, I was in Herm, not three miles away from Brecqhou, and though, for any benefit the knowledge was to me, I might as well have been in America itself, it still warmed my heart to think that Carette was there, and almost within sight but for that wretched wall of rock. If fiery longing could melt solid rock that barrier had disappeared in the twinkling of an eye.

The time passed very slowly with me. I spent most of it against the bars, peering out at the sea. Once or twice distant boats passed across my narrow view, and I wondered who were in them, and I thought sadly of the folk in Peter Port still looking hopefully for the *Swallow*, and following her possible fortunes, and wishing her good luck — and she and all her crew, except myself, at the bottom of the sea, as foully murdered as ever men in this world were.

Twice each day Torode himself brought me food and watched me steadfastly while I ate it. His oversight and interest never seemed to slacken. At first it troubled me, but there was in it nothing whatever of the captor gloating over his prisoner; simply, as far as I could make out, a gloomy desire to note how I took matters, which put me on my mettle to keep up a bold front, though my heart was heavy enough at times at the puzzling strangeness of it all.

I thought much of Carette and my mother, and my grandfather and Krok, and I walked each day for hours, to and fro, to and fro, to keep myself from falling sick or going stupid.   But the time passed slower than time had ever gone with me before, and I grew sick to death of that narrow cleft in the rock.

By a mark I made on the wall for each day of my stay there, it was on the tenth day that Torode first spoke to me as I ate my dinner.

"Listen!" he said, so unexpectedly, after his strange silence, that I jumped in spite of myself.   "Once you asked to join us and I refused.   Now you must join us — or die.   I have no desire for your death, but — well — you understand."

"When I asked to join you I believed you honest privateers.   You are thieves and murderers.   I would sooner die than join you now."

"You are young to die so."

"Go where you can, die when you must," I answered in our island saying.   "Better die young than live to dishonour."

He picked up my dishes and went out.   But I could not see why he should have kept me alive so long for the purpose of killing me now, and I would not let my courage down.

One more attempt he made, three days later, without a word having passed between us meanwhile.

"Your time is running out, mon gars," he said, as abruptly as before.   "I am loath to put you away, but it rests with yourself.   You love Le Marchant's girl, Carette.   Join us and you shall have her.   You will live with us on Herm, and in due time, when we have money enough, we will give up this life and start anew elsewhere."

"Carette is an honest girl — "

"She need not know — all that you know."

"And your son wants her — "

When you have had no one to speak to but yourself for fourteen days, the voice even of a man you hate is not to be despised. You may even make him talk for the sake of hearing him.

"I know it," said Torode. "I hear she favours you, but a dead man is no good. If you don't get her, as sure as the sun is in the sky the boy shall have her."

"Even so I will not join you."

"And that is your last word?"

"My last word. I will not join you. I have lived honest. I will die honest."

"Soit!" he growled, and went away, leaving me to somewhat gloomier thoughts.

CHAPTER XXI

HOW I FACED DEATHS AND LIVED

On the sixteenth day of my imprisonment, I had stood against my bars till the last faint glow of the sunset faded off a white cloud in the east, and all outside had become gray and dim, and my room was quite dark. I had had my second meal, and looked as usual for no further diversion till breakfast next morning. But of a sudden I heard heavy feet outside my door, and Torode came in with a lantern, followed by two of his men.

"You are still of that mind?" he asked, as though we had discussed the matter but five minutes before.

"Yes."

"Then your time is up," and at a word from him the men bound my hands and feet as before and a cloth over my eyes, and carried me off along the rocky way, — to my death I doubted not.

To the schooner first in any case, though why they could not kill a man on shore as easily as at sea surprised me. Though, to be sure, a man's body is more easily and cleanly disposed of at sea than on shore, and leaves no mark behind it.

I was placed in the same bunk as before, and fell asleep wondering how soon the end of the strange

business would come, but sure that it would not be
long.

I was wakened in the morning by the crash of the
big guns, and surmised that we had run across something. I heard answering guns and more discharges of
our own, then the lowering of a boat, and presently
my port hole was obscured as the schooner ground
against another vessel.

Then the unexpected happened, in a furious fusillade
of small arms from the other ship. Treachery had
evidently met treachery, and Death had his hands full.

From the shouting aboard the other ship I felt sure
they were Frenchmen, and glad as I was at thought
of these ruffians getting paid in their own coin, and fit
as it might be to meet cunning with cunning, I was
yet glad that the payment was French and not
English.

Of the first issue, however, I had small doubts in
view of Torode's long guns and merciless methods,
and though I could see nothing, with our own experiences red in my mind, I could still follow what happened.

The schooner sheered off, and presently the long
guns got to work with their barbarous shot, and pounded
away venomously till I could well imagine what the
state of that other ship must be.

When we ranged alongside again, no word greeted
us. There was traffic between the two ships, and
when we cast off I heard the crackling of flames.

Then there was much sluicing of water above my

head, as our decks were washed down, and presently
there came a rattling of boards which puzzled me
much, until the end of one dipped suddenly across my
porthole, and my straining wits suggested that Torode
was changing his stripes and becoming a Frenchman
once more.

The next day passed without any happening, and I
lay racking my brain for reasons why one spot of sea
should not be as good as another for dropping a man's
body into.

But on the day after that, Torode came suddenly in
on me in the afternoon, and looking down on me as I
lay, he said roughly:

"Listen, you, Carré! By every reason possible you
should die, but — well, I am going to give you chance
of life. It is only a chance, but your death will not lie
at my door, as it would do here. Now here is my last
word. You know more than is good for me. If ever
you disclose what you know, whether you come back
or not, I will blot out all you hold dear in Sercq from
top to bottom, though I have to bring the Frenchmen down to do it. You understand?"

"I understand."

"Be advised then and keep a close mouth."

I was blindfolded and carried out and laid in a waiting boat, which crossed to another vessel, and I was
passed up the side, and down a gangway amid the
murmur of many voices.

When my eyes and bonds were loosed I found myself
among a rough crowd of men in the 'tween decks of a

large ship. The air was dim and close. From the row of heavy guns and great ports, several of which were open, I knew her to be a battleship and of large size. From the gabble of talk all round me I knew she was French.

After the first minute or two no one paid me any attention. All were intent on their own concerns. I sat down on the carriage of the nearest gun and looked about me.

The company was such as one would have looked for on a ship of the Republic — coarse and free in its manners and loud of talk. They were probably most of them pressed men, not more than one day out, and looked on me only as a belated one of themselves. There was — for the moment at all events — little show of discipline. They all talked at once, and wrangled and argued, and seemed constantly on the point of blows, but it all went off in words and no harm was done. But to me, who had barely heard a spoken word for close on twenty days, the effect was stunning, and I could only sit and watch dazedly, while my head spun round with the uproar.

Food was served out presently, — well-cooked meat and sweet, coarse bread and a mug of wine to every man, myself among the rest. There was no lessening of the noise while they ate and drank, and I ate with the rest and by degrees found my thoughts working reasonably.

I was at all events alive, and it is better to be alive than dead.

I was on a French ship of war, and that, from all points of view, save one, was better than being on a King's ship.

The one impossible point in the matter was that I was an Englishman on a ship whose mission in life must to be to fight Englishmen. And that I never would do, happen what might, and it seemed to me that the sooner this matter was settled the better.

Discipline on a ship under the Republican flag was, I knew, very different from that on our own ships. The principles of Liberty, Equality, and Fraternity, if getting somewhat frayed and threadbare, still tempered the treatment of the masses, and so long as men reasonably obeyed orders, and fought when the time came, little more was expected of them, and they were left very much to themselves.

That was no doubt the reason why I had not so far, since I recovered my wits, come across anyone in authority, which I was now exceedingly anxious to do.

It was almost dark, outside the ship as well as inside, when I spied one who seemed, from his dress and bearing, something above the rest, and I made my way to him.

"Will you be so good as to tell me where I sleep, monsieur?" I asked.

"Same place as you slept last night, my son."

"I would be quite willing —"

"Ah, tiens! you are the latest bird."

"At your service, monsieur."

"Come with me, and I'll get you a hammock and show you where to sling it."

And as he was getting it for me, I asked him the name of the ship, and where she was going.

"The *Joséphine*, 40-gun frigate bound for the West Indies."

Then I proffered my request —

"Can you procure me an interview with the Captain, monsieur?"

"What for?"

"I have some information to give him — information of importance."

"You can give it to me."

"No — to the Captain himself, or to no one."

He looked at me critically and said curtly, "B'en, mon gars, we will see!" which might mean anything — threat or promise. But my thoughts during the night only confirmed me in my way.

Next morning after breakfast, the same man came seeking me.

"Come, then," he said, "and say your say," and he led me along to the quarter-deck, where the Captain stood with some of his officers. He was a tall, good-looking man, very handsomely dressed. I came to know him later as Captain Charles Duchâtel.

"This is the man, M. le Capitaine," said my guide, pushing me to the front.

"Well, my man," said the Captain, pleasantly enough. "What is the important information you have to give me?"

"M. le Capitaine will perhaps permit me to explain, in the first place, that I am an Englishman " said I with a bow.

"Truly, you speak like one, mon gars," he laughed.

"That is because I am of the Norman Isles, monsieur. I am from Sercq, by Guernsey."

"Well!" he nodded.

"And therefore, monsieur will see that it is not possible for me to fight against my own country." And I went on quickly in spite of the frown I saw gathering on his face. "I will do any duty put upon me to the best of my power, but fight against my country I cannot."

He looked at me curiously, and said sharply, "A sailor on board ship obeys orders. Is it not so?"

"Surely, monsieur. But I am a prisoner. And as an Englishman I cannot fight against my country. Could monsieur do so in like case?"

"This is rank mutiny, you know."

"I do not mean it so, monsieur, I assure you."

"And was this the important information you had to give me?"

"No, monsieur, it was this. The man who brought me prisoner on board here, — monsieur knows him?"

"Undoubtedly! He has made himself known."

"Better perhaps than you imagine, monsieur. The merchants of Havre and Cherbourg will thank you for this that I tell you now. Torode to the English, Main Rouge to the French — he lives on Herm, the next isle to Sercq, where I myself live. He is the most success-

ful privateer in all these waters. And why? I will
tell you, monsieur. It is because he robs French ships
as an English privateer, and English ships as a French
privateer. He changes his skin as he goes and plunders
under both flags."

"Really! That is a fine fairy tale. On my word it
is worthy almost of la Fontaine himself. And what
proof do you offer of all this, my man?"

"Truly, none, monsieur except myself — that I am
here for knowing it."

"And Main Rouge knew that you knew it?"

"That is why I am here, monsieur."

"And alive! Main Rouge is no old woman, my
man."

"It is a surprise to me that I still live, monsieur, and
I cannot explain it. He has had me in confinement
for three weeks, expecting to die each day, since he
sank our schooner and shot our men in the water as
they swam for their lives. Why, of all our crew, I live,
I do not know."

"It is the strongest proof we have that what you tell
me is untrue."

"And yet I tell it at risk of more than my life, monsieur. Torode's last words to me were that if I opened
my mouth he would smite my kin in Sercq till not one
was left."

"And he told me you were such an inveterate liar
and troublesome fellow that he had had enough of you,
and only did not kill you because of your people whom
he knows," he said with a knowing smile.

Torode's forethought staggered me somewhat, but I looked the Captain squarely in the face and said, "I am no liar, monsieur, and I have had no dealings with the man save as his prisoner." But I could not tell whether he believed me or not.

"And your mind is made up not to obey orders?" he asked, after a moment's thought.

"I cannot lift a hand against my country, monsieur."

"Place him under arrest," he said quietly, to the man who had brought me there. "I will see to him later," and I had but exchanged one imprisonment for another.

That was as dismal a night as ever I spent, with no ray of hope to lighten my darkness, and only the feeling that I could have done no other, to keep me from breaking down entirely.

What the result would be I could not tell, but from the Captain's point of view I thought he would be justified in shooting me, and would probably do so as a warning to the rest. He evidently did not believe a word I said, and I could not greatly blame him.

I thought of them all at home, but mostly of my mother and of Carette. I had little expectation of ever seeing them again, but I was sure they would not have had me act otherwise. It was what my grandfather would have done, placed as I was, and no man could do better than that. Most insistently my thoughts were of Carette and those bright early days on Sercq, and black as all else was, those remembrances shone like jewels in my mind. And when at times I thought of Torode and his stupendous treachery, my heart was

like to burst with helpless rage. I scarcely closed my
eyes, and in the morning felt old and weary.

About midday they came for me, and I was content
that the end had come. They led me to the waist of
the ship, where the whole company was assembled,
and there they stripped me to the waist, and bound my
wrists to a gun carriage.

It was little relief to me to know that I was to be
flogged, for the lash degrades, and breaks a man's
spirit even more than his body. Even if undeserved,
the brand remains, and can never be forgotten. It
seemed to me then that I would as lief be shot and
have done with it.

The captain eyed me keenly.

"Well," he asked, "You are still of the same mind?
You still will not fight?"

"Not against my own country — not though you
flog me to ribbons, monsieur."

The cat rested lightly on my back as the man who
held it waited for the word.

Then as I braced myself for the first stroke, which
would be the hardest to bear, the captain said quietly
to the officer next to him, "Perhaps as well end it at
once. Send a file of marines —" and they walked a
few steps beyond my hearing, for the blood belled in
my ears and blurred my eyes so that my last sight of
earth was like to be a dim one.

"Cast him loose and bandage his eyes," said the
captain, and they set me standing against the side of
the ship and tied a white cloth over my eyes.

I heard clearly enough now and with a quickened
sense.   I heard them range the men opposite to me, —
I heard the tiny clicking of the rings on the muskets as
the men handled them — the breathing of those who
looked on — the soft wash of the sea behind.   But as
far as was in me I faced them without flinching, for in
truth I had given myself up and was thinking only of
Carette and my mother and my grandfather, and was
sending them farewell and a last prayer for their good.

"Are you ready?" asked the captain.   "You will
fire when I drop the handkerchief.   You — prisoner
— for the last time — yes or no?"

I shook my head, for I feared lest my voice should
betray me.   Let none but him who has faced this
coldest of deaths cast a stone at me.

"Present! Fire!" — the last words I expected to
hear on earth.   The muskets rang out — but I stood
untouched.

The captain walked across to me, whipped off the
bandage, and clapped me soundly on the bare shoulder.
— "You are a brave boy, and I take as truth every
word you have told me.   If we come to fighting with
your countrymen you shall tend our wounded.   As to
Red Hand — when we return home we will attend to
him.   Now, mon gars, to your duty!" and to my
amazement I was alive, unflogged, and believed.

Perhaps it was a harsh test and an over cruel jest.
But the man had no means of coming at the truth, and
if he had shot me none could have said a word against
it.

For me, I said simply, "I thank you, monsieur," and went to my duty.

My shipmates were for making much of me, in their rough and excited way, but I begged them to leave me to myself for a time, till I was quite sure I was still alive. And they did so at last, and I heard them debating among themselves how it could be that an Englishman could speak French as freely as they did themselves.

I had no cause to complain of my treatment on board the *Joséphine* after that. The life was far less rigorous than on our own ships, and the living far more ample. If only I could have sent word of my welfare to those at home, who must by this time, I knew, be full of fears for me, I could have been fairly content. The future, indeed, was full of uncertainty, but it is that at best, and my heart was set on escape the moment the chance offered.

I went about my work with the rest and took a certain pride in showing them how a British seaman could do his duty. Our curious introduction had given Captain Duchâtel an interest in me. I often caught his eye upon me, and now and again he dropped me a word which was generally a cheerful challenge as to my resolution, and I always replied in kind. Recollections of those days crowd my mind as I look back on them, but they are not what I set out to tell, and greater matters lay just ahead.

With wonderful luck, and perhaps by taking a very outside course, we escaped the British cruisers, and arrived safely in Martinique, and there we lay for close on four months, with little to do but be in readiness for attacks which never came.

The living was good. Fresh meat and fruit were abundant, and we were allowed ashore in batches. And so the time passed pleasantly enough, but for the fact that one was in exile, and that those at home must be in sorrow and suspense, and had probably long since given up all hope of seeing their wanderer again. For this time was not as the last. They would expect news of us within a few weeks of our sailing, and the utter disappearance of the *Swallow* could hardly leave them ground for hope.

CHAPTER XXII

HOW THE JOSÉPHINE CAME HOME

I HAD ample time to look my prospects in the face while we kept watch and ward on Martinique, and no amount of looking improved them.

My greatest hope was to return to French and English waters in the *Joséphine*. I could perhaps have slipped away into the island, but that would in no way have furthered my getting home, rather would it have fettered me with new and tighter bonds. For in the end I must have boarded some English ship and been promptly pressed into the service, and that was by no means what I wanted. It was my own island of Sercq I longed for, and all that it held and meant for me.

I saw clearly that if at any time we came to a fight with a British warship, and were captured, I must become either prisoner of war as a Frenchman, or pressed man as an Englishman. Neither position held out hope of a speedy return home, but, of the two, I favoured the first as offering perhaps the greater chances.

As the weeks passed into months, all of the same dull pattern, I lost heart at times, thinking of all that might be happening at home.

Sometimes it seemed to me hardly possible that

Torode would dare to go on living at Herm and playing that desperate game of the double flags, while somewhere one man lived who might turn up at any time and blow him to the winds. And in pondering the matter, the fact that he had spared that man's life became a greater puzzle to me than ever. Depressing, too, the thought that if he did so stop on, it was because he considered the measures he had taken for his own safety as effective as death itself, and he was undoubtedly a shrewd and far-thinking man. That meant that my chances of ever turning up again in Sercq were small indeed. And, on the other hand, if a wholesome discretion drove him to the point of flitting, I had reason enough to fear for Carette. He had vowed his son should have her, and both father and son were men who would stick at nothing to gain their ends.

So my thoughts were black enough. I grew homesick and heart-sick, and there were many more in the same condition, and maybe, to themselves, with equal cause.

Just four months we had been there, when one morning an old-fashioned 20-gun corvette came wallowing in, and an hour later we knew that she had come to relieve us and we were to sail for home as soon as we were provisioned. Work went with a will, for every man on board was sick of the place in spite of the easy living and good faring, and we were at sea within forty-eight hours. The word between-decks, too, was, that Bonaparte was about to conquer England, and we were hurrying back to take part in the great invasion. The spirits and the talk ran to excess at times. I neither took part in it nor resented it. My alien standing was almost forgotten through the constant companionship of common tasks, and I saw no profit in flaunting it, though my determination not to lift a hand against my country was as strong as ever.

We had a prosperous voyage of thirty-five days, and were within two days' sail of Cherbourg, when we sighted a ship of war which had apparently had longer or quicker eyes than our own. She was coming straight for us when we became aware of her, and she never swerved from her course till her great guns began to play on us under British colours.

True to those colours, as soon as her standing was fixed, I made my way to Captain Duchâtel to claim performance of his promise.

I had no need to put it into words. The moment I saluted, he said, "Ah, yes. So you stick to it?"

I saluted again, without speaking.

"Bien! Go to the surgeon and tell him you are to help him. There will be work for you all before long."

And there was. The story of a fight, from the cockpit point of view, would be very horrible telling, and that is all I saw. I heard the thunder of our own guns, and the shouts of our men, and the splintering crash of the heavy shot that came aboard of us. But before long, when the streams of wounded began to come our way, I heard nothing but gasps and groans, and saw nothing but horrors which I would fain blot out of my memory, but cannot, even now.

I had seen wounded men before. I had been wounded myself. But seeing men fall, torn and mangled in the heat of fight, with the red fury blazing in one's own veins, and the smoke and smell of battle pricking in one's nostrils, and death in the very air — that is one thing. But tending those broken remnants of men in cold blood — handling them, and the pitiful parts of them, rent and torn out of the very semblance of humanity by the senseless shot — Ah! — that was a very different thing. May I never see it again!

If my face showed anything of what I felt, I must have looked a very sick man. But the surgeon's face was as white as paper and as grim as death, and when he jerked out a word it was through his set teeth, as though he feared more might come if he opened his mouth.

We worked like giants down there, but could not keep pace with Giant Death above. Before long all the passages were filled with shattered men; and with no distinct thought of it, because there was time to think of nothing but what was under one's hand, it seemed to me that the fight must be going against us, for surely if things went on so much longer, there would be none of our men left.

Then with a grinding crash, and a recoil that sent our broken men in tumbled heaps, the two ships grappled, and above our gasps and groans we heard the yells and cheers of the boarding parties and their repellers, and presently from among the broken men brought down to us, a rough voice, which still sounded homely to my ears, groaned:

'Oh, — you — Johnnies! One more swig o' rum an' I'd go easy," and he groaned dolorously.

I mixed a pannikin of rum and water and placed it to his lips. He drank greedily, looked up at me with wide-staring eyes, gasped, "Well —! my God!" — and died.

Captain Duchâtel, as I heard afterwards, and as we ourselves might then judge by the results that came down to us, made a gallant fight of it. And that is no less than I would have looked for from him. He was a brave man, and his treatment of myself might have been very much worse than it had been. But he was over-matched, and suffered too, when the time of crisis came, from the lack of that severe discipline which made our English ships of war less comfortable to live in but more effective when the time for fighting came. I had often wondered how all the miscellaneous gear which crowded our 'tween decks would be got rid of in case of a fight, or, if not got rid of, how they could possibly handle their guns properly. I have since been told that what I saw on the *Joséphine* was common elsewhere in the French ships of war, and often told sorely against them in a fight.

But in such matters Captain Duchâtel only did as others did, and the fault lay with the system rather than with the man. For myself I hold his name in highest gratitude and reverence for he crowned his good treatment of me by one most kindly and thoughtful act at the supremest moment of his life.

I was soaked in other men's blood from head to foot

and looked and felt like a man in a slaughter house. I was drawing into a corner, as decently as I could, the mangled remnants of a man who had died as they laid him down. I straightened my stiff back for a second and stood with my hands on my hips, and at that moment Captain Duchâtel came running down the stairway, with a face like stone and a pistol in his hand.

He glanced at me. I saluted. He knew me through my stains.

"Sauvez-vous, mon brave! C'est fini!" he said quietly through his teeth.

A great thing to do! — a most gracious and noble thing! In his own final extremity to think of another's life as not rightly forfeit to necessity or country.

I understood in a flash, and sped up the decks — with not one second to spare. The upper deck was a shambles. I scrambled up the bulwark straight in front and sprang out as far as I could. Before I struck the water I heard the roar of a mighty explosion behind, and dived to avoid the after effects. When I came up, the sea all round was thrashing under a hail of falling timbers and fragments, but mostly beyond me because I was so close in to the ship. I took one big breath and sank again, and then a mighty swirling grip which felt like death itself laid hold on me and dragged me down and down till I looked to come up no more.

It let me go at last, and I fought my way up through fathomless heights of rushing green waters, with the very last ounce that was in me, and lay spent on my back with bursting head and breaking heart, staring straight up into a great cloud of smoke which uncoiled itself slowly like a mighty plume and let the blue sky show through in patches.

After the thunder of the guns, and that awful final crash, everything seemed strangely still. The water lapped in my ears but I felt it rather than heard. Without lifting my head I could see, not far away, the ship we had fought, gaunt, stark, the ruins of the masterful craft that had raced so boldly for us two hours before. Her rigging was a vast tangle of loose ropes and broken spars, and some of her drooping sails were smouldering. Her trim black and white sides were shattered and scorched and blackened. It looked as though she had sheered off just a moment before the explosion and so had missed the full force of it, but still had suffered terribly. Some of her lower sails still stood, and her crew were busily at work cutting loose the raffle and beating out the flames. But damaged as their own ship was, they still had thought for possible survivors of their enemy, and two boats dropped into the water as I looked, and came picking their way through the floating wreckage with kneeling men in the bows examining everything they saw.

They promptly lifted me in, and from their lips I saw that they spoke to me. But I was encased in silence and could not hear a sound.

I had long since made up my mind that if we were captured I would take my chance as prisoner of war rather than risk being shot as a renegade or pressed into the King's service. For it seemed to me that the chances of being shot were considerable, since none would credit my story that I had been five months aboard a French warship except of my own free will. And as to the King's forced service, it was hated by all, and my own needs claimed my first endeavours.

So I answered them in French, in a voice that thundered in my head, that the explosion had deafened me and I could not hear a word they said. They understood and nodded cheerfully, and went on with their search.

Out of our whole ship's company six only were saved, and not one of them officers.

In the first moments of safety the lack of hearing had seemed to me of small account, compared with the fact that I was still alive. But, as we turned and made for the ship, the strange sensation of hearing only through the feelings of the body, grew upon me; the thought of perpetual silence began to appal me. I could feel the sound of the oars in the rowlocks, and the dash of the waves against the boat, but though I could see men's lips moving it was all no more to me than dumb show.

They were busily cleaning the ship when we came aboard, but I could see what a great fight the *Josephine* had made of it. A long row of dead lay waiting decent burial, and every second man one saw was damaged in one way or another.

My companions were all more or less dazed, and

probably deafened like myself. An officer questioned them, but apparently with small success. He turned to me and I told him I could hear nothing because of the explosion, but I gave him all particulars as to the *Joséphine*, — Captain's name, number of men and guns, and whence we came, and that was what he wanted.

In the official report the saving of six out of a crew of over three hundred was, I suppose, not considered worth mentioning. The *Joséphine* was reported sunk with all on board, and that, as it turned out, was not without its concern for me.

CHAPTER XXIII

THE ship we were on was the 48-gun frigate *Swift-sure*, and of our treatment we had no reason to complain. We were landed at Portsmouth two days later, drafted from one full prison to another, from Forton to the Old Mill at Plymouth, from Plymouth to Stapleton near Bristol, separated by degrees and circumstances, till at last I found myself one more lost soul in the great company that filled the temporary war prison, known among its inmates and the people of that countryside as Amperdoo.

It lay apart from humanity, in a district of fens and marshes, across which, in the winter time, the east wind swept furiously in from the North Sea, some thirty miles away. It cut like a knife — to the very bone. I hear it still of a night in my dreams, and wake up and thank God that after all it is only our own gallant Southwester, which, if somewhat unreasonably boisterous at times, and over-fond of showing what it can do, is still an honest wind, and devoid of treachery. For we were but ill-clad at best, and were always lacking in the matter of fuel, and many other things that make for comfort. Whatever we might be at other times, when the east wind blew in from the sea we were,

every man of us, *âmes perdues* in very truth, and I
marvel sometimes that any of us saw the winter through.

The prison was a huge enclosure surrounded by a
high wooden stockade. Inside this was another stockade, and between the two, armed guards paced day
and night. In the inner ring were a number of long
wooden houses in which we lived, if that could be
called living which for most was but a weary dragging
on of existence bare of hope and love, and sorely trying
at times to one's faith in one's fellows and almost in
God Himself. For the misery and suffering enclosed
within that sharp-toothed circle of unbarked posts were
enough to crush a man's spirit and sicken his heart.

In the summer, pestilential fevers and agues crept out
of the marshes and wasted us. In the winter, the east
winds wrung our bones and our hearts. And summer
and winter alike the government contractors, or those
employed by them, waxed fat on their contracts which,
if honestly carried out, would have kept us in reasonable content.

How some among my fellow-prisoners managed to
keep up their hearts, and to maintain even fairly cheerful faces, was a source of constant amazement to me.
They had, I think, a genius for turning to account the
little things of life and making the most of them, outwardly at all events. But the cheerfulness of those
who refused to break down, even though it might be
but skin-deep and subject to sudden blight, was still
better than the utter misery and despair which prevailed elsewhere.

Outwardly, then, when the sun shone and one's bones were warm, our company might seem almost gay at times, joking, laughing, singing, gambling. But these things covered many a sick heart, and there were times when the heart-sickness prevailed over all else, and we lay in corners apart, and loathed our fellows and wished we were dead.

I say we, but in truth, in these, and all other matters, except the regular routine of living, I was for a considerable time kept apart from my fellows by the deafness brought on by the explosion. I lived in a little soundless world of my own with those dearest to me — Carette, and my mother, and my grandfather, and Krok, and Jeanne Falla and George Hamon. And, if I needed further company, I could people the grim stockade with old friends out of those four most wonderful books of my grandfather's. And very grateful was I now for the insistence which had made me read them times without number, and for the scarcity which had limited me to them, till I knew parts of them almost by heart.

Outwardly, indeed, I might seem loneliest of the company, for cards and dice had never greatly attracted me, and to risk upon a turn of the one or a throw of the other the absolute necessaries of life, which were the only things of value we possessed as a rule, seemed to me most incredible folly. Possibly the personal value of the stakes added zest to the game, for they wrangled bitterly at times, and more than once fought to the death, over the proper ownership of articles which would have been dearly bought for an English shilling. But the loss of even these trifling things, since they meant starvation, inside or out, made all the differences in the world to the losers, and cut them to the quick, and led to hot disputations.

And, though I strove to maintain a cheerful demeanour, which was not always easy when the wind blew from the east, my deafness relieved me of any necessity of joining in that mask of merriment, which, as I have said, as often as not covered very sick hearts. For, though a merry face is better than a sad one, I take it to be the part of an honest man to bear himself simply as he is, and the honest sad faces drew me more than the merry masked ones through which the bones of our skeletons peeped grisly enough at times.

Thoughts of escape occupied some of us, but for most it was out of the question. For, even if they could have got out of the enclosure and passed the sentries, their foreign speech and faces must have betrayed them at once outside.

To myself, however, that did not so fully apply. In appearance I might easily pass as an English sailor, and the English speech came almost as readily to my tongue as my own. It was with vague hopes in that direction, and also as a means of passing the long dull days, that I began carving bits of bone into odd shapes, and, when suitable pieces offered, into snuff-boxes, which I sold to the country folk who came in with provisions. At first my rough attempts produced but pence, and then, as greater skill came with practice, shillings, and so I began to accumulate a small store of money against the time I should need it outside.

In building the prison in so marshy a district, advantage had been taken of a piece of rising ground. The enclosure was built round it so that the middle stood somewhat higher than the sides, and standing on that highest part one could see over the sharp teeth of the stockade and all round the country-side.

That wide view was not without a charm of its own, though its long dull levels grew wearisome to eyes accustomed only to the bold headlands and sharp scarps of Sercq, or to the ever-changing sea. For miles all round were marshes where nothing seemed to grow but tussocks of long wiry grass, with great pools and channels of dark water in between. Far away beyond them there were clumps of trees in places, and further away still one saw here and there the spire of a church a great way off.

When we came there the wiry grass was yellow and drooping, like bent and rusted bayonets, and the pools were black and sullen, and the sky was gray and lowering and very dismal. And in Sercq the rocks were golden in the sunshine, the headlands were great soft cushions of velvet turf, the heather purpled all the hillsides, and the tall bracken billowed under the west wind. And on the gray rocks below, the long waves flung themselves in a wild abandon of delight and shouted aloud because they were free.

Then the east winds came, and all the face of things blanched like the face of death, with coarse hairs sticking up out of it here and there.   The pools and ditches were white with ice, and all the country-side lay stiff and stark, a prisoner bound in chains and iron.   To stand there looking at it for even five minutes made one's backbone rattle for half a day.   And yet, even then in Sercq the sun shone soft and warm, the sky and sea were blue, the fouaille was golden-brown on the hillside, the young gorse was showing pale on the Eperquerie, and the Butcher's Broom on Tintageu was brilliant with scarlet berries.

To any man — even to our warders — Amperdoo was a desolation akin to death.   To many a weary prisoner it proved death itself and so the gate to wider life.   To one man it was purgatory but short removed from hell, and that he came through it unscathed was due to that which he had at first regarded as a misfortune, but which, by shutting him into a world of his own with those he loved, kept his heart sweet and fresh and unassoiled.

In time, indeed, my hearing gradually returned, and long before I left the prison it was quite recovered. But, before it came back, the habit of loneliness had grown upon me, and there was little temptation to break through it, and I lived much within myself.

Many the nights I sought my hammock as soon as the daylight faded, and lay there thinking of them all at home.   To open my eyes was to look on a mob of crouching figures by the distant fire, wrangling as it seemed — for I could not hear them — over their cards and dice.   But — close my eyes, and in a moment

I was in Jeanne Falla's great kitchen at Beaumanoir, with Carette perched up on the side of the green-bed, swinging her feet and knitting blue wool, and Aunt Jeanne herself, kneeling in the wide hearth in the glow of the flaming gorse, seeing to her cooking and flashing her merry wisdom at us with twinkling eyes. Or — in the glimmer of the dawn my eyes would open drearily on the rows and rows of hammocks in the long wooden room, every single hammock a stark bundle of misery and suffering. And I would close them again and draw the blanket tight over my head, and — we were boy and girl again, splashing barefoot in the warm pools under the Autelets; or we were lying in the sunshine in the sweet short herbs of the headlands, with kicking heels and light hair all mixed up with dark, as we laid our heads together and plotted mischiefs; or, side by side, with gleaming brown faces, and free unfettered limbs as white as our thoughts, we slipped through the writhing coils of the Gouliot, and hung panting to the honeycombed rocks while the tide hissed and whispered in the long tresses of the sea-weed.

My clearest and dearest recollections were of those earlier days, before any fixed hopes and ideas had brought with them other possibilities. But I thought too of Jeanne Falla's party, and of young Torode, and I wondered and wondered what might be happening over there, with me given up for dead and Torode free to work his will so far as he was able.

Some comfort I found in thought of Aunt Jeanne, in whose wisdom I had much faith; and in George

Hamon, who knew my hopes and hated Torode; and in my mother and my grandfather and Krok, who would render my love every help she might ask, but were not so much in the way of it as the others. But, if they all deemed me dead — as by this time I feared they must, though, indeed, they had refused to do so before — my time might already be past, and that which I cherished as hope might be even now but dead ashes.

At times I wondered if Jean Le Marchant had not had his suspicions of Torode's treacheries, and how he would regard the young Torode as suitor for Carette in that case. I was sure in my own mind that her father and brothers would never yield her to anything but what they deemed the best for her. But their ideas on that head might differ widely from my own, and I drew small comfort from the thought.

And Carette herself? — I hugged to myself the remembrance of her last farewell. I lived on it. It might mean nothing more than the memory of our old friendship. It might mean everything. I chose to believe it meant everything. And I knew that even if I were dead she would never listen to young Torode if a glimmer of the truth came to her ears, for she was the soul of honour.

Then came a matter which at once added to my anxieties, and set work to my hands which kept my mind from dwelling too darkly on its own troubles.

So crowded were all the war prisons up and down the land, and so continuous was the stream of captives brought in by the war-ships, that death no sooner made a vacancy amongst us than it was filled at once from the overflowing quarters elsewhere.

We had fevers and agues constantly with us, and one time so sharp an epidemic of small-pox that every man of us, willy nilly, had to submit to the inoculation then newly introduced as a preventive against that most horrible disease. Some of us believed, and rightly I think, that as good a preventive as any against this or any ailment was the keeping of the body in the fittest possible condition, and to that end we subjected ourselves to the hardest exercises in every way we could contrive, and suffered I think less than the rest.

As the long hard winter drew slowly past, and spring brightened the land and our hearts and set new life in both, my mind turned again to thoughts of escape. While that bleak country lay in the grip of ice and snow it had seemed certain death to quit the hard hospitality of the prison. It was better to be alive inside than dead outside. But now the stirrings of life without stirred the life within towards freedom, and I began to plan my way.

CHAPTER XXIV

HOW I CAME ACROSS ONE AT AMPERDOO

I HAD worked hard at my carvings, and had become both a better craftsman and a keener bargainer, and so had managed to accumulate a small store of money. I could see my way without much difficulty over the first high wooden stockade, but so far I could not see how to pass the numberless sentries that patrolled constantly between it and the other fence.

And while I was still striving to surmount this difficulty in my own mind, which would I knew be still more difficult in actual fact, that occurred which upset all my plans and tied me to the prison for many a day.

Among the newcomers one day was one evidently sick or sorely wounded. His party, we heard, had come up by barge from the coast. The hospital was full and they made a pallet for the sick man in a corner of our long room.

He lay for the most part with his face to the wall and seemed much broken with the journey.

I had passed him more than once with no more than the glimpse of a white face. An attendant from the hospital looked in now and again, at long intervals, to minister to his wants. The sufferer showed no sign of requiring or wishing anything more, and while his forlornness troubled me, I did not see that I could be of any service to him.

It was about the third day after his arrival that I caught his eye fixed on me, and it seemed to me with knowledge. I went across and bent over him, then fell quickly to my knees beside him.

"Le Marchant! Is it possible?"

It was Carette's youngest brother, Helier.

"All that's left of him, — hull damaged," he said, with a feeble show of spirit.

"What's wrong?"

"A shot 'twixt wind and water — leaking a bit."

"Does it hurt you to talk?"

He nodded to save words, but added. "Hurts more not to. Thought you were dead."

"I suppose so. Now you must lie quiet, and I'll look after you. But tell me — how were they all in Sercq the last you heard — my mother and grandfather — and Carette? And how long is it since?"

"A month — all well, far as I know. But we —" with a gloomy shake of the head — "we are wiped out."

"Your father and brothers?"

"All in same boat — wiped out."

I would have liked to question him further, but the talking was evidently trying to him, and I had to wait. It was much to have learnt that up to a month ago all was well with those dearest to me, though his last words raised new black fears.

I hung about outside till the hospital attendant paid his belated visit, and then questioned him.

"A shot through the lung," he told me, "and a bout of fever on top of it. Lung healing, needs nursing. Do you know him?"

"He is from my country. If you'll tell me what to do I'll see to him."

"Then I'll leave him to you. We've got our hands full over there," and he gave me simple directions as to treatment and told me to report to him each day.

And so my work was cut out for me, and for the time being all thought of escape was put aside.

It was as much as I could do to keep Le Marchant from talking, but I insisted and bullied him into the silence that was good for him, and had my reward in his healing lung and slowly returning strength.

To keep him quiet I sat much with him, and told him by degrees pretty nearly all that had happened to me. In the matter of Torode I could not at first make up my mind whether to disclose the whole or not, and so told him only how John Ozanne and the *Swallow* encountered Main Rouge, and came to grief, and how the privateer, having picked me up, had lodged me on board the *Joséphine*.

I thought he eyed me closely while I told of it, and then doubted if it was not my own lack of candour that prompted the thought.

His recovery was slow work at best, for the wound had brought on fever, and the fever had reduced him terribly, and when the later journeying renewed the wound trouble he had barely strength to hang on. But he was an Islandman, and almost kin to me for the love I bore Carette, and I spared myself no whit in his service, thinking ever of her. And the care and attention I was able to give him, and perhaps the very fact of companionship, and the hopes I held out of escape together, when he should be well enough, wrought mightily in him. So much so that the hospital man, when he looked in, now and again, to see how we were getting on, told me he would want my help elsewhere as soon as my present patient was on his feet again, as I was evidently built for tending sick men.

As soon as Le Marchant's lung healed sufficiently to let him speak without ill consequences, I got out of him particulars of the disaster that had befallen them.

They were running an unusually valuable cargo into Poole Harbour when they fell into a carefully arranged trap. They flung overboard their weighted kegs and made a bolt for the open, and found themselves face to face with a couple of heavily armed cutters converging on the harbour evidently by signal. Under such circumstances the usual course, since flight was out of the question, would have been a quiet surrender, but Jean Le Marchant, furious at being so tricked, flung discretion after his kegs, and fought for a chance of freedom.

"But we never had a chance," said Helier bitterly, "and it was a mistake to try, though we all felt as mad about it as he did. I saw him and Martin go down. Then this cursed bullet took me in the chest, and I don't remember things very clearly after that, till I came to myself in the prison hospital at Forton, with a vast crowd of others. Then we were bustled out and anywhere to make room for a lot of wounded from the King's ships, and I thought it best to play wounded sailor than wounded smuggler, and so I kept a quiet tongue and they sent me here. The journey threw me back, but I'm glad now I came. It's good to see a Sercq face again."

"And the others?" I asked, thinking, past them all, of Carette.

"Never a word have I heard," he said gloomily, "They were taken or killed without doubt. And if they are alive and whole they are on King's ships, for they're crimping every man they can lay hands on down there."

"And Carette will be all alone, and that devil of a Torode — my God, Le Marchant! — but it is hard to sit here and think of it! Get you well, and we will be gone."

"Aunt Jeanne will see to her," he said confidently. "Aunt Jeanne is a cleverer woman than most."

"And Torode a cleverer man — the old one at all events," and under spur of my anxiety, with which I thought to quicken his also, I told him the whole matter of the double-flag treachery, and looked for amazement equal to the quality of my news. But the surprise was mine, for he showed none.

"It's a vile business," he said, "but we saw the possibilities of it long since and had our suspicions of Torode himself. I'm not sure that he's the only one

at it either. They miscall us Le Marchants behind
our backs, but honest smuggling's sweet compared
with that kind of work. And so Torode is Main
Rouge! That's news anyway. If ever we get home,
mon beau, we'll make things hot for him. He's a
treacherous devil. I'm not sure he hadn't a hand in
our trouble also."

"If he had any end to serve I could believe it of
him."

"But what end?"

"Young Torode wants Carette."

He laughed as though he deemed my horizon bounded
by Carette, as indeed it was. "No need for him to
make away with the whole of her family in order to get
her," he said. "It would not commend him to her."

And presently, after musing over the matter, he said,
"All the same, Carré, what I can't understand is why
you're alive. In Torode's place now, I'd surely have
sunk you with the rest. Man! His life is in your
hands."

"I understand it no more than you do. I can only
suppose he thought he'd finally disposed of me by shipping me aboard the *Joséphine*."

"A sight easier to have shipped you into the sea with
a shot at your heels, and a sight safer too."

"It is so," I said. "And how I come to be here,
and alive, I cannot tell."

As soon as the lung healed, and he was able to get
about in the fresh air, he picked up rapidly, and we
began to plan our next move.

We grew very friendly, as was only natural, and our minds were open to one another. The only point on which I found him in any way awanting was in a full and proper appreciation of his sister. He conceded, in brotherly fashion, that she was a good little girl, and pretty, as girls went, and possessed of a spirit of her own. And I, who had never had a sister, nor indeed much to do with girls as a class, could only marvel at his dulness, for to me Carette was the very rose and colour of life, and the simple thought of her was a cordial to the soul.

I confided to him my plans for escape, and we laid our heads together as to the outer stockade, but with all our thinking could not see the way across it. That open space between, with its hedge of sentries, seemed an impossible barrier.

We were also divided in opinion as to the better course to take if we should get outside. Le Marchant favoured a rush straight to the east coast, which was not more than thirty miles away. There he felt confident of falling in with some of the free-trading community who would put us across to Holland or even to Dunkirk, where they were in force and recognised. I, on the other hand, stuck out for the longer journey right through England to the south coast, whence it should be possible to get passage direct to the islands. Whichever way we went we were fully aware that our troubles would only begin when the prison was left behind us, and that they would increase with every step we took towards salt water. For so great had been the waste of life in the war that the fleets were short-handed, and everything in the shape of a man was pounced on by the press-gangs as soon as seen, and flung aboard ship to be licked into shape to be shot at.

Le Marchant urged, with some reason, that on the longer tramp to the south his presence with me would introduce a danger which would be absent if I were alone. For his English was not fluent, and he spoke it with an accent that would betray him at once. He even suggested our parting, if we ever did succeed in getting out — he to take his chance eastward, while I went south, lest he should prove a drag on me. But this I would not hear of, and the matter was still undecided, when our chance came suddenly and unexpectedly.

CHAPTER XXV

WE were well into the summer by the time Le Marchant was fully fit to travel, and we had planned and pondered over that outer stockade till our brains ached with such unusual exercise, and still we did not see our way. For the outer sentries were too thickly posted to offer any hopes of overcoming them, and even if we succeeded in getting past any certain one, the time occupied in scaling the outer palisades would be fatal to us.

Then our chance came without a moment's warning, and we took it on the wing.

It was a black, oppressive night after a dull, hot day. We had been duly counted into our long sleeping-room, and were lying panting in our hammocks, when the storm broke right above us. There came a blinding blue glare which lit up every corner of the room, and then a crash so close and awful that some of us, I trow, thought it the last crash of all. For myself, I know, I lay dazed and breathless, wondering what the next minute would bring.

It brought wild shouts from outside, and the rush of many feet, the hurried clanging of a bell, the beating of a drum, and then everything was drowned in a furious downpour of rain, which beat on the roof like whips and flails.

What was happening I could not tell, but there was confusion without, and confusion meant chances.

I slipped out of my hammock, unhitched it, and stole across to Le Marchant.

"Come! Bring your hammock!" I whispered, and within a minute we were outside in the storm, drenched to the skin, but full of hope.

One of the long, wooden houses on the other side of the enclosure was ablaze, but whether from the lightning or as cover to some larger attempt at escape we could not tell. Very likely the latter, I have since thought, for the soldiers were gathering there in numbers, and the bell still rang and the drum still beat.

Without a word, for all this we had discussed and arranged long since, we crept to the palisade nearest to us. I took my place solidly against it. Le Marchant climbed up on to my shoulders, flung the end of his hammock over the spiked top till it caught with its cordage, and in a moment he was sitting among the teeth up above. Another moment, and I was alongside him, peering down into the danger ring below, while the rain thrashed down upon us so furiously that it was all we could do to see or hear. We could, indeed, see nothing save what was right under our hands, for the dead blackness of the night was a thing to be felt.

There was no sound or sign of wardership. It seemed as though what I had hardly dared to hope had come to pass — as though, in a word, that urgent call to the other side of the enclosure, to forestall an escape or assist at the fire, had bared this side of guards.

We crouched there among the sharp points, listening intently, then, taking our lives in our hands, we dropped the hammock on the outside of the palisade and slipped gently down.

My heart was beating a tattoo as loud as that in the soldiers' quarters, as we sped across the black space which had baffled us so long, and not another sound did we hear save the splashing of the rain.

My hammock helped us over the outer palisade in the same way as the other, and we stood for a moment in the rain and darkness, panting and shaking,—free men.

We made for the void in front, with no thought but of placing the greatest possible distance between ourselves and the prison in the shortest possible time. We plunged into bogs and scrambled through to the further side, eager bundles of dripping slime, and sped on and on through the rain and darkness — free men, and where we went we knew not, only that it was from prison.

For a time the flicker of the burning house showed us where the prison lay, and directed us from it. But this soon died down, and we were left to make our own course, with no guide but the drenching rain. We had headed into it when we loosed from the palisade and we continued to breast it.

No smaller prize than freedom, no weaker spur than the prison behind, would have carried men through what we underwent that night. We ran till our breath came sorely, and then we trudged doggedly, with set teeth, and hands clenched, as though by them we clung to desperate hope. Twice when we plunged into black waters we had to swim, and Le Marchant was not much of a swimmer. But there I was able to help him, and when we touched ground we scrambled straight up high banks and went on. And the darkness, if it gave us many a fall, was still our friend.

But my recollections of that night are confused and shadowy. It was one long plunge through stormy blackness, water above, water below, with tightened breath and shaking limbs, and the one great glowing thought inside that we were free of the cramping prison and that now everything depended on ourselves.

Scarce one word did we speak, every breath was of consequence. Hand in hand we went, lest in that blackness of darkness we should lose one another and never come together again. For the thick streaming blackness of that night was a thing to be felt and not to be forgotten. Never had I felt so like a lost soul condemned to endless struggle for it knew not what. For whether we were keeping a straight course, or were wandering round and round, we had no smallest idea, and we had not a single star to guide us.

It was terribly hard travelling. When we struck on tussocks of the wiry grass we were grateful, but for the most part we were falling with bone-breaking jerks into miry pitfalls, or tumbling into space as we ran and coming up with a splash and a struggle in some deep pool or wide flowing ditch.

There is a limit, however, to human endurance, even where liberty is at stake. We trod air one time, in that disconcerting way which jarred one more than many a mile of travel, and landed heavily in the slime below, and Le Marchant lay and made no attempt to rise. I groped till I found him, and hauled him to solider ground, and he lay there coughing and choking, and at last sobbing angrily, not with weakness of soul, but from sheer lack of strength to move.

"Go on! Go on!" he gasped, as soon as he could speak. "I'm done. Get you along!"

"I'm done too," I said, and in truth I could not have gone much farther. "We'll rest here till daybreak, till we can see where we are."

He had no breath for argument, and we lay in the muddy sedge till our hearts had settled to a more reasonable beat, and we had breath for speech.

"How far have we come, do you think?" Le Marchant asked.

"It felt like fifty miles, but it was such rough work that it's probably nearer five. But it can't be long to daylight. Then we shall know better."

We struggled to a drier hummock and lay down again. The rain had ceased, and presently, while we lay watching for the first flicker of dawn in front or on our left, an exclamation from Le Marchant brought me round with a jerk, to find the sky softening and lightening right behind us. The ditches and the darkness and our many falls had led us astray. Instead of going due east we had fetched a compass and bent round to the north; instead of leaving our prison we had circled round it. And as the shadows lightened on the long, dim flats we saw in the distance the black ring of the stockade on its little elevation.

"Let us get on," said Le Marchant, with a groan at the wasted energies of the night.

"I believe we're safer here. If they seek us it will be farther away. They'd never think we'd be such fools as to stop within a couple of miles of the prison."

And, indeed, before I had done speaking, we could make out the tiny black figures of patrols setting off along the various roads that led through the swamps, and so we lay still, and watched the black figures disappear, to the east and south and north.

So long as we kept hidden I had no great fear of them, for the swamps were honeycombed with hiding-places, and to beat them thoroughly would have required one hundred men to every one they could spare.

"I'm not at all sure it's us they're after," I said, by way of cheer for us both. "All that turmoil last night and the fire makes me think some of the others in Number 3 were on the same job."

"Like enough, but I don't see that it helps us much. Can we find anything to eat?"

But we had come away too hurriedly to make any provision, and we knew too little of the roots among which we lay to venture any of them. So we lay, hungry and sodden, in spite of the sun which presently set the flats steaming, and did not dare to move lest some sharp eye should spy us. We could only hope

for night and stars, and then sooner or later to come
across some place where food could be got, if it was
only green grain out of a field, for our stomachs were
calling uneasily.

Twice during the day we heard guns at a distance,
and that confirmed my idea that others besides ourselves, had escaped, and by widening the chase it gave
me greater hopes.   But it was weary work lying there,
and more and more painful as regards our stomachs,
which from crying came to clamour, and from clamour
to painful groanings, and a hollow clapping together
of their empty linings.

Not till nightfall did we dare to move, and very
grateful we were that the night was fine with a glorious
show of stars.   By them we steered due east, but still
had to keep to the marsh lands and away from the
roads.   And now, from lack of food, our hearts were
not so stout, and the going seemed heavier and more
trying.   It brought back to me the times we had in the
Everglades of Florida, and I told Le Marchant the
story, but it did not greatly cheer him.

Once that night, in our blind travelling, we stumbled
out into a road, and while we stood doubtful whether
we might not dare to use it for the easement of our
bodies, there came along it the tramp of men and the
click of arms, and we were barely in the ditch with
only our noses above water when they went noisily
past us in the direction of the prison.

We made a better course that night, in the matter
of direction at all events, but our progress was slow

for we were both feeling sorely the lack of food, and our way across the flats was still full of pitfalls, into which we fell dully and dragged ourselves out doggedly. We had been thirty hours without a bite and suffered severe pains, probably from the marsh water we had drunk and had to drink.

"Two hundred kegs of fine French cognac we dropped overboard outside Poole Harbour," groaned Le Marchant, one time, "and a mouthful of it now —!" Ay, a mouthful of it just then would have been new life to us. We stumbled on like machines because our spirits willed it so, but truly at times the weariness of the body was like to master the spirit.

"We must come across something in time," I tried to cheer him with — feeling little cheer myself.

"If it's only the hole they'll find our bodies in," he said down-heartedly.

And a very short while after that, as though to point his words, we fell together into a slimy ditch, and it seemed to me that Le Marchant lay unable to rise.

I put my arms under him, and strove to lift him, and felt a shock of horror as another man's arms round him on the other side touched mine, and I found another man trying to lift him also.

"Bon Dieu!" I gasped in my fright, and let the body go, as the other jerked out the same words, and released his hold also, and the body fell between us.

"Dieu-de-dieu, Carré! But I thought this was you," panted Le Marchant, in a shaky voice.

"And I thought it was you."

We bent together and lifted the fallen one to solid ground, but it was too dark to see his face.

"Is he dead?"

"He is dead," I said, for I had laid my hand against his heart, and it was still, and his flesh was clammy cold, and when we found him he was lying face down in the mud.

"He escaped as we did, and wandered till he fell in here and was too weak to rise. Let us go on," and we joined hands, for the comfort of the living touch, and went on our way more heavily than before.

We kept anxious lookout for lights or any sign of humanity. And lights indeed we saw at times that night, and cowered shivering in ditches and mudholes as they flitted to and fro about the marshes. For these, we knew, were no earthly lights, but ghost flares tempting us to destruction — stealthy, pale flames of greenish blue which hovered like ghostly butterflies, and danced on the darkness, and fluttered from place to place as though blown by unfelt winds. And one time, after we had left the dead man behind, one such came dancing straight towards us, and we turned and ran for our lives, till we fell into a hole. For Le Marchant vowed it was the dead man's spirit, and that the others were the spirits of those who had died in similar fashion. But for myself I was not sure, for I had seen similar lights on our masts at sea in the West Indies, though indeed there was nothing to prove that they also were not the spirits of drowned mariners.

CHAPTER XXVI

But — " pas de rue sans but!" as we say in Sercq — there is no road but has an ending. And, just as the dawn was softening the east, and when we were nigh our last effort, we stumbled by sheerest accident on shelter, warmth, and food, — and so upon life, for I do not think either of us could have carried on much longer, and to have sunk down there in the marsh, with no hope of food, must soon have brought us to an end.

It was Le Marchant who smelt it first.

"Carré," he said suddenly. "There is smoke," and he stood and sniffed like a starving dog. Then I smelt it also, a sweet, pleasant smell of burning, and we sniffed together.

Since it came to us on the wind we followed up the wind in search of it, and nosed about hither and thither, losing it, finding it, but getting hotter and hotter on the scent till we came at last to a little mound, and out of the mound the smoke came.

A voice also as we drew close, muffled and monotonous, but human beyond doubt. We crept round the mound till we came on a doorway all covered with furze and grasses till it looked no more than a part of the mound. We pulled open the door, and the voice inside said, "Blight him! Blight him! Blight him!" and we crept in on our hands and knees.

There was a small fire of brown sods burning on the ground, and the place was full of a sweet pungent smoke. A little old man sat crouched with his chin on his knees staring into the fire, and said, "Blight him! Blight him! Blight him!" without ceasing. There was no more than room for the three of us, and we elbowed one another as we crouched by the fire.

He turned a rambling eye on us but showed no surprise.

"Blight him! Blight him! Blight him!" said the little old man.

"Blight him! Blight him! Blight him!" said I, deeming it well to fall in with his humour.

"Ay — who?" he asked.

"The one you mean."

"Ay — Blight him! Blight him! Blight him!" and he lifted a bottle from the ground between his knees, and took a pull at it, and passed it on to me. I drank and passed it to Le Marchant, and the fiery spirit ran through my veins like new hot life.

"We are starving. Give us to eat," I said, and the old man pointed to a hole in the side of the hut. I thrust in my hand and found bread, dark coloured and coarse, but amazingly sweet and strengthening, and a lump of fat bacon. We divided it without a word, and ate like famished dogs. And all the time the old man chanted "Blight him!" with fervour, and drank every now and then from the bottle. We drank too as we ate, but sparingly, lest our heads should go completely, though we could not believe such hospitality a trap.

It was a nightmare ending to a nightmare journey, but for the moment we had food and shelter and we asked no more. When we had eaten we curled ourselves up on the floor and slept, with "Blight him! Blight him! Blight him!" dying in our ears.

I must have slept a long time, for when I woke I felt almost myself again. I had dim remembrances of half-wakings, in which I had seen the old man still crouching over his smouldering fire muttering his usual curse. But now he was gone, and Le Marchant and I had the place to ourselves, and presently Le Marchant stretched and yawned, and sat up blinking at the smoke.

"Where is the old one?" he asked. "Or was he only a dream?"

"Real enough and so was his bread and bacon. I'm hungry again," and we routed about for food but found only a bottle with spirits in it, which we drank.

We sat there in the careless sloth that follows too great a strain, but feeling the strength grow as we sat.

"Is he safe?" asked Le Marchant at last. "Or has he gone to bring the soldiers on us? And is it night or day?" and he felt round with his foot till it came on the door and let in a bright gleam of daylight.

We crawled out into the sunshine and sat with our

backs against the sods of the house, looking out over the great sweep of the flats. It was like a sea whose tumbling waves had turned suddenly into earth and become fixed. Here and there great green breakers stood up above the rest with bristling crests of wire grass, and the darker patches of tiny tangled shrubs and heather and the long black pools and ditches were like the shadows that dapple the sea. The sky was almost as clear a blue as we get in Sercq, and was so full of singing larks that it set us thinking of home.

Away on the margin of the flats we saw the steeples of churches, and between us and them a small black object came flitting like a jumping beetle. We sat and watched it, and it turned into a man, who overcame the black ditches, and picked his way from tussock to tussock by means of a long pole, which brought him to us at length in a series of flying leaps.

"Blight him! Blight him! Blight him!" he said as he landed. "So you are awake at last."

"Awake and hungry," I said.

He loosed a bundle from his back and opened it, and showed us bread and bacon.

"Blight him! Eat!" he said, and we needed no second bidding.

"You are from the cage?" he asked as he sat and watched us.

I nodded.

"All the birds that come my way I feed," he said. "For once I was caged myself. Blight him!"

"Whom do you blight?" I asked.

"Whom?" he cried angrily, and turned a suspicious eye on me. "The Hanover rat, — George! . . . And the blight works — oh, it works, and the brain rots in his head and the maggots gnaw at his heart. And they wonder why! . . . an effectual fervent curse! — Oh, it works! For years and years I've cursed him night and day and—you see! 'Keep him in the dark,' they said. 'Let no man speak to him for a twelvemonth and a day,' they said. And no man spoke, but I myself, and all day long and all night I cursed him out loud for the sound of my own voice, since no other might speak to me. For the silence and the darkness pressed upon me like the churchyard mould, and I kept my wits only by cursing. Blight him! Blight him! And now they say . . . But they may say what they will so they leave me in peace, for I know — and you know —" and he bent forward confidentially — "it's the King that's mad, and soon everyone will know it. Blight him! Blight him! Oh — an effectual fervent curse indeed!"

"We are grateful to you," I said, "for food and shelter. We have money, we will pay."

"As you will. Those who can, pay. Those who can't, don't. All caged birds, I help. Blight him! Blight him!"

"We would rest till night, then you can put us on our way to the coast. This is an ill land to wander in in the dark. Last night we came on one who had strayed and died."

"Where away?" he asked quickly.

"In the marshes — over yonder — about a mile away, I should say."

"Was he clothed?" he snapped.

"Yes, he was clothed."

And he was off with his pole across the flats, in great bounds, while we sat wondering. We could see his uncouth hops as he went to and fro at a distance, and in time he came back with a bundle of clothes tied on his back.

"Food one can always get for the herbs of the marshes," he said, "and drink comes easy when you know where to get it. But clothes cost money and the dead need them not. Blight him!"

Le Marchant begged me to ask if he had any tobacco and a pipe, and I did so. He went inside and came out with a clay pipe and some dried brown herb.

"It is not what you smoke, but such as it is it is there," he said, and Le Marchant tried a whiff or two but laid the pipe aside with a grunt.

"He speaks as do the others from the cage. How come you to speak as we do?"

"I am from Sercq. It is part of England."

"I never heard of it. Why did they cage you?"

"I was a prisoner on a French ship which they captured. I let them believe me French rather than be pressed on board a King's ship."

"Blight him! Blight him!"

That long rest made men of us again. Our host had little to say to us except that the King was mad, and we concluded that on that subject he was none too

sane himself, though in other matters we had no fault
to find with him.

We got directions for our guidance out of him during
the day, and as soon as it was dark he set off with us
across the marshes, and led us at last on to more trustworthy ground and told us how to go. We gave him
money and hearty thanks, and shook him by the hand
and went on our way. The last words we heard from
him out of the darkness were the same as we heard
first in the darkness, — "Blight him! Blight him!
Blight him!" and if they did another old man no harm
they certainly seemed to afford great satisfaction to
this one.

All that night we walked steadily eastward, passing
through sleeping villages and by sleeping farmhouses,
and meeting none who showed any desire to question
us. In the early morning I bought bread and cheese
from a sleepy wife at a little shop in a village that was
just waking up, and we ate as we walked, and slept
in a haystack till late in the afternoon. We tramped
again all night, and long before daylight we smelt salt
water, and when the sun rose we were sitting on a cliff
watching it come up out of the sea.

CHAPTER XXVII

WE wandered a great way down that lonely coast before a fishing village hove in sight. At regular intervals we came upon watchmen on the lookout for invaders or smugglers, and to all such we gave wide berth, by a circuit in the country or by dodging them on their beats. It was only towns we feared, and of those there were fortunately not many. In the villages we had no difficulty in buying food, and to all who questioned, we were on our way to the Nore to join a King's ship and fight the Frenchmen. To cover Le Marchant's lack of speech, we muffled his face in flannel and gave him a toothache which rendered him bearish and disinclined for talk. And so we came slowly down the coast, with eyes and ears alert for chance of crossing, and wondered at the lack of enterprise on the part of the dwellers there which rendered the chances so few.

Many recollections crowd my mind of that long tramp along the edge of the sea. But greater matters press and I may not linger on these. We had many a close shave from officious village busybodies, whose patriotism flew no higher than thought of the reward which hung to an escaped prisoner of war or to any likely subject for the press-gang.

One such is burnt in on my mind, because thought of him has done more to make me suspicious of my fellows, especially of such as make parade of their piety, than any man I ever met.

He was a kindly-looking old man with white hair and a cheerful brown face, and his clothes were white with flour dust which had a homely, honest flavour about it. He was in a small shop, where I went for food one evening, engaged in talk with the woman who kept it, and he began to question me as soon as I opened my mouth.

I told him our usual story, and he seemed much interested in it.

"And you're going to the fleet! Well, well! A dreadful thing is war, but if it has to be it's better on sea than on the land here, and the fleet must have sailors, I suppose. But every night I pray for wars to cease and the good times of universal peace to come."

"Yes," I said, "Peace is very much the best for everyone. It is those who have seen war who know it best."

"Surely! Yet one hears enough to know how terrible it is. You have seen service then?"

"In the West Indies, both battle and shipwreck," I said, having no wish to come nearer home.

"A wonderful land, I'm told, and very different from this country."

"Very different."

"Where do you rest to-night?" he asked in the kindest way possible.

"We are pushing on to lose no time. The fleet wants men."

"Brave men are always wanted, and should be well-treated. A few hours will not hurt the fleet. You shall sup and sleep with me, and to-morrow I will put you on your way in my gig. It is but a step to the mill."

He seemed so gentle and straightforward, and the prospects of a bed and an ample meal were so attractive, that we went with him without a thought of ill.

The mill stood on rising ground just off the village street. I have never passed under the gaunt arms of a mill since without a feeling of discomfort.

The miller's house, however, was not in the mill itself, but just alongside, under its great, bony wings. There was a light in the window and a sweet, whole-some smell all about.

He introduced us to his wife, a very quiet woman, and much less cheerful and hospitable than himself, and bade her hasten the supper and prepare a bed, and we sat and talked while they were getting ready. He showed great concern too, on Le Marchant's account, and insisted on his wife applying a boiling lotion of herbs, which very soon made his face look as bad as anyone could have wished; and in consequence of some hasty words the sufferer dropped during this infliction, I found it necessary to explain that we were from the Channel Islands, but good Englishmen, although our native speech was more akin to French. The old miller was very much interested and asked many questions about the islands, and the land and crops there.

We had an excellent hot supper, with home-brewed ale to drink, and then the old man read a chapter out of the Bible, and prayed at length — for us, and for peace and prosperity, and much more besides. Then we had a smoke, and he showed us to the most comfortable bed I had seen since I left home.

Le Marchant was not in the best of humours. He chose to regard the old man's hospitality with suspicion, and even went the length of casting doubts upon his piety. But I put it down to the heat of the herb lotion, which had made his face like a full blown red rose, and had doubtless got into his blood.

I was very sound asleep when a violent shaking of the arm woke me, and Le Marchant's whisper in my ear — "Carré, there's something wrong. Don't speak! Listen!" — brought me all to myself in a moment, and I heard what he heard — the hushed movement of people in the outer room off which our bedroom opened, the soft creak of a loose board in the flooring.

"Outside the window a minute ago," he murmured in my ear.

Then a sound reached us that there was no mistaking, the tiny click of the strap-ring of a musket against the barrel, and a peaceful miller has no need of muskets.

We had but a moment for thought. I feared greatly

that we were trapped, and felt the blame to myself.
There would be men outside the window but more in
the room, for they looked to catch us sleeping. I had
no doubt, in my own mind, that it was a press-gang,
in which case their object was to take us, not to kill us.
And, thinking it over since, I have thought it possible
that the treacherous old miller may have signaled
them by a light in the top of the mill which would be
seen a very long way.

I peeped out of the window. Three men with muskets and cutlasses stood there watching it. We were
trapped of a surety. Carette and Sercq seemed to
swing away out of sight, and visions of the routine and
brutality of the King's service loomed up very close
in front.

We had no weapons except my sailor's knife, which
would be little use against muskets and cutlasses.
But there was a stout oak chair by the bedside, and at
a pinch its legs might serve.

We could do nothing but wait to see what their move
would be, and that waiting, with the gloomiest of
prospects in front, was as long and dismal a time as
any I have known.

It was just beginning to get light when a tap came
on the door, and the voice of the villainous old miller:

"Your breakfast is ready. We should start in half
an hour."

"Hello?" I asked, in as sleepy a fashion as I could
make it.

He repeated his message, and Le Marchant, with

his ear against the door, nodded confirmation of our fears. The breakfast we were invited to consisted of muskets and cutlasses and hard blows.

It was Le Marchant's very reasonable anger at this treacherous usage that saved us in a way we had not looked for. But possibly there was in him some dim idea of chances of escape in what might follow. Chance there was none if we walked into the next room or tried the window.

Our comfortable bed consisted of sweet, soft hay inside the usual covering. He suddenly ripped this open, tore out the hay in handfuls and flung it under the bedstead, then pulled out his flint and steel and set it ablaze. The room was full of smoke in a moment, and we heard startled cries from the outer room. Taking the stout oak chair by opposite legs we pulled till they parted, and we were armed.

The door burst open and the miller went down headlong under Le Marchant's savage blow.

"Next!" he cried, swinging his club athwart the doorway. But, though there were many voices, no head was offered for his blow.

The flames burned fiercely behind us. With a crack of my chair leg I broke both windows, and the smoke poured out and relieved us somewhat, and the fire blazed up more fiercely still. The flooring was all on fire and the dry old walls behind the bed, and we stood waiting for the next man to appear.

"Better give in, boys," cried some one in the outer room. "You'll only make things worse for yourselves."

But we answered never a word, and stood the more cautiously on our guard.

Then they began throwing buckets of water in at the door, and we heard it splashing also on the outer walls, but none came near the fire, since the bed was not opposite the door.

We were scorched and half smothered, but the draught through the door and out at the window still gave us chance to breathe.

The bedstead fell in a blazing heap, the flames crept round the walls. We could not stand it much longer. We would have to lay down our chair-legs and surrender.

Then a very strange thing happened.

Le Marchant saw it first and grabbed my arm.

The portion of the blazing bedstead nearest the wall sank down through the floor and disappeared, and at a glance we saw our way, though how far it might lead us we could not tell.

"Allons!" said Le Marchant, and without a moment's hesitation leaped down into the smoke that came rolling up out of the hole, and I followed.

We landed on barrels and kegs covered with blazing embers. Le Marchant gave a laugh at sight of their familiar faces, and, by way of further payment to the miller, dashed his heel through the head of a keg and sped on, while the flames roared out afresh behind us.

For a short way we had the light of the blaze, but soon we were past it and groping in darkness down a narrow tunnel way. It seemed endless, but fresh blowing air came puffing up to us at last, and of a sudden we crept out into the night through a clump of gorse on the side of a cliff. Below us was the sea, and on the shingle lay a six-oared galley such as the preventive men use.

"Devil's luck!" laughed Le Marchant, and we slipped and rolled down the cliff to the shore, with never a doubt as to our next move. We set our shoulders to the black galley, ran it gaily down the shingle, and took to the oars. As we got out from under the land, we saw the house blazing fiercely on the cliff. There was a keg in the boat and a mast with a leg of mutton sail. We stepped the mast and set the sail and drew swiftly out to sea.

I do not think either of us ever found a voyage so much to our liking as this. Our craft was but a custom's galley, twenty feet long and four feet in beam, it is true, and we were heading straight out into the North Sea. We had not a scrap of food, but we had fared well the night before, and the keg in the bows suggested hopes. But we were homeward bound, and we had just come through dire peril by the sheer mercy of Providence.

"The old one is well punished for his roguery," said Le Marchant with a relish. "And after his prayers too! Diable, but he stinks!"

"He gave us a good supper, however."

"So that we might breakfast en route for a King's ship! Non, merci! No more mealy mouths for me." And to me also it was a lesson I have never forgotten.

Our first idea had been to run due east till we struck the coast of Holland, which we knew must be something less than one hundred and fifty miles away. But Le Marchant, who knew the smuggling ports better than I, presently suggested that we should run boldly south by east for Dunkerque or Boulogne, and he affirmed that it was little if any farther away than the Dutch coast, and even if it was, we should land among friends and save time and trouble in the end. So, as the weather and wind seemed like to hold, we turned to the south, and kept as straight a course as we could, and met with no interference. The setting sun trued our reckoning and we ran on by the stars.

The keg in the bows contained good Dutch rum, and we drank sparingly at times for lack of other food. Once during the night we heard guns, and our course carried us close enough to see the flashes, but we were content therewith and went on about our business glad to be of small account and unseen.

When the sun rose, there stole out of the shadows on our right white cliffs and a smiling green land, which Le Marchant said was the coast of Kent, so we ran east by south and presently raised a great stretch of sandy dunes, along which we coasted till the ramparts and spires of Dunkerque rose slowly before us.

Le Marchant knew his way here and took us gaily over the bar into the harbour, where many vessels of all shapes and sizes were lying, and he told me what I had heard spoken of on the *Joséphine*, that Bonaparte was said to be gathering a great fleet for the invasion of England.

We landed in a quiet corner without attracting observation, and Le Marchant led the way to a quarter of the town which he said was given up entirely to the smuggling community, and where we should meet with a warm welcome. But, we found, on arriving there, that the free-traders had been moved in a body down the coast to Gravelines, half-way to Calais, all but a stray family or two of the better behaved class. These however, treated us well on hearing our story, and we rested there that day, and left again as soon as it was dark with all the provisions we could carry. We crept quietly out of the harbour and coasted along past the lights of Gravelines, and Calais, and weathered with some difficulty the great gray head of Gris Nez, and were off the sands of Boulogne soon after sunrise.

We kept well out, having no desire for forced service, but only to get home and attend to our own affairs. But even at that distance, and to our inexperienced eyes, the sight we saw was an extraordinary one. The heights behind the town were white with tents as though a snow-storm had come down in the night, and for miles each way the level sand flats flashed and twinkled with the arms of vast bodies of men, marching to and fro at their drill, we supposed.

We dropped our sail to avoid notice and rowed slowly past, but time and again found ourselves floating idly, as we gazed at that great spectacle and wondered what the upshot would be.

Then we were evidently sighted by some sharp lookout on one of the round towers, for presently a white sail came heading for us, and we hastily ran up our own and turned and sped out to sea, believing that they would not dare to follow us far. They chased us till the coast sank out of our sight, and could have caught us if they had kept on, but they doubtless feared a trap and so were satisfied to have got rid of us. When they gave it up we turned and ran south for Dieppe, and sighted the coast a little to the north of that small fishing port just before sunset.

Here Le Marchant was among friends, having visited the place many times in the way of business, and we were welcomed and made much of. We were anxious to get on, but the wind blew up so strongly from the southwest that we could have made no headway without ratching all the time to windward, and the sea was over high for our small boat. So we lay there three days, much against our will, though doubtless to the benefit of our bodies. And I have wondered at times, in thinking back over all these things, whether matters might not have worked out otherwise if the wind had been in a different quarter. Work out to their fully appointed end I knew they had to do, of course. But that three days' delay at Dieppe brought us straight into the direst peril conceivable, and an hour either way— ay, or ten minutes for that matter — might have avoided it. But, as my grandfather used to say, and as I know he fervently believed, a man's times and courses are ordered by a wisdom higher than his own, and the proper thing for him to do is to take things as they come, and make the best of them.

After three days the wind shifted to the northwest, and we said good-by to our hosts and loosed for Cherbourg, well-provisioned and in the best of spirits, for Cherbourg was but round the corner from home.

We made a comfortable, though not very quick passage, the wind falling slack and fitful at times, so that it was the evening of the next day before we slipped in under the eastern end of the great digue they were building for the protection of the shipping in the harbour. It was at that time but a few feet above water level, and its immense length gave it a very curious appearance, like a huge water snake lying flat on the surface of the sea.

We pulled in under an island which held a fort, and keeping along that side of the roadstead, ran quietly ashore, drew our boat up, and went up into the town.

CHAPTER XXVIII

HOW WE WALKED INTO THE TIGER'S MOUTH

CHERBOURG was at that time a town of mean-looking houses and narrow streets, ill-paved, ill-lighted, a rookery for blackbirds of every breed. It was a great centre for smuggling and privateering, the fleet brought many hangers-on, and the building of the great digue drew thither rough toilers who could find, or were fitted for, no other employment.

Low-class wine-shops, and their spawn of quarrellings and sudden deaths, abounded. Crime in fact attracted little attention so long as it held no menace to the public peace. Life had been so very cheap, and blood had flowed so freely, that the public ear had dulled to its cry.

Le Marchant led the way through the dark, ill-smelling streets to a café in the outskirts.

The Café Au Diable Boiteux looked all its name and more. It was as ill-looking a place as ever I had seen. But here it was that the free-traders made their headquarters, and here, said Le Marchant, we might find men from the islands, and possibly even from Sercq itself, and so get news from home.

The café itself opened, not directly off the road, but off a large courtyard surrounded by a wall, which tended to privacy and freedom from observation.

It was quite dark when we turned in through a narrow slit of a door, in a larger door which was chained and bolted with a great cross beam. There were doubtless other outlets known to the frequenters.

Le Marchant led the way across the dark courtyard which was lighted only by the red-draped windows of the café, and opened a door out of which poured a volume of smoke and the hot reek of spirits, and a great clash of talk and laughter.

The room was so thick with smoke that, coming in out of the darkness, I could only blink, though there was no lack of lamps, and the walls were lined with mirrors in gilt frames which made the room look almost as large as the noise that filled it, and multiplied the lights and the smoke and the people in a bewildering fashion.

Three or four men had risen in a corner and were slowly working their way out, with back-thrown jests to those they were leaving. Following close on Le Marchant's heels, I stepped aside to let them pass, and in doing so bumped against the back of a burly man who was leaning over the table in close confidential talk with one opposite him.

"Pardon!" I said, and looking up, saw two grim eyes scowling at me, through the smoke, out of the looking-glass in front.

I gave but one glance and felt as if I had run my head against a wall or had received a blow over the heart. For those fierce black eyes were full of menace. They had leaped to mine as blade leaps to blade,

touches lightly, slides along, and holds your own with
the compelling pressure that presages assault. They
were like thunder-clouds charged with blasting lightnings. They were full of understanding and dreadful
intention, and all this I saw in one single glance.

I gripped Le Marchant's jacket.

"Out quick!" I whispered, and turned and went.

"What — ?" he began.

"Torode of Herm is there."

"The devil! Did he see you?"

"I think so. Yes; he looked at me through the
looking-glass."

"No time to lose then!" and he sped down the yard,
and through the slit of a door, and down the dark road,
and I was not a foot behind him.

"You are quite sure, Carré?" he panted, as we ran.

"Quite sure. His eyes drew mine, and I knew him
as he knew me."

"Never knew him to go there before. Devil's luck
he should be there to-night."

I think it no shame to confess to a very great fear,
for of a surety, now, the earth was not large enough
for this man and me. I held his life in my hand as
surely as though he were but a grasshopper, and he
knew it. And he was strong with the strength of many
purposeful men behind him, every man as heartless
as himself, and Le Marchant and I were but two.
My head swam at thought of the odds between us and
hope grew sick in me.

My sole idea of escape, under the spur of that great

fear, had been to get to the boat and make for home.
But Le Marchant, having less at stake — so far as
he knew at all events — had his wits more in hand,
and used them to better purpose. For, supposing we
got away all right in the dark, Torode's schooner could
sail four feet to our one, and if he sighted us we should
be completely at his mercy, a most evil and cruel
thing to trust to. Then, too, there was La Hague,
with its fierce waves, and beyond it the wild Race
of Alderney with its contrarieties and treacheries
— ill things to tackle even in a ship of size. Le
Marchant thought on these things, and before we
were into the town he panted them out, and turned
off suddenly to the left and made for the open
country.

"We'll strike right through to Carteret," he jerked.
"The boat must go. . . . He'll look for us in the town
and the wind's against him for La Hague. . . . We
must get across before he can get round."

"How far across?"

"Less than twenty miles. . . . There soon after
midnight. . . . Steal a boat if necessary."

We settled down into a steady walk and got our
wind back, and my spirits rose, and hope showed head
once more. If we could get across to Sercq before
Torode could lay us by the heels, we would be safe
among our own folks, and unless I was very much
mistaken, he would no more than visit Herm and away
before I could raise Peter Port against him.

Neither of us had travelled that land before, but we

knew the direction we had to take, and the stars kept us to our course.

We pressed on without a halt, for every moment was of importance, and for the most part we went in silence. For myself, I was already in my thoughts clasping my mother and Carette in my arms once more, and then speeding across to Peter Port to rouse them there with the news of Torode's murderous treachery.

Le Marchant was the more practical man of the two. As we passed some windmills, and came swinging down towards the western coast, soon after midnight, he gave a cheerful "Hourra!" and in reply to my stare, cried, "The wind, man! It's as dead as St. Magloire. Monsieur Torode will never get round La Hague like this."

"It will come again with the sun, maybe," I said.

"Then the quicker we get home the better," and we hurried on.

When we came out at last on the cliffs the sea lay below us as smooth as a clouded mirror. It would mean a toilsome passage, but toil was nothing compared with Torode. We walked rapidly along till we came to a village, which we learned afterwards was not Carteret but Surtainville. There were boats lying on the shore, and we slipped down the cliff before we reached the first house, and made our way towards them. One of those boats we had to use if we had to fight for it, but we had no desire to fight, only to get away at once, without dispute and without delay.

We fixed on the one that seemed the least heavy

and clumsy, though none were much to our liking, and while Le Marchant punted up a pair of spare oars in case of accident, I found a piece of soft white stone and scrawled on a board — "Boat will be returned in two days, keep this money for hire" — and emptied all I possessed on to it. Then we ran the clumsy craft into the water and settled down to a long seven hours' pull.

But labour was nothing when so much — everything — waited at the other end of the course. We bent to it with a will, and I do not suppose that old boat had ever moved so rapidly since she was built.

We had been rowing hard for, we reckoned, close on three hours when the sun rose. The gray shadows drew slowly off the face of the sea, and we stood up and scanned the northern horizon anxiously. But there was no flaw upon the brimming white rim. Torode had evidently not been able to get round La Hague, and a man must have been blind indeed not to see therein the hand of Providence; for a cap full of wind and he would have been down on us like a wolf on two strayed lambs. But now Sercq lay straight in front of our boat's nose, like a great gray whale nuzzling its young, and every long pull of the oars brought it nearer.

There was time indeed for catastrophe yet, and our anxieties would not be ended till Creux harbour was in sight. For, from Cherbourg to Sercq was but forty miles, — but fortunately for us, forty miles which included La Hague and The Race — and if Torode could pick up a fair wind he could do it in four hours —

or, with all obstacles, in five, or at most six — whereas, strain as we might, and we were not fresh to begin with, we could not possibly cover the distance in less than seven hours.   So, given a wind, the race might prove a tight one, and, as we rowed, our eyes were glued to the northern sky-line, where La Hague was growing dimmer with every lurch of the boat, and our hearts were strong with hope if not entirely free from fear.

We toiled like galley-slaves, for though the danger was not visible — as yet, for aught we knew it might appear above the horizon at any moment, and then our chances would be small indeed.   Had any eye watched our progress it must have deemed us demented, for we rowed across a lonely sea as though death and destruction followed close in our wake.

For myself, I know my heart was just one dumb prayer for help in this hour of need.   We had come through so much.   We had escaped so many perils; so very much depended on our winning through to Sercq; and failure at this last moment would be so heart-breaking.   Yes, my heart boiled with unspoken prayers and strange vows, which I fear were somewhat in the nature of bargainings — future conduct for present aid — but which did not seem to me out of place at the moment, and which, in any case, did me no harm, for a man works better on prayers than on curses, I'll be bound.

Sercq at last grew large in front of us, and our hearts were high.   When we jerked our heads over our shoulders we could see the long green slopes of the

Eperquerie beckoning us on, and the rugged brown crests of the Grande and Petite Moies bobbing cheerfully above the tumbling waves, and Le Tas on the other side standing like a monument of Sercq's unconquerable stubbornness.

And these things spoke to us, and called to us, and braced us with hope, though our flanks clapped together with the strain of that long pull, and our legs trembled, and our hands were cramped and blistered.

Then, of a sudden, Le Marchant jerked a cry, and I saw what he saw — the topsail of a schooner rising white in the sun above the sky line, and to our hearts there was menace in the very look of it.

We looked round at Sercq, at the cracks in the headlands, and the green slopes smiling in the sunshine, and the white tongues of the waves as they leaped up the cliffs.

" Five miles!" gasped Le Marchant.

"She must be twelve or more.   We'll do it."

"Close work!"

And we bent and rowed as we had never rowed in our lives before.

The schooner had evidently all the wind she wanted. She rose very rapidly.   To our anxious eyes she seemed to sweep along like a sungleam on a cloudy day. . . . Both her topsails were clear to us. . . . We could see her jibs swollen with venom, and past them the great sweep of her mainsails with the booms well out over the side to take the full of the wind. . . . The sweat poured down us, the veins stood out on us like cords. . . .

Once, in the frenzy of my thoughts, the gleaming white sails on our quarter, and the crisp green waves alongside, and the dingy brown boat, and Le Marchant's fiery crimson neck all shot with red for a moment, and I loosed one hand and drew it over my brow to see if it was blood or only sweat that trickled there.

On and on she came a marvel of beauty, though she meant death for us, and showed it in every graceful venomous line, from the sharp white curl at her forefoot to the swelling menace of her sails.

Her long black hull was clear to us now, and still we had a mile to go. The breath whistled through our nostrils. Le Marchant's face when he glanced across his shoulder was twisted like a crumpled mask. We swung up from our seats and slewed half round to get every pound we could out of the thrashing oars.

We rushed in between the Moie des Burons and the Burons themselves and drove straight for the harbour. For a moment the schooner was hid from us. Then she came racing out again. The tide was running like a fury. We drove swirling through it.

"Ach!" burst out from both of us, as a puff of white smoke whirled from the schooner's bows and a crash behind told us that a point of rock had saved us. . . . The coils of the current, which runs there like a mill-race, gripped our rounded bottom and dragged at us like very devils. . . . It was life and death and a question of seconds. . . . We were level with the remnant of the old breakwater. . . . As we tore frantically at the oars to round it, the puff of smoke whirled out again, ... a crash behind us and chips of granite came showering into the smooth water inside, and a boat that lay just off the shore in a line with the opening scattered into fragments before our straining eyes. . . . We lay doubled over our oars, panting and sobbing and laughing. We had escaped — but as by fire.

A moment for breath, and we slipped over the side, grateful for the cold bracing of the water on our sweltering skins, struggled through the few yards to the mouth of the tunnel, and crept through to the road. We lay there prone till our strength came back, and one full heart, at all events, — nay, I will believe two — thanked God fervently for escape from mighty peril. For no man may look death so closely in the face as that without being stirred to the depths.

"A close thing!" breathed Le Marchant, as we got on to our feet and found the solid earth still rolling beneath us.

"God's mercy!" I said, and we sped up the steep Creux Road, among the ferns and flowers and over-hanging trees.

My heart was leaping exultantly. For Carette and my mother and home and everything lay up the climbing way, and I believed, poor fool, that I had got the better of a man like Torode of Herm.

At sight of us one came running down from Les Lâches where he had gone at sound of the firing, and greeted us with amazement.

"Bon Gyu, Phil Carré! And we thought you dead!

And Helier Le Marchant! Where do you come from? Where have you been all the time?"

"Prisoners of war. We came across from France there. There's a boat in the harbour, Elie, that we borrowed and promised to return. Will you see to it for us?" and we sped on, to meet many such welcomes, and staring eyes and gaping mouths, till we came to Beaumanoir, and walked into the kitchen.

"Oh, bon Dieu!" gasped Aunt Jeanne, and sat down suddenly on the green-bed at sight of us, believing we were spirits bearing her warning.

But I flung my arms round her neck and kissed her heartily, and asked only, "Carette? — and my mother?"

And she said, "But they are well, mon gars," and regarded me with somewhat less of doubt, but no less amazement. And I kissed her again, and said, "Helier will tell you all about it, Aunt Jeanne," and ran off across the knoll, past Vieux Port, to Belfontaine.

I looked across at Brecqhou as I came in sight of the western waters, and said to myself, "In an hour I will be over there to see Carette," and my heart leaped with joy. Away up towards Rondellerie I thought I saw my grandfather in the fields. I jumped over the green bank and came down to the house through the orchard. The door stood wide and I went in. My mother looked up in quick surprise at a visitor at so unusual an hour, and in a moment she was on my neck.

"My boy! my boy!" she cried. "Now God be praised!" and sobbed and strained me to her, and I felt all her prayers thrill through her arms into my own heart.

It was quite a while before we could settle to reasonable talk, for, in spite of her repeated assertions that she had never really given me up, she could still hardly realise that I was truly alive and come back to her, and every other minute she must fling her arms round my neck to make sure.

Then up she jumped and set food before me, in quantity equal almost to the time I had been away, as though she feared I had eaten nothing since I left home. And I had an appetite that almost justified her, for the night had been a wasteful one.

And while I ate, I told her briefly where I had been, and what had kept me so long, and touched but lightly on the matter of Torode, for I saw that was not what she would care to hear.

"And Carette?" I asked. "I know she is well, for Aunt Jeanne told me so"; and she looked up quickly, and I hastened to add: "We had to pass Beaumanoir and I left Helier Le Marchant there. I only stopped long enough to ask if you were all right — and Carette." If I had told her I had kissed Aunt Jeanne before herself, I really believe she would have felt hurt, though I had never thought of it so when I did it.

But her nature was too sweet, and her heart too full of gratitude, to allow long harbourage to any such thoughts.

"Carette," she said with a smile, "has been much

with me. But —" and her face saddened — "you do not know what has befallen them."

"Helier feared they were wiped out."

"Almost. Monsieur Le Marchant and Martin, the eldest boy, got home sorely wounded. They are still there on Brecqhou and Carette is nursing them back to life. But I think —" and there was a touch of pride in her pleasure at it —"she has been here every time she has come across to see Jeanne Falla. She is a good girl . . . and I think she is prettier than ever." But for myself I thought that was perhaps because she saw her with new eyes.

"And my grandfather? — and Krok?"

"Both well, only much troubled about you. I do not think they ever expected to see you again, my boy. Your grandfather has blamed himself, I think, for ever letting you go, and it has aged him. Krok gave you up too, I think, but he has never ceased to keep an eye on Carette for you. I doubt if he has missed going over to Brecqhou any single day, except when the weather made it quite impossible."

"God bless him for that!"

And even as I spoke the door opened and Krok came in, but a Krok that we hardly knew.

He was in a state of most intense agitation. I thought at first that it was on my account, — that he had heard of my arrival. But in a moment I saw that it was some greater thing still that moved him.

At sight of me he stopped as if doubting his senses, —

or tried to stop, for that which was in him would not let him stand still. He was bursting with some news and my heart told me it was ill news. His eyes rolled and strained, his dumb mouth worked, he fairly gripped and shook himself in his frantic striving after communication with us.

My mother was alarmed, but yet kept her wits. Truly it seemed to me that unless he could tell us quickly what was in him something inside must give way under the strain. She ran quickly to a drawer in her dresser, and pulled out a sheet of paper and a piece of charcoal, and laid them before him on the table. He jumped at them, but his hand shook so that it only made senseless scratches on the paper. I heard his teeth grinding with rage. He seized his right hand with his left, and held it and quieted himself by a great effort. And slowly and jerkily he wrote, in letters that fell about the page, — "Carette — Torode —" and then the charcoal fell out of his hand and he rolled in a heap on the floor.

My heart gave a broken kick and fell sickly. It dropped in a moment to what had happened. Failing to end us, Torode had swung round Le Tas and run for Brecqhou, where Carette, alone with her two sick men, would be completely at his mercy. He would carry her off, gather his gear on Herm, and be away before Peter Port could lift a hand to stop him. If I held his life in my hand, he held in his what was dearer far than life to me. And I had been pluming myself on getting the better of him!

"See to him, mother. I must go. Carette is in danger," and I kissed her and ran out.

I went down the zig-zag at Port à la Jument in sliding leaps, tumbled into the boat from which Krok had just landed, and once more I was pulling for life and that which was dearer still.

CHAPTER XXIX

THE race was running furiously through the Gouliot, but I would have got through it if it had been twice as strong. There was a wild fury in my heart, at thought of Carette in Torode's hands, which ravened for opposition — for something, anything, to rend and tear and overcome.

If I had come across Torode himself I would have hurled myself at his throat, though all his ruffians stood between, and had I clutched it they had hacked my hands off before I had let go.

I whirled up to the Galé de Jacob before prudence told me that two men armed are of more account than one man with nothing but a heart on fire, and that it would have been good to run round for Le Marchant. But my one thought had been to get to the place where Carette was in extremity, and the fire within me felt equal to all it might encounter.

I climbed the rocky way hot-foot, and sped down through the furze and golden-rod to the house. The door was open and I ran in. A drawn white face, with grizzled hair and drooping white moustache, and two dark eyes like smouldering fires, jerked feebly up out of a bunk at the far end, and then sank down again. It was Jean Le Marchant.

There was no sign of disorder in the room. In the next bunk another man lay apparently asleep.

"Where is Carette?" I asked hastily, but not without hope, from the lack of signs of disturbance.

"Where is she?" he asked feebly, with a touch of impatience.

"Is she not here?"

"She went out. I thought I heard a shot. Where is she?"

"I will go and see," and I ran out again, still not unhopeful. It might be that Krok had seen Torode's ship and his fears for Carette had magnified matters.

I searched quickly all round the house. I cried "Carette! Carette!" But only a wheeling gull squawked mockingly in reply. Then I ran along the trodden way to their landing-place. There was a boat lying there with its nose on the shore, — no sign of outrage anywhere. Could Krok be mistaken? Could Carette just have rowed over to Havre Gosselin for something she was in need of?

I went down to the boat doubtful of my next move.

In the boat that nosed the shore lay Helier Le Marchant, my comrade in prison, in escape, in many perils, with a bullet hole in his forehead — dead. And I knew that Krok was right and my worst fears were justified.

Torode had landed, had caught Carette abroad, in carrying her off they had met Le Marchant hastening to her assistance, and had slain him, — the foul cowards that they were.

There was nothing I could do for him. I lifted him gently out on to the shingle, and turned to and pulled out of the harbour. Others I knew would soon be across to Brecqhou, and would see to him and the rest. My work lay on Herm, and as like as not might end there, for death as sudden and certain as Helier Le Marchant's awaited me if Torode set eyes on me, and that I knew full well.

Had my brain been working quietly I should probably have doubted the wisdom of crossing to Herm in daylight. But all my thoughts were in a vast confusion, with this one thought only overtopping all the rest, — Carette was in the hands of Torode and I must get there as quickly as possible.

There are times when foolish recklessness drives headlong through the obstacles which reason would bid one avoid, and so come desperate deeds accomplished while reason sits pondering the way.

I have since thought that the only possible reason why I succeeded in crossing unseen was that the boiling anxiety within drove me to the venture at once. I followed so closely on their track that they had not yet time to take precautions, which presently they did. But at the time, my one and only thought — the spring and spur of all my endeavour was this — Carette was on Herm and I must get there too.

The toil of rowing, however, relieved my brain by degrees to the point of reasonable thinking. One unarmed man against a multitude must use such strategy as he can devise, and so such little common

sense as was left me took me in under the Fauconnière
by Jethou, and then cautiously across the narrow
channel to the tumbled masses of dark rock on the
eastern side of Herm. Here were hiding-places in
plenty, and I had no difficulty in poling my boat up
a ragged cleft where none could see it save from the
entrance. And here I was safe enough, for all the
living was on the other side of the island, the side which
lay towards Guernsey.

Instinct, I suppose, and the knowledge of what I
myself would have done in Torode's place, told me
what he would do. And, crawling cautiously about
my hiding-place, and peering over the rocks, I presently saw a well-manned boat row out from the channel
between Herm and Jethou, and lie there in wait for
anything that might attempt the passage from Sercq
to Peter Port.

Nothing would pass that day, that was certain, for
Torode would imagine Sercq buzzing with the news
of his treacheries and bursting to set Peter Port on
him. I had got across only just in time.

On the other side of the island I could imagine all
that was toward — the schooner loading rapidly with
all they wished to take away, the bustle and traffic
between shore and ship, and Carette prisoner either
on board or in one of the houses, — or, as likely as
not, to have her out of the way, in my old cleft in the
rock.

I wondered how long their preparations would take,
for all my hopes depended on that. If they cleared

out before dark I was undone. If they stayed the night I might have a chance.

It was about midday now. Could they load in time to thread their way through the maze of hidden rocks that strew the passages to the sea, and try the skilful pilot even in the daytime? I thought not. I hoped not. He would be a reckless or a sorely pressed man who attempted it. And with his boat on the watch there, and no word able to get to Peter Port unless after dark, and the time necessary for an organized descent on Herm, I thought Torode would risk it and lie there quietly till perhaps the early morning.

It was a time of weary waiting, with nothing to do but think of Carette's distress, and watch the white clouds sailing slowly along the blue sky, while my boat rose high and fell low in the black cleft, now ten feet up with a rush and a swirl, then as many feet down, with deep gurglings and rushing waterfalls from every ledge. She was getting sorely bruised against the rough rock walls in spite of all my fendings, but there was no help for it.

I could make no plans till I knew where Carette was lodged, and that I could not learn until it was dark, and I remembered gratefully that the new moon was not due for several days yet.

In thinking over things while I lay waiting, I took blame to myself, and felt very great regret, that I had not taken the time to see my grandfather and tell him about Torode. For if the night saw the end of me, as it very well might, no other was cognisant of the matter and Torode would go unpunished. But go he would I felt sure, for he would never believe that it was all still locked up in me. Of course Helier Le Marchant might have told Jeanne Falla. But even then Jeanne Falla would only have on hearsay from Helier what he had heard from me, whereas I was an eye-witness, and could swear to the facts. And yet I could not but feel that if I had not got across to Herm when I did, I should not have got across at all, and Carette's welfare was more to me than the punishment of Torode.

That day seemed as if it never would end. Sercq and Brecqhou lay basking in the sun, as though no tragedies lurked behind their rounded bastions. The sun seemed fixed in the sky. The shadows wheeled so slowly that only by noting them against the seams in the rocks could I be sure that they moved at all. Then even that was denied me, as the headland, in a cleft of whose feet I lay, cut off the light, and flung its shadow out over the sea.

"But — pas de rue sans but." At last the red beams struck level across the water, and all heads of Sercq and the black rocks of Brecqhou were touched with golden fire. I could see the Autelets flaming under the red Saignie cliffs; and the green bastion of Tintageu; and the belt of gleaming sand in Grande Grève; and the razor back of the Coupée; and the green heights above Les Fontaines; and all the sentinel rocks round Little Sercq.

And then the colours faded and died, and Brecqhou

became a part of Sercq once more, and both were folded softly in a purple haze, and soon they were shadows, and then they were gone. And I could not but think that I might never see them again; and if I did not, that was just how I would have wished to see them for the last time.

CHAPTER XXX

HOW I FOUND MY LOVE IN THE CLEFT

I WAITED till the night seemed growing old to me, for the waiting in that dark cleft was weary work, with the water, which I could no longer see, swelling and sinking beneath me, carrying me up and up and up, bumping and grinding against the unseen rocks, then down and down and down into the depths, wet and wallowing, and fearful every moment of a wound beyond repair to my frail craft.

But at last I could wait no longer. With my hands on the rough wet walls I hauled out of the cleft and started on my search for Carette.

The shore thereabouts was a honeycomb of sharp-toothed rocks. I took an oar over the stern and sculled slowly and silently out from the land. I turned to the north and felt my way among the rocks, grazing here, bumping there, but moving so gently that no great harm was done.

I knew at last, by the changed voice of the sea on the shore, that I had come to the first beach of shells, and there I turned the boat's nose in and ran her softly aground.

Here, where the heights of Herm run down in green slopes to the long flat beaches, I drew the boat well up and crept to the other side of the island, keeping as close to the high ground as I dared.

As soon as I came out on the western side I saw that work was still going on busily in the little roadstead, and so far I was in time. The rocky heights sloped gradually on that side also. The schooner had to lie in the roads, and everything had to be conveyed to her by boat. There was much traffic between her and the shore, and the work was carried on by the light of many lamps.

Now where would they have stowed Carette? On the ship? In one of the cottages? In the natural prison where they had kept me? The only three possibilities I had been able to think of. To reduce them to two I would try the least hazardous first, and that was the prison in the rock.

I had been carried to and from it blindfolded, but from what I had seen from its windows I had formed a general idea as to where it lay. So I crept back halfway towards the shell beach and then struck cautiously up towards the tumbled masses of rock on the eastern side of the island.

It was chancy work at best, with a possible stumble up against death at every step. But life without Carette — worse still, life with Carette in thrall to young Torode — would be worse to me than death, and so I take no credit to myself for risking it for her. It was hers already, it did but seek its own.

In daylight I could have gone almost straight to that cleft, steering my course by the sea rocks I had noted

from the window. But in the dark it was different.
I could only grope along in hope with many a stop to
wonder where I had got to, and many a stumble and
many a bruise. Stark darkness is akin to blindness,
and blindness in a strange land, and that a land of
rocks and chasms, is a vast perplexity. I wandered
blindly and bruised myself sorely, but suffered most
from thought of the passing minutes. For the minutes
in which I might accomplish anything were numbered
and they passed with no result.

I was half minded to give up search for the cleft and
steal down to the houses and see what I could learn
there. And yet I was drawn most strongly to that
cleft in the rock.

If only I could find it and satisfy myself!

My wandering thoughts and wandering body came
to sudden and violent pause at bottom of a chasm. I
had stepped incautiously and found myself a mass of
bruises on the rocks below. I felt sore all over, but I
could stand and I could stretch my arms, so no bones
were broken.

I rubbed the sorest bruises into some approach to
comfort, and wondered where I had got to. I could
feel rock walls on either side, and the rocks below
seemed roughly levelled. With a catch of the breath,
which spelled a mighty hope, I began to grope my way
along, and found that the way sloped up and down.
I turned and groped up it. On, and on, and on, and
at last I brought up suddenly against iron bars, and
knew where I was. And never sure to any man was

the feel of iron bars so grateful as was the touch of these to me.

I shook them gently, but the gate was locked. I strained my ears for any sound inside, strained them so that I heard the breaking of the waves on the rock below the window at the other end of the rock chamber.

Then I cried softly, "Carette!" — and listened — and thought I heard a movement.

"Carette!" I cried again.

And out of that blessed darkness, and the doubt and the bewilderment, came the sweetest voice in all the world, in a scared whisper, as one doubtful of her own senses.

"Who is it? Who calls?"

"It is I, Carette — Phil Carré," — and in a moment she was against the bars, and my hands touched hers and hers touched me.

"Phil!" she cried, in vast amazement, and clung tight to my hands to make sure. "Is it possible? Oh, my dear, is it truly, truly you? I knew your voice, but — I thought I dreamed, and then I thought it the voice of the dead. You are not dead, Phil?" with a doubtful catch in her breath as though a doubt had caught her suddenly by the throat.

"But no! I am not dead, my dear one," and I drew the dear, little hands through the bars and covered them with hot kisses.

"But how come you here, Phil? What brings you here?"

"You yourself, Carette. What else?"

"Bon Dieu, but it is good to hear you again, Phil! Can you get me out? They carried me off this morning —"

"I know. I reached Sercq this morning, and Krok brought us the word an hour later. I have been trying ever since to find where you were. I knew this place for I was prisoner here myself for many weeks."

"You, Phil?"

"Truly, yes. This Torode is a murderer and worse. He fights under both flags. He is Main Rouge in France and Torode of Herm. He slaughtered John Ozanne and all our crew before my eyes, and why my life was spared I know not."

"If he sees you he will kill you."

"Or I kill him."

"Phil, he will kill you. Oh, go! — go quick and rouse the Sercq men and Peter Port. You need not fear for me. I will never wed with young Torode — not if they kill me for it —"

And my heart was glad in spite of its heaviness and perplexity.

"When will they come to you again, Carette? And who is it comes?"

"A woman — Madame, I suppose. She brought me my supper. I think they are going away."

"Yes, they are going. They are going because I have come back alive, and Torode knows the game is up if I get to Peter Port."

And that started her off again on that string, but I understood the tune of it quite well.

"That is it," she urged. "Get across to Peter Port, Phil, and rouse them there, and stop their going." But she only said it to get me away out of danger, and I knew it.

"Peter Port can wait the news, and Torode can wait his dues. I am not going till I take you with me, Carette."

"They will kill you," she cried, and let go my hands to wring her own.

"Not if I can help it," I said stubbornly. "I want to live and I want you, and God fights on the right side. If they do get you away, Carette, remember that if I am alive I will follow you to the end of the world."

"They will kill you," she repeated.

"They are very busy loading the schooner. If the woman comes to you in the morning I shall be able to get you out. My boat waits on the shell beach."

"You would do better to get round to Peter Port," she persisted.

"Torode would be off before they would be ready. If it was one man to convince he would act, but where there are many time is wasted. I will see you safe first and then see to Torode," and seeing that I was fixed on this she urged my going no more.

She gave me her hands again through the bars and I kissed them, and kissed them again and again, and would not let them go. That which lay just ahead of us was heavy with possibilities of separation and death, but I had never tasted happiness so complete as I did through those iron bars. The rusty bars could keep us apart, but they could not keep the pure hot love that filled us from head to foot from thrilling through by way of our clasped hands.

"Kiss me, Phil!" she said, of a sudden.

And I pressed my face into the rough bars, and could just touch her sweet lips with mine.

"We may never come closer, dear," she said. "But if they kill you I will follow soon, and — oh, it is good to feel you here."

When the first wild joy of our uncovered hearts permitted us to speak of other things, she had much to ask and I much to tell. I told her most of my story, but said no word as yet of her brother Helier, for she had quite enough to bear.

And through all her askings I could catch unconscious glimpses of the faith and hope and love she had borne for me all through those weary months. She had never believed me dead, she said, though John Ozanne and all his men had long since been given up in Peter Port.

"Your mother and I hoped on, Phil, in spite of them all, for the world was not all dark to us, and if you had been dead I think it would have been."

"And it was thought of you, Carette, — of you and my mother, that kept my heart up in the prison. It was weary work, but when I thought of you I felt strong and hopeful."

"I am glad," she said simply. "We have helped one another."

"And we will do yet. I am going to get you out of this."

"The good God help you!"

When the night began to thin I told her I must go, though it would not be out of hearing.

"Be ready the moment I open the gate," I said, "for every second will be of consequence. Now, good-by, dearest!" and we kissed once more through the rusty bars, and I stole away.

The passage in the rock which led up to the gate was a continuation of the natural cleft which formed the chamber. The slope of the rocks left the gateway no more than eight or nine feet high, though, at the highest point inside, the roof of the chamber was perhaps twenty feet above the floor. The same slope continued outside, so that the side walls of the passage were some eight or nine feet high, and fell almost straight to the rock flooring. Both cleft and passage were made, I think, like the clefts and caves on Sercq, by the decay of a softer vein of rock in the harder granite, so leaving, in course of time, a straight cleavage, which among the higher rocks formed the chamber, and on the lower slope formed the passage up to it.

My very simple plan was to lie in wait, crouched flat upon the top wall of the passage close to the gateway, and from there to spring down upon the unsuspecting warder whoever it might be — Torode, or his wife, or any other. And by such unlooked for attack I hoped to win the day, even though it should be Torode himself who came. But I did not believe it would be Torode, for he had his hands full down below, and Carette was to him only a very secondary matter.

I half hoped it might be young Torode, for the hurling of my hatred on him would have been grateful to me. But I thought it would be the mother, and in that case, though I would use no more violence than might be necessary, nothing should keep me from Carette.

I lay flat on the rough rock wall and waited.

"Carette!" I whispered.

"Phil!"

"I am here just above you, dearest. When you hear them coming, be ready."

The thin darkness was becoming gray. In the sky up above, little clouds were forming out of the shadows, and presently they were flecked with pink and all reached out towards the rising sun. The rocks below me began to show their heads. It was desperately hard work waiting. I hungered anxiously for some one to come and let me be doing.

What if they left her till the very last, and only came up, several of them, to hurry her on board the schooner? The possibility of that chilled me more than the morning dews. My face pinched with anxiety in accord with my heart. I felt grim and hard and fit for desperate deeds.

And now it was quite light, and I could see across

the lower slope of rocks to St. Sampson's Harbour and the flat lands beyond it.

Would they never come? Hell is surely an ever-lasting waiting for something that never comes.

I was growing sick with anxiety when at last the blessed sound of footsteps on the rocky path came to me, and in a moment I was Phil Carré again, and Carette Le Marchant, the dearest and sweetest girl in all the world, was locked behind iron bars just below me, and I was going to release her or die for it.

But my heart gave a triumphant jump, and there was no need to think of death, for the coming one was a woman, and she came up the ascent with bent head and carried food in her hands.

I let her get right to the gate, then, from my knees, launched myself on to her and she went down against the bars in a heap, bruising her face badly. But Carette was all my thought. Before the woman knew what had struck her, I had her hands tied behind her with twisted strips of her own apron, and had gagged her with a bunch of the same, and had the key in the lock, and Carette was free.

The woman was dazed still with her fall. We bound her feet with a strip of blanket and laid her on the bed, locked the gate again behind us, and sped down the rocky way till a gap let us out into the open. Then swiftly among the humps of rock, hand in hand, down the slope, towards the shell beach where the boat lay. I had left it close under the last of the high ground, and had drawn it well up out of reach of the tide, as I believed. But there was no boat there. The beach lay shining in the sun, bare and white, and my heart gave a jerk of dismay.

"There it is," panted Carette, pointing the opposite way along the shore. And there, among a tumbled heap of rocks, whose heads just showed above the water, I saw my boat mopping and mowing at me in the grip of the tide.

I ran along to the nearest point on the beach, calling over my shoulder to Carette, — "If they come after you, take to the water. I will pick you up," — and dashed in as we used to do in the olden days, till the water tripped me up, and then swam my fastest for the boat, and thanked God that swimming came so natural to me.

I had the boat back to the beach and Carette aboard within a few minutes, and we each took an oar and pulled for Brecqhou with exultant hearts. We thought our perils were past—and they were but just beginning.

For as we cleared the eastern point which juts out into the sea, and opened Jethou and the dark channel between the two islands, our eyes lighted together on a boat which was just about to turn the corner into the Herm Roadstead. Another minute and it would have been gone and we should have been free.

I stopped rowing and made to back in again out of sight, but it was not to be. They sighted us at the same moment, and in an instant were tugging at their oars to get their boat round while we bent and pulled for our lives.

Fortunately for us the tide was running swiftly between the islands, and the time it took them to get round gave us a start.   Moreover, their course, till they got clear of the land, was set thick with perils, and they had to go cautiously, while nothing but clear sea lay between us and Brecqhou.

CHAPTER XXXI

HOW I HELD THE NARROW WAY

AND so, once again I was pulling for dear life, and now indeed for more than life, with death, and more than death, coming on astern in venomous jerks and vicious leaps.

Carette's soft hands were not equal to work of this kind, and she saw it. There were but the two oars in the boat. I bade her hand me hers and she did it instantly, sliding it along to my rowlock and losing but a single stroke.

The odds were somewhat against us, but not so much as I feared. For, if I was single-handed against their six oars, their boat was heavier, and carried four armed men in addition to the oarsmen.

But I saw that Brecqhou would be impossible to us, and, moreover, must prove but a cul-de-sac if we got there, for at best there were but two sick men there, and they could give us no help. The house indeed might offer us shelter for a time, but the end would only be delayed. So I edged off from Brecqhou, thinking to run for Havre Gosselin, and then, with senses quickened to the occasion, I saw that Havre Gosselin would serve us no better.

Port és Saies, Grande Grève, Vermandés, Les Fontaines, Port Gorey, — I ran them rapidly through my mind and saw the same objection to all. For in all the ascent to the high lands was toilsome and difficult, and one, so climbing, could be picked off with a musket from below as easily as a rabbit or a sitting gull. And that any mercy would be shown, to one of us at all events, I did not for one moment delude myself. I saw again the round hole bore itself in John Ozanne's forehead, and Helier Le Marchant's dead body lying in the boat.

But past Gorey, where the southwest gales have bitten deep into the headlands, there were places where a quick leap might carry one ashore at cost of one's boat, and then among the ragged black rocks a creeping course might be found where bullets could not follow.

So I turned for Little Sercq, and rowed for dear life and that which was dearer still, and the venomous prow behind followed like a hound on the scent.

The black fangs of Les Dents swept past us. La Baveuse lay ahead. If I could get past Moie de Bretagne before they could cripple me I would have good hope, for thereabouts the sea was strewn with rocks and I knew my way as they did not.

They were gaining on me, but not enough for their liking. I saw the glint of a musket barrel in the sun.

"Lie down, dearest," I said sharply.

But she had seen it too and understood.

"I will not," she said. "The wind is with us and I help."

But in her mind she believed they would not shoot her, and she sat between me and them.

It was no time for argument. Safety for both of us lay in my arms and legs, and their power to gain a landing and get up the slope before the others could damage them. I accepted her sacrifice, and set my teeth, and strove to pull harder still.

Young Torode himself was distinguishable in the boat behind, and I knew his passion for her, and did not believe he would deliberately attempt her life. Nor do I now. Possibly his intent was only to frighten us, but when bullets fly, lives are cheap.

Torode himself stood up in the stern of his boat, and levelled at us, and fired. But the shot went wide, and I only pulled the harder, and was not greatly in fear, for shooting from a jumping boat is easy, but hitting a jumping mark is quite another matter.

We drove past Moie de Bretagne, with the green seas leaping up its fretted sides and lacing them with rushing white threads as they fell. How often had Carette and I sat watching that white lacery of the rocks and swum out through the tumbling green to see it closer still. Good times they were, and my thought shot through them like an arrow as we swung past Rouge Cane Bay and opened Gorey.

But these times were better, even though death came weltering close behind us. For, come what might, we were man and woman, and all the man within me, and what there might be of God, clave to this sweet woman who sat before me — who sat of her own choice between me and death — and I knew that she loved me as I loved her, and my heart was full and glad in spite of the hunting death behind.

We were in among the tumbled rocks. I knew them like a book. We swept across the dark mouth of Gorey. In among the ragged heads and weltering white surf of the Pierres-à-Beurre; past the sounding cave where the souffleur blows his spray a hundred feet into the southwest gale. We swung on a rushing green-white swirl towards a black shelf, behind which lies a deep, dark pool in a mighty hollow worn smooth and round with the ceaseless grinding of the stones that no tide can ever lift.

"Ready!" I cried.

And at the next wave we leaped together, and the hand that I held in mine was steadier than my own, for mine was all of a shake with the strain.

Without a look behind we dived in among the black rocks, and a bullet spatted white alongside.

Now we were hidden from them for the moment, until they should land and follow. We scrambled up the yellow grit above, joined hands, and raced along the rabbit tracks, through waist-high bracken and clumps of gorse, for the Coupée.

"If they follow . . ." I panted as I ran, ". . . I will hold them at the Coupée. . . . No danger. . . . Behind pillar. . . . You run on and rouse neighbours. . . . Our only chance. . . . They can shoot us as we run."

She had been going to object, but saw that I was

right, and on we went — past the old mill, past the
old fort, and a bullet buzzed by my head like a droning
beetle. Down the narrow way to the razor of a path
that led to Sercq, and half the way along it, I ran with
her. Then —

"Go!" I panted, and flung myself behind the great
rock pillar that buttressed the path on the Grande
Grève side and towered high above me.

She ran on obediently, and one shot followed her, for
which I cursed the shooter and heard young Torode
do the same. I was their quarry; but one, in the lust
of the chase, had lost his head.

I leaned panting against the rock, and saw Carette's
skirts disappear over the brow of the common at the
Sercq end with thankfulness past words. For myself
I was safe enough. No shot could reach me so long
as I kept cover. From no point on Little Sercq could
they snap at me by any amount of climbing. I was
as safe as if in a fortress, and Carette was speeding to
rouse the neighbours, and all was well.

I had no weapon, it is true, and if they had the sense
and the courage to come in a body along the narrow
way, things might go ill with me. The first comer,
and the second, I could dispose of, but if the others
came close behind they could end me, as I fought.
But I did not believe they would have the courage,
even though they saw it was the only possible chance.
For that knife-edge of a path, — two hundred yards
in length and but two feet wide in places, with the
sea breaking on the rocks three hundred feet below

on each side — set unaccustomed heads swimming, and put tremors into legs that were steady even at sea.

My sudden disappearance had puzzled them. They were discussing the matter with heat, and I could hear young Torode's voice above the rest urging them forward and girding at their lack of courage. Their broken growls came back to me also.

"Girl's yours, 'tis for you to follow her."

"Fools!" said Torode. "If he escapes, your necks are in the noose."

"He's down cliff and she ran on."

"We'd have seen him fall. He's behind one of them stacks, an' —"

"Not me — on an edge like that — and ne'er a rope to lay hold of."

"Rope-walking's no part of a seaman's duty" — and the like, while Torode stormed between whiles and cursed them for cowards.

"Bien!" I heard at last. "If you are all such curs I'll go myself. If he shows, shoot him. You're brave enough for that. He can't hurt you."

I heard his steps along the narrow path, and wrenched out a chunk of rock from the crumbling pillar to heave at him.

He came on cautiously, and I stood with the missile poised to hurl the moment he appeared. He was evidently in doubt as to my hiding-place. I pressed away round the pillar as far as I dared — till another step must have landed me on the rocks below. I wanted him in sight before I showed myself, for one chance was all I could expect.

The men behind watched him in silence now. I held my breath. A second or two would decide the matter between us.

A musket barrel came poking round my bastion, but I was balanced like a fly on the seaward side. Then Torode's dark eyes met mine as he peered cautiously round the corner. He fired instantly, and my footing was too precarious to let me even duck. My left arm tingled and went numb, but before he could draw a pistol I stepped to safer ground and launched my rock at him. It caught him lower than I intended, but that was the result of my insecure foothold. I meant it for his head. It took him between neck and shoulder. He dropped like an ox, and his musket went clattering down the steep. He lay still across the path, very near to the place where, as I looked, I could see again Black Boy's straining eyes and pitiful scrabbling feet as he hung for a moment before falling into the gulf.

A howl and a burst of curses from the cautious ones behind greeted his fall, but I heard no sound of footsteps coming to their leader's assistance.

With another rock I could have smashed him where he lay, and at small risk to myself; but hurling rocks in hot blood is one thing, and smashing fallen men is another; and Torode, lying on his face, was safer from harm than Torode on his feet with his gun in his hand.

There was excited discussion among his followers,

the necessity of securing the wounded man evidently prompting them to an attempt, but no man desirous of first honours.

But presently I heard a shuffling approach along the path, hands and knees evidently, and Torode's body was pulled slowly out of my sight. And then, along the narrow way that leads up into Sercq, there came the sound of many feet and I knew that all was well.

They came foaming up over the brow, an urgent crowd — Abraham Guille from Clos Bourel, and Abraham Guille from Dos D'Ane, William Le Masurier from La Jaspellerie, Henri Le Masurier from Grand Dixcart, Thomas Godfray from Dixcart, and Thomas De Carteret from La Vauroque — just as Carette had come across them and told them of my need. They had snatched their guns from the hanging rocks and come at once.

They gave a shout at sight of me behind the stack, and Torode's body being dragged slowly up the path. The Herm men gave them a hasty volley and went off over Little Sercq towards Gorey, two of them carrying young Torode between them, and the Sercq men came running across the Coupée to greet me.

"Sercq wins," cried one.

"Wounded, Phil?" asked another, at sight of my arm which hung limp and bleeding.

"A scratch on the shoulder. Torode fired and I downed him with a rock."

"Shall we follow them, and give them a lesson?"

"Let them go," I said. "I have got all I wanted, since Carette is safe."

"Come, then. She is just round the corner there getting her breath. We wouldn't let her come any nearer. And here comes your grandfather."

My grandfather took me to his arms with much emotion.

"Now, God be thanked!" he said, in his great, deep voice, which shook as he said it. "You are come back as from the dead, my boy. I had given you up before, and when I knew you had gone across to Herm I gave you up again. Jeanne Falla told me what poor Helier Le Marchant had told her."

"Jean Le Marchant and Martin were lying sick on Brecqhou —"

"They are safe at Beaumanoir."

"Carette does not know about Helier yet."

"Better so for the present. We buried him yesterday on Brecqhou. She believed him dead long since, as did the others."

Carette jumped up out of the heather, at sound of our voices, and came running towards us.

"Oh, Phil!" she cried, and flung her arms about my neck before them all, and made me a very happy and satisfied man.

"You are wounded?" she cried, at sight of blood on my sleeve. "Oh, what is it?"

"It is only a trifle, and you have spoiled your sleeve."

"I will keep it so always. Dear stain!" and she bent and kissed the mark my blood had left.

I thanked the neighbours for coming so promptly to my help, and as we stood for a moment at the road leading to Dos D'Ane, where Abraham Guille would break off to get back to his work, my grandfather stopped them.

"Phil brings us strange and monstrous news," he said weightily. "It is well you should know, for we may need your neighbourly help again. John Ozanne's ship was sunk by the French privateer, *Main Rouge*, and John Ozanne himself and such of his men as tried to save themselves were shot in the water as they swam for their lives, and that was cold-blooded murder. Phil here saw what was toward and saved his life by floating under a spar and sail. And this Main Rouge who did this thing is Torode of Herm —" At which they broke into exclamations of astonishment. . . "He fought under both flags. No wonder he waxed so fat. He knows that Phil has his secret. I fear he will give us no rest, and it is well the matter should be known to others, in case, — you understand."

"He is preparing to leave Herm," I said. "They were loading the schooner all night long. I ought to have gone across to Peter Port to lay my information before them there, but, you understand, Carette was more important to me. But, surely Sercq need fear nothing from Herm," I said looking round on them.

"Ah, you don't know," said my grandfather. "We are but few here just now. So many are away — to the wars and the free-trading. How many men does Torode carry?"

"With those on Herm, sixty to eighty, I should say."

"He could harry us to his heart's content, if he knew it," and Abraham Guille went off soberly to Dos D'Ane, and the rest of us went on to our homes.

My grandfather was full of thought, and I saw that he was anxious on our account. And, now that the excitement was over, my shoulder began to throb and shoot. Every movement was painful to it and I felt suddenly worn out and very weary. Carette must have seen it in my face, for she said:

"Lean on me, Phil, dear. Aunt Jeanne will doctor you as soon as we get there"; and I leaned on her, for the touch of her was very comforting to me, and my right arm was happy if my left was not, and I was content.

"Go on to Jeanne Falla, you two," said my grand-father, when we came to La Vauroque, "and ask her to see to your arm, Phil. She is a famous doctor. I must see George Hamon."

Aunt Jeanne cut away the sleeves of my coat and shirt, and saw to my wound with the tenderest care, and many a bitter word for the cause of it. The bullet had gone clean through the muscles and had probably grazed the bone, she thought, but had not broken it. She washed it, and bound it up with soft rags and simples of her own compounding, while Carette fetched and carried for her. Then she set my arm in a sling, and but for the fact that I had only one arm to use, and so felt very lopsided, and deadly tired still, I was in much greater content than two whole arms and the highest of spirits had ever found me.

I was also feeling very empty, though with no great appetite for food. But she insisted on my eating and drinking, and saw to it herself in her sharp, masterful way.

She was tying the sling behind my neck when my grandfather and George Hamon came in together.

Uncle George gave me very hearty greeting, and they complimented Aunt Jeanne on her handiwork, and then asked her advice, and all the while I was in fear lest some incautious word from one or the other should weight Carette's heart with over-sudden news of her brother's death.

"Jeanne Falla, we want your views," said my grandfather. "It is in my mind that Torode will come back for these two. Phil holds his life in his hand. What others know is hearsay, but Phil can swear to it. I cannot believe he will rest while Phil lives. He can bring sixty or eighty ruffians down on us, and I doubt if we can put thirty against them. What does your wit suggest?"

"Ma fé!" said Aunt Jeanne. "You are right. Torode will be after them, and they are not safe here. Can you not get them over to Peter Port, or to Jersey?"

"They are watching the ways," I said, for I was loth to start on any fresh voyaging now that Carette and home were to my hand. "Their boats were out all night on the lookout."

"We might get through one way or another, if we started at once," said my grandfather, looking doubtfully at me.

"I can't do another thing till I've had some rest," I said. "It is so long since I slept that I cannot remember when it was," and, indeed, what with want of food, and want of sleep, and loss of blood, now that the excitement was over I was feeling weary unto death.

"Then hide them," said Aunt Jeanne. "George Hamon knows hiding-places, I trow —" at which Uncle George grinned knowingly. "And if Torode comes, swear they are safe in Peter Port. One does not cut gorse without gloves, and lies to such as Torode don't count. Bon Gyu, non!"

"That is right," said Uncle George, "and what I advised myself. Philip thinks we might hold them at arms' length, but —"

"It would mean many lives and to no purpose, may be, in the end," said Aunt Jeanne, shaking her head.

"I can hide them where none will ever find them," said Uncle George.

"Ma fé! it does not sound too tempting," said Carette.

"Since we are together, I am content," I said, for rest and the assurance of Carette's safety were the only things I cared about just then.

"Bien! So am I," said Carette. "When will you put us in the hole?"

"At once. Torode is not the man to waste time when so much is at stake."

"And how long will you keep us there?" she asked.

"That may depend on Torode," said Uncle George. "But no longer than is necessary."

"Ma fé, it may be days! We must take food —"

"There is a pie and a ham, and I made bread and gâche to-day," said Aunt Jeanne, picking up a big basket and beginning to pack it with all she could think of and lay hands on.

"Water?" asked Carette.

"Plenty of water, both salt and fresh," said Uncle George.

"All the same, a can of milk won't hurt," said Aunt Jeanne. "Carette, my fille, fill the biggest you can find."

"And Mistress Falla will give us two sacks of hay to soften the rocks," said Uncle George, "and a lantern and some candles, lest they get frightened of one another in the dark," — which I knew could never happen. All the same Carette asked, "Is it dark there *all* the time?"

"Not quite dark all the time, but a light is cheerful."

"Lend me a pipe, Uncle George," I said, and the good fellow emptied his pockets for me.

CHAPTER XXXII

HOW WE WENT TO EARTH

So presently we set out, all laden to the extent of our powers, and went first to Belfontaine since our way lay past it. And there my mother fell gratefully on Carette and me, as though she had feared she might never see either of us again, and I was well pleased to see the tender feeling that lay between these two who were dearest to me in all the world.

"Wherever George Hamon puts you, you will be safe," said my mother, at which Uncle George's face shone happily, "and I hope it will not be for long."

"Not for long," nodded my grandfather with assurance. "We must give Monsieur Torode business of his own to attend to nearer home. Once Peter Port knows all we know, his fat will be in the fire."

"And the sooner the better," said Carette.

"And Krok?" I asked, tardily enough, though not through lack of thought of him.

"Your grandfather thinks he must have broken a blood-vessel yesterday. He is in there."

And I went in and found him sitting up in great excitement at all the talking. I shook him very heartily by the hand, and clapped him on the back and told him how much we were indebted to him, and how it was his prompt warning that enabled me to get across to Herm before they set their patrol boats — and very briefly of what had passed and was toward, and so left him, content and cheerful.

My mother would have added to our supplies, but we had as much as we could carry, and enough, we thought, for the term of our probable imprisonment. So we bade her farewell, and went on across the fields, past La Moinerie towards the Eperquerie.

"We are going to the Boutiques," I said.

"My Boutiques," said Uncle George, with a laugh. And, instead of going on to that dark chasm, whose steep black walls and upstanding boulders lead one precariously into the caves with which we were familiar, he turned aside to another narrower gash in the tumbled rocks, and we stood on the brink wondering where he would take us. For, well as we knew the nooks and crannies thereabouts, we had never found entrance here.

We stood looking down into the narrow chasm. The tide was still churning among its slabs and boulders and the inner end showed no opening into the cliff, nothing but piles of rounded pebbles and stranded tangles of vraic. We thought he had made a mistake.

But he looked quietly down into the boiling pot below, and said, "We have still an hour to wait. The tide is higher than I thought." So we sat on the short salt turf and waited.

"Tiens!" said Carette, pointing suddenly. And looking, we saw three boats pull out from the channel, between Herm and Jethou. One came past us towards the northeast, and Uncle George made us lie flat behind gorse cushions till it was out of sight, round Bec du Nez, though by crawling a little way up the head we could see it lying watchfully about a mile away. Another went off round Little Sercq to stop any communication with Jersey. The third lay in the way between Sercq and Peter Port.

"M. Torode shuts the doors," said my grandfather tersely. "B'en! we will try in the dark."

Between the softness of the turf and the heat of the sun and my great weariness, I was just on the point of falling asleep, when Uncle George came back from a look at his cleft, and picked up his loads, and said, "Come!" and five minutes later we were standing behind him in the salt coolness of the little black chasm, among the slabs and boulders and the fresh sea pools. And still we saw no entrance.

But he went to the inner side of a great slab that lay wedged against the wall of the chasm, and, stooping there, dragged out rock after rock, cunningly piled so that the waves could not displace them, until a small opening was disclosed behind the leaning slab. It was no more than three feet high and we had to creep in on our hands and knees, which my grandfather, from his size and stiffness, found no easy matter.

The tunnel led straight in for a space of twenty feet or so, and then struck upwards, with a very rough floor which made no easy crawling ground, and a roof set with ragged rocks for unwary heads. The

little light that came in round the corner of the slab
in the dark chasm very soon left us, and we crawled
on in the dark, hoping, one of us at all events, that the
road was not a long one.   And suddenly we breathed
more freely and found a welcome space above our
heads.

Uncle George struck flint and steel and lit a candle,
and we found ourselves in a long narrow chamber,
which looked just a fault in the rocks, or the space out
of which the softer stuff had sunk away.   The roof we
could not see, but from the slope of the walls on either
side I thought they probably met at a point a great
way up, and the narrow crack of a cave ran far beyond
our sight.

"My Boutiques," said Uncle George, "and no man
— no living man but myself, has ever been here till
now, so far as I know."   And round the walls we saw
a very large number of neatly piled kegs and packages,
at which my grandfather said, "Ah, ha, mon beau!"
and Uncle George smiled cheerfully in the candle-light.

"The Great Boutiques lie over there," he said,
pointing.   "There are communications, high up along
the cross shelves.   But they need not trouble you.   I
am quite certain no man but myself knows them.   So
if you hear the waves tumbling about in the big cave
you don't need to be frightened."

"And how far does this go?" asked my grandfather,
trying to see the end.

"Right through the Eperquerie.   It runs into a
water-cave there.   Its mouth is below tide level, but

sometimes the light comes through. If you want brandy, Phil, broach a keg. If you want more tobacco, open a package."

"And water?" asked Carette.

"About fifty yards along there on the right in a hollow place. You can't miss it."

"Keep your hearts up, my children," said my grandfather. "You will be quite safe here. Our work lies outside and we must get back. George will come to you as soon as the way is clear. God be with you!"

"You are quite sure there are no ghosts about, Uncle George?" asked Carette in a half-scared whisper, for she was still a devout believer in all such things.

"I've never seen the ghost of one," said Uncle George with a laugh. "Here, Phil! Take this!" and he handed me from his pocket an old flint-lock pistol, of which I knew he had a pair. "You won't need it but it makes one feel bolder to carry it. If you see any ghosts blaze away at them, and if you hit them we'll nail their bodies up outside to scare away the rest."

Then, still laughing, to cheer us I think, they bade us good-bye, and went off down the tunnel.

Carette was already spreading out the hay, which Uncle George and my grandfather had got through the narrow ways with difficulty. Their voices died away and we were alone, and I was so heavy that, from sitting on the hay, I rolled over on it and was asleep before I lay flat.

CHAPTER XXXIII

HOW LOVE COULD SEE IN THE DARK

CARETTE says I slept through three days and nights, but that is only one of her little humours. When I woke, however, I was in infinitely better case than before, and as she herself was fast asleep she may have been so all the time.

It was quite dark. The candle had either burned out or she had extinguished it. But in the extraordinary silence of that still place I could hear her soft breathing not far away, and I lay a long time listening to it. It was so calm and regular and trustful, as though no harmful and threatening things were in the world, that it woke a new spirit of confident hope in me, and I lay and listened, and thought sweet warm thoughts of her.

It seemed a long time, and yet not one whit too long, before the soft breathing lost its evenness, and at last I could not hear it at all, and knew she was waking. And presently she stirred, and after a time she said softly:

"Phil . . . are you awake?"

"Yes, my dear," I said sitting up, and feeling first for her, for love of the feel of her, and then in my pockets for my flint and steel.

"How still it is, and how very dark!" she whispered.

"I'll soon see how you're looking," and my sparks caught in the tinder and I lit a candle.

"You slept very sound," said she, blinking at the light.

"I had not slept for nearly ninety hours and they had held more for me than any ninety weeks before. But it was rude of me to go off like that and leave you all alone."

"You could no more help it than I can help being very hungry. You have slept three days and three nights, I believe. I wonder George Hamon is not back for us."

"Let's look at the milk," I said, and tasted it and found it sweet.

"That's because the air here is so cool and even," said Carette.

"Well, I feel all the better, anyway, and so do you, I'll be bound. I'm beginning to think, you know, that we were over fearful, perhaps, and that we need not have come hiding here at all."

"We'll know better when we hear what's going on outside. Your grandfather and George Hamon are not men to be over fearful and they thought it well."

"That is so," I said, feeling better at that.

"I wonder if it is day or night, and how long we've really been in here."

"Long enough to be hungry, anyway," I said, heartily ready to eat. And we fell to on Aunt Jeanne's ham and rabbit pie, Carette cutting up all I ate into small pieces with my knife, since we had forgotten to bring any other. We drank up the milk out of the big-bellied tin can, and never was there sweeter milk or sweeter can, for Carette had first drink. And then, lest it should get foul, we started off to find the fresh water to wash it out and bring back a supply.

There was no mistaking the hollow place where the fresh water was. The light of the lantern fell on many a narrow rift in the walls of rock on either side, all sharp cracks and fissures, with rough-toothed edges as though the solid granite had been split with mighty hammer-strokes. The seams were all awry, and the lines and cracks were all sharp and straight, though running into one another and across in great confusion. And, of a sudden, in the midst of this tangle of straight clefts and sharp-pointed angles, we came on a little rounded niche where the wall was scooped out in a graceful curve from about our own height to the ground. It was all as smooth and softly rounded as if wrought by a mason's chisel, and as we stood looking at it with surprise, because it was so different from all the rest, a movement of the lantern showed us a greater wonder still. At our feet, in a smooth round basin, bubbled the spring, and looked so like a great dark eye looking up at us in a dumb fury that we both stood stark still staring back at it.

The dark water rushed up from below in coils and writhings like the up-leap of the tide in the Gouliot Pass, and our lantern set golden rings in it which floated brokenly from the centre to the sides, and gave to it a strange look of life and understanding. So strong was the pressure from below that the centre of the little pool seemed higher than the sides. It looked as though the pent-up force within was striving all the time to shoot up to the roof and any moment might succeed.

But the strangest thing of all was that with all this look of hidden power there was no sound, and no drop of water overflowed the hollow basin. The ground we stood on was a slab of solid rock and dry as bone, — no splash, no sound, no drop outside, — only the silent and powerful up-thrust of the water from below, the silent golden rings that tumbled to the sides of the basin, and the constant expectation of something more which never came.

It was Carette's quick undertsanding that named it.

"It is like Krok," she whispered, and the word was said. It was all as like Krok — not the outside man, but the inner Krok, dumb and powerful, silently doing his appointed work — as anything that could be imagined.

"Yes," I said. "It is like Krok. It is very wonderful — running like that all through the ages — since the cave was made any way — very wonderful."

She stooped to dip her hand and taste it, and then drew back.

"It looks as if it would bite," she said, and I took off the lid of the can and scooped up a draught and drank it.

"The sweetest water I ever tasted, and cold as ice. It is as good as the water at La Tour."

Then she drank also, and then she washed out the milk can, but would not pour the dirty water back into the basin. "It would be an offence," she said simply, and I felt the same.

Then we left our can there and went on along the cleft, which grew narrower and narrower till we could only go singly. And so we came at last into a sound of waters in front, and going cautiously, found ourselves in a somewhat wider place, with dull waves tumbling hollowly at our feet.

Carette crept to my side and I held the lantern up and out, but we could see only a rough, black arched roof and ragged rock walls, and a welter of black waves which broke sullenly against the shelving path on which we stood, as though driven in there against their will.

"This is the water-cave Uncle George spoke of, but I don't see any light."

"Perhaps it's night outside," said Carette in a whisper. "Let us get back, Phil. I don't like this place. The waves look as if they were dead."

So we went back the way we had come, and she pressed still closer to me as we passed the little hollow in which the spring churned on, noiseless, and ceaseless, and untiring, and seemed to look up at us with a knowing eye as our lantern set the yellow gleams writhing and twisting in it. We watched it for a time, it looked so like breaking into sound every next moment. But no sound came and we picked up our can and went on.

"I do wish I knew if it is to-day or to-morrow," said Carette.

"Without doubt it is to-day."

"I don't believe it, Phil. It's either to-morrow or the day after, or the day after that."

"But that milk would never have kept sweet."

"It would keep sweet a very long time here. The air is so fresh and cool."

"Well, even if it's to-morrow it's still to-day," I argued.

"I know. But what I want to know is — how long we've been in here, and it feels to me like days and days."

But it was impossible to say how long we had slept, and until we got some outside light on the matter we could not decide it.

So we gathered our beds into cushions and sat there side by side, and since our supply of candles was not a very large one, and I could feel her in the dark quite as well as in the light, I lit my pipe and put the lantern out. And bit by bit she began to tell me of the dreary days when they waited for news of me, and hope grew sick in them, but they would not let it die.

"Your mother was an angel and a saint, and a strong tower, Phil, — so sweet and good. How she made me long for a mother of my own!"

"You shall have a share of mine!"

"I've made sure of my share, already. It made the

ache easier just to be with her, and so I went often to Belfontaine, and she never failed me. She was always full of hope and confidence. 'He will come back to us, my dear,' she would say. 'And when we get him back we must try to keep him, though that is not so easy in Sercq.'"

"But you know why I went, Carette."

"Don't go again, Phil. It is very hard on the women to have their men folk go. All the fear and the heart-ache are ours."

"But it is for you we go — to win what we can for you."

"Ah, what is it all worth? — Just nothing at all. It's not what you bring in your hands, but what is in your hearts for us, Phil. Better a cottage on Sercq, with our hearts together like this" — and I could feel her sweet heart beating through as she nestled up against me with my right arm round her neck — "than all the plunder of Herm."

"Then I will never leave you again, my sweet," and I sealed that pledge in kisses. "But how we are to live —"

"Aunt Jeanne will tell you, and I will tell you now. We are to live at Beaumanoir. She says she is getting too old for the farming, and must have help, and so —"

"So you have arranged it all among you, though for all you knew it was a dead man you were planning for."

"It kept our hearts alive to plan it, and, besides, we knew you were not dead. I think we would have felt it if you had been."

"A woman's heart is the most wonderful thing in the world and the most precious. But it may deceive itself. It believes a thing is because it wishes it to be sometimes, I think, and it won't believe a thing because it wishes it not to be."

"Well, that is as it should be, and you are talking like one of your grandfather's books, Phil," she said lightly, not guessing what was in my mind. For it had seemed to me that I ought to tell her of her brother's death, lest it should come upon her in a heap outside.

"Your father and brothers now," I asked. "Did you look to see them back?"

"Surely! Until my father and Martin came alone telling us the rest were gone. It was sore news indeed."

"Unless they saw them lying dead they may still live. You have thought them dead. But, dear, Helier was with me in the prison in England. He came there sorely wounded, and I helped to nurse him back to life. We escaped together and got home together —" Her hands had clasped in her excitement, and the white glimmer of her face was lifted hopefully to mine, and I hurried on to crush her hope before it grew of size to die hard.

"We got home together that morning they carried you off. He went to Aunt Jeanne's and I went home. When Krok burst in with the news about you, I hurried across to Brecqhou. On the shore of the bay was a boat, and in it Helier lay dead with a bullet through his head."

"Oh, Phil!" in a voice of anguish, for Helier had been her favourite. . . . "And who — ?"

"Those who took you without doubt."

"Ah, the wretches! I wish —" and I was of the same mind.

"I could do nothing, for he was dead. So I took his boat and followed you to Herm. Those who followed me to Brecqhou buried him there. But if he had not come I could not have got to Herm before they set their watch boats. So he helped, you see, though he did not know it."

"My poor Helier! . . . They had muffled my head in a cloak so that I could neither hear nor see. I had just gone outside —"

"Your father and Martin were in a great state about you, but I could not wait to explain. Anything I could have said would only have added to their anxiety, and that was not as great as my own, for I had my own fears of what had happened and they knew nothing."

"Yes, yes. You could have done no other," and she fell silent for a time, refitting her thoughts of Helier, no doubt.

So far, the most striking things in our rock parlour had been the silence and the darkness, but before long we had noise and to spare.

First, a low, harsh growling from the tunnel by which we had entered, and that was the returning tide churning among the shingle and boulders in the rock channels outside. Then it grew into a a roar which rose and fell as the long, western waves plunged into the Boutiques, and swelled and foamed along its echoing sides, and then sank back with a long, weltering sob, and rose again higher than before, and knew no rest. We could hear it all so clearly, that none could doubt the existence of passages between the two caves.

We sat and listened to it, and ate at times, but could not talk much for the uproar. But for me it was enough to sit with Carette inside my arm and close against my heart, and there was something in that long, swelling roar and sighing sob which, after a while, set weights on the eyelids and the senses and disposed one to sleep. For a time we counted the coming of the larger wave, and then the countings grew confused and we fell asleep.

As a matter of fact, we lost all count of time in that dark place. When we woke we ate again by lantern light, and though either one of us alone must have fallen into melancholy as black as the place, being together, and having that within us which made for glad hearts, we were very well content, though still hoping soon to be out again in the free air and sunshine.

My arm gave me little pain. Aunt Jeanne's simples had taken the fire out of the wound, and kept the muscles of an even temper. And whenever the bandages got dry and stiff Carette soaked them in fresh water and tied me up again, and seemed to like the doing of it.

Mindful of Uncle George's saying that the water-

cave held light at times, we visited it again, and yet
again, until coming down the sloping path one time,
we saw the narrow roof above us and the rough walls
on either side tinged with a faint, soft light, and hastening down like children into a forbidden room, we
found ourselves in a curious place.

The tide was very far out, and the black cave, in
which we had hitherto seen only sulky waves tumbling
unhappily, had become a wonder equal to those Krok
used to open to us in the Gouliots.

We could now go quite a long way down the shelving
side of the rock, and the water that lay below was no
longer black but a beautiful living green, from the light
which stole up through it by means of an archway at the
farther end. The arch was under water, but the light
streamed through it, soft and mellow and glowing, so
that the whole place seemed to throb with gentle life.
Outside I judged it was early morning, with the sun
shining full on the sea above the archway.

And here we found what Krok had shown us in the
Gouliots as their chiefest beauties — the roof and walls
were studded with anemones of every size and colour,
green and crimson, and brown and pink, and laven-
der and white and orange — so completely was the
rock clothed with them that it was not rock we saw
but masses and sheets and banks of the lovely clinging
things, all closed up within themselves till the water
should return, and shining like polished gems in the
ghostly green light.

The boulders that strewed the sloping sides of the

cave-floor were covered with them also, and in the glowing green water they were all in full bloom and waving their arms merrily to and fro in search of food.

There, too, a leprous thing with treacherous gliding arms crawled after prey, and at sight of it Carette gripped my arm and murmured "Pieuvre," as though she feared it might hear her. She had always a very great horror of those creatures, though in speaking of them when they were not present she had at times assumed a boldness which she did not really feel. This, however, was a very small monster, and, indeed, they do not grow to any very great size with us.

This softly glowing place was very pleasant to us after the darkness and lantern light of the other cave. We sat for a long time, till the glow faded somewhat and the water began whiffling against the rock walls, and climbed them slowly till at last all the cave was dark again, and we groped back along the cleft to our sleeping-place with the sound of great waters in our ears from the Boutiques.

After that we sought the sea-cave each time we woke, and whenever the light was in it we sat there, and ate, and talked of all we had done, and thought, and feared, and hoped during those long months when we were apart. And once and again Carette fell on earlier times still, and we were boy and girl together under the Autelets and Tintageu, or swimming in Havre Gosselin, and trembling through the Gouliot caves behind Krok's tapping stick. And we talked of Aunt Jeanne's party, and our Riding-Day, and Black

Boy, and Gray Robin. And she told me much of the Miss Maugers, and their school, and her school-fellows. And at times she fell silent, and I knew she had sudden thought of her brother Helier. But, you see, she had so long thought of him as dead, that the fact that he had died later than she had supposed had not the power to cloud her greatly. And perhaps the fact that we were together, and going to part no more, was not without its effect on her spirits.

And I told her more fully than I had done, of all that had happened to me on Herm, and on the French ship in the West Indies, and at Amperdoo, and of our escape into France in the preventive officers' boat, and of that last desperate pull across from Surtainville.

"But, mon Gyu, Phil, what a strange man!" she said of Torode. "Why should he let you live one time, and try his hardest to kill you another?"

"I do not know. I have puzzled over it to no purpose. Now I have given it up."

"He is perhaps mad," she suggested.

"He did not seem so, except in not making an end of me when he had the chance, and that truly was madness on his part."

The time was never long with us, for we were strangely set apart from time and its passage. We ate and slept and talked and walked, just whenever the inclination came, and measurements of time we had none. But Aunt Jeanne's pie was finished, and we were down to the ham bone, and what little bread and gâche we had

left was growing hard, and by that Carette said we had
been there at least three days, and we looked for George
Hamon's coming at any moment, except when the
tunnel was growling and the Boutiques roaring and
sobbing.

CHAPTER XXXIV

I WOKE from a very sound sleep with a start, and lay with a creeping of the back and half asleep still, wondering what I had heard.

It was dark, with a blackness of darkness to be felt, and all was very still, which meant that the tide was out, so it was probably early morning. But it seemed to me that a sound unusual to the place lingered in my ear, and I lay with straining senses.

It was not such a sound, it seemed to me, as Carette might have made in her sleep or in wakening, but something altogether foreign and discordant.

Whether, in my sudden wakening, I had made some sound, I do not know, but there had been heavy silence since. And in that thick silence and darkness I became aware of another presence in the place besides our own, — by what faculty I know not, but something told me that we were not alone. My very hair bristled, but I had the sense to lie still, and there was in me a great agony of fear lest Carette should move and draw upon herself I knew not what.

Safety seemed to lie in silence, for I knew that other, whatever it was, was listening as I was.

I held my breath, but my heart was thumping so

that it seemed impossible that it should not be heard. From the place where Carette lay I could not hear a sound, not even the sound of her breathing.

I think I must have burst soon if that state of matters had continued. Every drop of blood in my body seemed throbbing in my head just back of my ears, and all the rest of me was cold and tense with the strain. It was like waiting on a fearsome black day of thunder for the storm to break.

Then I heard a movement close to me where I lay on the ground, and, like the lightning out of the thunder cloud, there came the click of steel on flint, and I breathed soundlessly. It was, at all events, human.

And then my breath caught again. For the tiny lightning flash that came out of the flint lit, with one brief gleam, the face of the man to whom my death was as necessary as the breath of life, — whose presence there held most dreadful menace for us both, — Torode of Herm.

For one moment life stood still with me. For here, in this close darkness, were we three within arm's length of one another; — the man I had reason to fear and hate above any other on earth, and the price of whose life was my own, a price I would not pay; the woman whose life was dearer to me than my own, for whom I would gladly pay any price, even the utmost; and myself, by force of circumstances, the unwilling link that had brought them both there, and the menace to both their lives, for Torode came for me and Carette came with me.

The wheels of life began to turn for me again, and my hand felt stealthily along the ledge at my side, where George Hamon's pistol had lain ever since he gave it to me.

Thoughts surged in my brain like the long western waves in the Boutiques, all in a wild confusion. This man had spared my life. He had come to take it. Carette was at stake.

I knew what I had to do — if I could do it.

He struck again with the steel, and as he bent to blow the tinder into flame his eye caught the gleam of it on Aunt Jeanne's polished milk-can. I know not what he thought it. Possibly his nerves were over-strung with what he had been going through. With an oath he dropped the tinder, and snatched out a pistol, and fired in the direction of the can. And as the blaze lit up the great black bulk of him, I stood up quickly and fired also, — and, before God, I think I was justified, for it was his life or ours.

The place bellowed with the shots, and the air was thick with smoke and the sharp smell of powder. No sound came from the floor, and I stood holding the pistol by the muzzle to strike him down again if he should rise. But he did not move, and my fears were not for him.

"Carette!" I cried. "Carette!"

And my love rose suddenly with a cry and fell sobbing into my arms.

"Oh, Phil! Phil! What is it? I thought you were dead."

"Dieu merci, it is he who is dead, I think. We will see," and I managed a light with my flint and steel, and knelt down by the fallen man.

"Who is it?" asked Carette, breathless still.

"It is Monsieur Torode."

"Torode!" she gasped, and bent with me to make sure. "Bon Dieu, how came he here?"

"That I don't know. This seems not the hiding-place Uncle George supposed. I was awakened by his trying to strike a light, and I thought he was a ghost."

I hoped he was dead, and so an end to all our fears from him. But I found him still breathing, though but faintly, and he had not his senses. I dragged him across to my bed and sought for his wound, and found it at last in the head. Either the old pistol had cast high, or my sudden up-jump, or his down-bending, had upset my aim. For the shot had entered the side of his head at the back, just above the ear, and as I could find no hole whence it had issued it was probably in his head still. The wound had bled very little, but beyond his slow heavy breathing he gave no sign of life.

On the floor, where he had fallen, I found a seaman's torch, which had been lighted, but was now sodden with water. He had probably dropped it or dragged it in some pool as he made his way into the cave.

And now that the hot anger and the fear of the man were out of me, and he lay under my hand helpless to do us further harm, I found myself ready to do what I could for him, since, unfortunately, he was not dead.

I took Uncle George at his word, and broached one of his little kegs, and found it most excellent French cognac, and mixing some with water in the lid of the can, I prevailed on Carette to drink some too.   We had both been not a little shaken by these happenings, and the fiery life in the spirit pulled us together and braced the slackened ropes.   I dropped a little into Torode also, and it ran down his throat, but he showed no sign of appreciation, and I doubted the fine liquor was wasted.

Then, as there was no chance of sleep, I lit my pipe and found comfort in it, and regretted that Carette had no similar consolation of her own, though I do not take to women smoking as I have seen many of them do abroad.   But there was not even a crust to eat, so we sat and talked in whispers of the very strange fate, or chance, or the leading of God, that had brought Torode to us in this remote place into which we had fled to escape him.

" But, Phil, however did he get here? " asked Carette.   " For Uncle George said that no living man —"

" It was that made me think him a ghost," I said, " until I heard his flint and steel, which no ghost needs."

" Did he come in the way we did ? "

" He was standing just there when I woke.   I'll go and look," and I crept away down the narrow way till I found myself against the piled stones which blocked it, and felt certain that no one had passed that way since George Hamon went out and closed the door behind him.   I heard the in-coming tide gurgling in the channel outside and returned to Carette much puzzled.

"He must have come by way of the Boutiques," I said, "for those stones have not been moved."

"And yet Uncle George seemed certain that no one besides himself knew of this place. 'No living man' — that is what he said."

"He'll be the more surprised when he comes," I said, and we left it there.

The sight of M. Torode lying there like a dead man was not a cheerful one, so we left him and went to our usual place by the water-cave. And, when we came to the well, Carette said, "Ugh! it looks as if it knew all about it," and the bulging eye of the spring goggled furiously at us as we passed.

We had nothing to eat all that day, but drinks of water, mixed now and then with a little cognac. For myself it did not matter much, for I had my pipe, but I felt keenly for Carette. She would not admit that she was hungry, but during the afternoon she fell asleep leaning against me, and I sat very still lest I should waken her to her hunger. And her face as it lay against my arm was like the face of a saint, so sweet and pure and heedless of the world.

It was I awoke her after all.

I was pondering whether we should not make our way out by the tunnel, for if we stopped there much longer we should starve. And the idea had struck me all of a heap, that if any ill had befallen George Hamon or my grandfather we might wait in vain for their coming, when a shout came pealing down the long and narrow cleft of the cave:

"Carré!   Phil Carré!"

I thought it was George Hamon's voice, and the start I gave woke Carette, and we set off for the rock parlour.

Before we got there the shouts had ceased, and in their place we heard a torrent of amazed oaths, and knew that Uncle George had lighted on Torode.

"Dieu-de — dieu-de-dieu-de-dieu-de-dieu!" met us, as we drew near.   "What in the name of the holy St. Magloire is this?" cried he, as soon as he saw us.   He had lit his lantern, his head was bound round with a bloody cloth, and he was bending over the bed.

"We had a visitor," I said jauntily, for the sight of him was very cheering, even though he seemed all on his beam ends, and maybe the sight of a basket he had dropped on the ground went no small way towards uplifting my spirits.

"Thousand devils," he said furiously — and I had never in my life seen him so before — "A visitor! — Here!   But it is not possible —"

I pointed to the wounded man.   "It is Monsieur Torode from Herm.   We had a discussion, and he got hurt."

"Torode!" he said, and knelt hastily, and held his lantern so that the light fell full on the dark face, and peered into it intently, while we stood wondering.

His eyes gleamed like venomous-pointed tools.   He stared long and hard.   Then he did a strange thing.

He put his hand under Torode's black moustache and folded it back off his mouth, and drew back himself to arm's length, and stared and stared, and we knew that some strange matter was toward.

And then of a sudden he sprang back with a cry, — a great, strange cry.

"My God! My God! it is he himself! — Rachel!" and he reeled sideways against the wall.

"Who?" I asked. And he looked very strangely at me, and said:

"Your father, — Paul Martel," and I deemed him crazy.

"My poor Rachel!" he groaned. "We must hide it. She must not know. She must never know. My God! Why did I tell you?"

"Uncle George!" I said soothingly, and laid my hand on his shoulder, for I made sure his wound had upset his brain.

"Give me time, Phil. I am not crazy. Give me time. Mon dieu! mon dieu!" and he sat down heavily with his head in his hands.

And we, not understanding anything of the matter, but still much startled at the strangeness of his words and bearing, nevertheless found the size of our hunger at sight of the basket he had brought, and fell to on its contents, and ate ravenously.

CHAPTER XXXV

HOW WE HEARD STRANGE NEWS

"WHATEVER is it all, Phil?" whispered Carette as we ate.

"There has evidently been fighting outside, and he has got a knock on the head, and his wits are astray." But that strange thing he had said ran in my head, and made such play there that I began to be troubled about it.

You must remember I had never heard the name of Paul Martel, and of my father I knew nothing, save that he was dead. So that this strange word of George Hamon's was to me but empty vapouring brought on by that blow on the head. But against that there was the tremendous fact which had so exercised my mind, that this man Torode had spared my life at risk of his own, when every other soul that could have perilled him had been slaughtered in cold blood.

If — the awful import of that little word! — if there was — if there could be, any sense in George Hamon's words, the puzzle of Torode's strange treatment of me was explained. I saw that clearly enough, but yet the whole matter held no sense of reality to me. It was all as obscure and shadowy as the dim cross-lights in which we sat, and ate because we were starving.

Torode lay like a log, breathing slowly, but with no other sign of life. George Hamon presently knelt beside him again and gazed long into his face, and then examined his wound carefully. Then he stood up and sighed to us to follow him, and we went along the cleft to the water-cave, and sat down there in the dim, green light that filtered through the water.

"Mon gars," he said very gravely. "I have done you a wrong. I ought to have kept it to myself. It was the suddenness of it that upset me. I told you no living man besides myself knew of this place, and that was because I believed this man dead — dead this twenty years. He was partner with me in the free-trading for a time, until we fell out —"

"You said just now that he was my father," I broke in, and eyed him closely to see if his wits were still astray. "What did you mean?"

"It is true," he said gloomily. "I am sorry. It slipped out."

"But he is Torode, and you called him Martel, and I am Phil Carré."

"All that, but, all the same, it is true, mon gars. He is your father, Paul Martel."

"I have always been told my father was dead."

"We believed so. He went away twenty years ago, and never came back. We believed him dead — we wished him dead. He was better dead than alive."

"I don't understand," I said doggedly, still all in a maze. "You call him Martel, and say he is my father, but I am Phil Carré."

"Yes. We were sick of Martel, and sick of his name. We did not wish you to be weighted with it. . . . Now see, mon gars, I was in the wrong to slip it out, but — well, there it is — I was wrong. But, since it is done, and we must keep it to ourselves, I will tell you the rest. You are old enough to know. And Carette — eh bien! it is you yourself, and not your father —"

"Ma fé, one does not choose one's father," said Carette, and slipped her hand through my arm, and clung tightly to it through all the telling.

And George Hamon told us briefly that which I have set forth in the beginning of my story. We two talked of it many times afterwards, and it was at such odd times that he told me all the rest. And I think it like enough that you, who have read it all in the order in which I have written it, may long since have guessed that thing which had puzzled me so much — Torode's strange sparing of my life when he murdered all my comrades. But to me, who had never known anything of my father, and had grown to know myself only as Phil Carré, the whole matter was amazing, and up-setting beyond my power to tell.

"And what are we to do now, Uncle George?" I asked dispiritedly, for the sudden tumbling into one's life of a father, whom all honest men must hate and loathe, darkened all my sky like a thunder-cloud on a summer day.

"If he dies, we will bury him here and in our three hearts, and no other must know. It would only break your mother's life again as it was broken once before."

"And if he lives?" I asked gloomily, and, unseemly though it might be, it was perhaps hardly strange that I could not bring myself to wish anything but that he might die.

"If he lives," said Uncle George, no whit less gloomily — and stopped in the slough. . . . "I do not know. . . . His life is forfeit . . . and yet — you cannot give him up . . . nor can I. . . . But perhaps he will die . . ." he said hopefully.

"And I shall have killed him."

"Mon dieu, yes! — I forgot. . . . But you did not know, and if you had not, he would certainly have killed you . . . and Carette also without doubt."

"All the same —"

"Yes, I know," he nodded. "Well, we must wait and see. I wonder now what Philip would do" — meaning my grandfather, in whose wisdom he had implicit faith, as all had who knew him. "I'm inclined to think he would give him up, you know. He would never loose him on the world again. . . . However, he may die."

"Where is he, — my grandfather? And what has been doing outside, and when can we get out?"

"He is away to Peter Port, but he had to go by way of Jersey, and by night, to avoid their lookout boats. He has got there all right, for there is fighting on Herm. We heard the sound of the guns, and the Herm men are getting back there as fast as they can go."

"What day is this?"

"To-day is Thursday."

"Thursday!" echoed Carette. "And we came in
here on Tuesday! Is it Thursday of this week or
Thursday of next week, Uncle George?"

"This week," he said with surprise, for he could not
possibly understand how completely we had lost count
of time. "Torode came across himself with four big
boat-loads of rascals, with carronades in their boats too,
and they have turned the island upside down in search
of you. He thought, you see, without doubt, that if
he could lay hands on you there was no one else could
swear to anything but hearsay. But the Peter Port
men will take your grandfather's word for it, as they
would take no one else's. And that word concerning
John Ozanne and his men would set them in a flame
if anything could. He was very loth to go, but he saw
it was the surest way of ending the matter. So he
slipped away with Krok in the dark, and they were to
swim out to a boat off Les Lâches and make their
way by Jersey. Now, if you have eaten, we will get
out to the light."

"Dieu merci!" said Carette heartfully.

"And what about him?" I asked, nodding towards
the wounded man.

"He must wait. Can he eat?"

"I have dropped brandy down his throat two or
three times, and he seems to swallow it."

"We will give him some more, and decide afterwards.
Mon dieu! But I wish Philip was here."

"Would you tell him?"

"Surely! But not your mother, Phil," he said anxiously, and I knew again how truly he loved her. "She must not know. She must never know."

"What about Aunt Jeanne?" I asked.

He shook his head. "The fewer that know the better." So we dropped some more brandy and water into the wounded man's mouth, and gathered our few belongings, and crept down the tunnel after Uncle George.

Oh, the blessedness of the sweet, salt, sunlit air, as we stood in the water-worn chasm and blinked at the light, while Uncle George carefully closed his door. We took long, deep draughts of it, and felt uplifted and almost light-headed.

"It is resurrection," said Carette, and as we climbed out of the cleft and took our way quickly among the great gorse cushions along Eperquerie, the dull sound of firing on Herm came to us on the west wind.

CHAPTER XXXVI

"THANK God, you have escaped them!" was my mother's grateful greeting as we came into Belfontaine. "But you have suffered! You are starving?"

"Not a bit, little mother," chirped Carette, as they kissed very warmly. "We have been quite happy, though, ma fé, it was as dark and still as the tomb, and there is a spring in there that is enough to frighten one into a fit. And George Hamon here is trying to make us believe this is only Thursday, and it is certain we have been in there at least a week."

"It is only Thursday," smiled my mother. "But the time must have seemed long in the dark and all by yourselves."

"Oh, we didn't mind being by ourselves, not a bit, and we never quarrelled once. But, ma fé, yes, it was dark, and so still. I could hear Phil's heart beat when I couldn't see him."

"You both look as if you had been seeing ghosts. Is it that your arm is paining you, Phil, mon gars?"

"Hardly at all. Carette saw to it."

"Bien! You are bleached for lack of sunshine then."

"Mon dieu, yes," said Carette. "I felt myself

getting whiter every minute, and we were almost starving when Uncle George came. We had been days without food, you know, although you all say it is only Thursday," and my mother smiled and began to spread the table, but we showed her it was only Carette's nonsense.

But if she was relieved on our account, she was still very anxious about her father.

"They are fighting over there, George," she said, looking anxiously out over the water to where Herm lay peacefully in the afternoon sunshine, and as we stood listening, the dull sound of guns came to us again. "That means that he got there all right?"

"Trust Philip to get there all right. And to come back all right, too. I hope they'll make an end of them," said Uncle George stoutly.

"You can never tell what will happen when fighting's afoot," she sighed.

"He'll take care of himself. Don't you worry, Rachel."

"Shall I put a fresh bandage on your head? It is hurting you, I can see."

"No, no," he said hastily, and then, "Well, yes, truly, it is hard and dry — if you will," and she steeped his bandage in cold water and carefully bound up his head again. And all the time we were all in mortal fear lest some chance word from one or the other should disclose that which was hidden in the cave, that which would blight her life again if it got out.

"Did they trouble you, mother?" I asked.

"The young Torode came with a party of his men, and searched every corner of the place. And in reply to his questionings all I said was that you were gone. Then George and your grandfather came up and would have turned them out, and the young man and George fell out—"

"He drew a pistol on me and gave me this and I knocked him down," said Uncle George. "And then the men dragged him away."

"It's well it was no worse," said my mother. "I do not like that young man," and little she knew how small cause indeed she had to like him.

We went on along the cliffs to Beaumanoir, to show ourselves to Aunt Jeanne, and ever and again the sound of the guns came to us on the wind, and more than once Uncle George stopped with his face turned that way, as though his thoughts were more there than here.

"Ah, v'là! So here you are, my little ones. I hope you had a pleasant time in Jersey," cried Aunt Jeanne, as soon as she caught sight of us. "I have been risking my salvation by swearing through thick and thin that you went to Jersey on Tuesday. But that young Torode only scoffed at me. Bad manners to say the least of it, after eating one's gâche and drinking one's cider, and nearly dancing holes in one's floor. I believe you're hungry, you two," and she made for her cupboards.

"No, truly, auntie," said Carette, "we have done nothing but eat and sleep since ever Uncle George shut

us up in his hole. But, mon dieu, you cannot imagine
how dark and still it is in there. Each time we slept
was a night, and each time we woke was a day, and we
were there about three weeks."

"Ma fé, you look it," nodded Aunt Jeanne.

"And the father and Martin?" asked Carette.

"So, so. Give them time. They have kept asking
for you."

Uncle George was standing looking over at Herm
again, and something of what was in his face was in
Aunt Jeanne's, as she said to him:

"Ma fé, yes! But they are getting it hot over there.
If you take my advice, George Hamon, you will muster
all the men you can and have them ready."

"How, then?" he said quickly, "You think —?"

"I think what you are thinking, my friend. If they
are beaten over there — and they will be, unless the
Guernsey men are bigger fools than they used to be —
we may see some of them across here again and in a
still worse temper. If they make a bolt at the last
they'll make for France, and ten to one they'll take a
bite at us in passing. They came to stop trouble
before, now they'll come to make it."

"It's what was in my mind. I'll see Amice Le
Couteur at once."

"B'en! and give the word to all you see, George,"
she called after him. "And bid the women and children to the Gouliots, if they hear they are coming, —
the upper chamber above the black rock. It won't be
just hide and seek this time."

"Good idea!" Uncle George called back over his shoulder.

"Common sense," said Aunt Jeanne. "I'd undertake to hold the Gouliots against the lot of them if the tide was at flood."

"And you really think they may come across here again, Aunt Jeanne?" I asked.

"Ma fé, yes, I do. They were angry men before, but if the Guernsey men have smoked them out they'll be simply devils, and it's just as well to look ahead. How is that arm of yours?"

"The other one's all right. I can do my share."

"You'll be wanted if they come. I doubt if we can muster more than thirty men at most, and there may be more than that left of them and madmen at that."

"We won't let them land."

"You can't close every door with thirty men, mon gars."

"One at the Coupée, if they make for Gorey. Three at Dos d'Ane. Three at Havre Gosselin. Half a dozen at the Creux —"

"Ta-ta! What about Eperquerie and Dixcart, my boy? Those are the open doors, and they know it just as well as you do. They're not going to climb one by one when they can come all in a heap. Mon Dieu, non!" she said, shaking her head ominously. "If they come there'll be rough work and the readier we are for it the better."

Carette's face had shadowed at this gloomy talk, when she had been hoping that our troubles were over.

And I could find little to reassure her, for it seemed to me more than likely that Aunt Jeanne's predictions would be fulfilled.

"I'll go along to Moie de Mouton, and keep a look-out," I said.

"I also," said Carette, and we went off over the knoll together.

We sat in the short sweet grass of the headland, just as we had sat many a time when we were boy and girl, when life was all as bright as the inside of an ormer shell and we were friends with all the world.

The sun was dropping behind Herm into a dark bank of clouds, which lay all along the western sky. Behind the clouds the heavens seemed ablaze with a mighty conflagration. Long level shafts of glowing gold streamed through the rifts, like a hot fire through the bars of a grate, and our faces and all the bold Sercq cliffs were dyed red. The sun himself looked like a fiery clot of blood. Everything was very still, as with a sense of expectation.

Tintageu, and the Platte, and Guillaumesse, and the gleaming Autelets, and La Grune, and on the other side the great black Gouliot Rocks, and Moie Batarde, and the long dark side of Brecqhou all seemed straining with wide anxious eyes to learn what was coming. There was a dull growl of surf from below, and low harsh croakings and mewings from the gulls down in Port à la Jument. And we seemed to be all waiting for what should come out of Herm along the red path of the sun.

Carette shivered inside my arm.

"Cold, dearest?" I asked.

"My heart is heavy.   Oh, but I wish it was the day after to-morrow, Phil."

"It will come.   But we look like having a storm first.   Those black clouds —"

"God's storms I do not mind.   It is that black Herm — Hark!" and we heard the sound of guns again along the wind.   "Do you think they will come here, Phil?"

"I think it quite likely, dear.   But we are forearmed and we fight for our homes.   If they come they are a beaten crew bent only on mischief.   We shall beat them again."

"You won't go and get yourself killed, Phil dear, just when you've come back to me?"

"That I won't.   And when they've come and gone" — and I comforted her with warmer things than words. And Tintageu, and the black Gouliot rocks, and all the straining headlands seemed to look at us for a moment, and then turned and stared out anxiously at Herm.

And then I jumped up quickly, and stood for a moment staring as they stared.

"Tiens! — Yes — they are coming! Allons, ma chérie!" and we set off at a run for Beaumanoir to give the alarm.   For, out of the shadow of Herm, half a dozen black objects had crept and were making straight for Sercq, and I understood that the lookout boat, and the boats of those who had hurried across from

Sercq, had been left on the shell beach because the
channel was probably blocked, and that the broken
remnants of Herm had fled across the island and were
coming down to take a bite at us, as Aunt Jeanne had
predicted.

A dozen of the neighbours, who had gathered about
the gate of Beaumanoir, came running to meet us —
the two Guilles from Dos d'Ane, and Clos Bouret,
Thomas de Carteret from La Vauroque, Thomas Godfray of Dixcart, and Henri Le Masurier from Grand
Dixcart, Elie Guille from Le Carrefour, Jean Vaudin,
and Pierre Le Feuvre, and Philippe Guille from La
Genétière. George Hamon and Amice Le Couteur,
the Sénéchal from La Tour, were just coming down
the lane, and every man carried such arms as he could
muster.

"They're coming!" I shouted, and Amice Le Couteur, panting with his haste from the north, took command in virtue of his office, since Peter Le Pelley, the
Seigneur, was away in London.

"How many, Phil Carré?" he asked.

"I counted six boats, but they were too far off to see
how many in them."

"So! Run on, you, Jean Vaudin and Abraham
Guille, and tell us how they are heading. They won't
try to land hereabouts. They may try Gorey, but not
likely. They have tasted the Coupée already. All the
same, you, Pierre, run and warn the folks on Little
Sercq. They had better come over here. Then stop
on the Coupée and let no man across. I have bidden

the women and children to the Gouliots here.   Thomas
Hamon of Le Fort is collecting them.   The rascals are
most likely to try the Eperquerie or Dixcart.   You,
Elie Guille, see them all safely into the upper cave
above the black rock, and sit in the mouth and let no
one in.   But I don't think you will be troubled.   We
shall beat them off.   Now, my friends, to the Head
and watch them, and let every man do his duty by
Sercq this night!" and they moved off in a body to
Moie de Mouton, while Carette and I went on into
Beaumanoir, she to join Aunt Jeanne, I to find a
weapon, which I was doubtful of finding at home.

"Must I go underground again, Phil?" asked
Carette.   "I would far sooner stop here and take the
risk if there is any."

"You must go with the rest, my dear.   We may
have our hands full.   It will be a vast relief to know
you are all safe out of sight.   If any of these rascals
should get past us they will spare no one.   Their only
idea in coming is to pay off scores because they are
beaten.   They will be very angry men."

Aunt Jeanne, as might have been expected, was
packing baskets of food with immense energy.

"Ah, — b'en!" she cried at sight of us.   "Carry
those baskets down to Saut de Juan, you two.   I'll be
with you in a minute."

"Give me something to fight with, Aunt Jeanne."

"There's my old man's cutlass, and there are his
pistols, but, mon Dieu, they haven't been loaded this
twenty years, and moreover, there's no powder."

I strapped the cutlass round me and stuck the pistols in the belt.

"What about M. Le Marchant and Martin?" I asked.

"They are in the cellar. No one will find them. The Gouliot was too far for them."

Women and children were running past towards Saut de Juan, the women anxious for their men, the children racing and skipping as if it were a picnic. I handed over my basket to willing hands, at the head of the path that leads down by the side of the gulf to the Gouliots, and gave Carette a hearty kiss before them all, which set some of the women smiling in spite of their forebodings.

"Ah-ha!" chuckled one old crone. "Bind the faggot if it's only for the fire."

"Faggot without band is not complete," I laughed. "See you take care of my faggot, Mère Tanquerel, or I'll want to know why," and I ran on along the heights to fetch my mother from Belfontaine.

As I came down the slope towards Port à la Jument I met her and George Hamon hurrying along, and her face was full of anxious surprise still, while Uncle George's had in it a rare tenderness for her which I well understood.

"I was just coming for you, mother," I said.

"It is good to be so well looked after," she smiled through her fears. "If only we knew that your grand-father was all right —"

"Philip will be here before long," said Uncle George

confidently. "When he sees which way they've taken he will guess what they're up to and will bring on some of the Guernsey men. If we can't keep them at arm's length till then we're a set of lubbers."

"You'll be careful of yourselves," she said wistfully, as we stood at the top of the slope. "I — we can't spare either of you yet."

We promised every possible caution, and she went on to join the other women, while Uncle George and I ran across to the men standing in a dark clump on the Moie de Mouton.

CHAPTER XXXVII

HOW WE HELD OUR HOMES

THERE was no need to ask how the boats were heading. All eyes were fixed anxiously on them as they came straight for the north of the island, and just as we came up Amice Le Couteur gave the word to move on to Eperquerie.

Stragglers from the more distant houses were coming up every few minutes. He left one to send them all on after us, and we straggled off, past Belfontaine and Tintague and the Autelets and Saignie Bay, and so into the road to the Common, and took our stand on the high ground above the Boutiques, and as we went Thomas Godfray loaded my pistols for me from his own flask.

The colours had long since faded out of the sky, and the bank of clouds in which the sun had set was creeping heavily up the west. Both sky and sea were gray and shadowy. The sea was flawed with dark blurs of sudden squalls, and the waves broke harsh and white on La Grune and Bec du Nez.

The six boats came on with steady venom. They kept well out round Bec du Nez, and we ran across the broken ground to meet them on the other side of the island, and lay down there by the Sénéchal's orders.

There was always the chance that they were making straight for the French coast. It would have been well for some of them if they had. That hope died as they turned inside the Pécheresse rock and came sweeping down towards Eperquerie landing.

We could see them better now, and estimate our chances. Three of the boats were of large size, holding ten to twelve men each, and carrying a small carronade in the bows. The others held six to eight, and they were all as evil and scowling a set as ever I set eyes on.

"They will try here," said Amice Le Couteur. "I will warn them once not to land, then do you be ready to fire. Take advantage of the rocks and let no man expose himself unnecessarily."

They came thrashing along, with no show of order but much of the spirit that was in them. There is no dog so ready to snap at anything that offers as the one that is running from a fight. Their lust for mischief came up to us in hoarse growls and curses and tightened our grip on our weapons.

The first boat ground on the shingle, and the next ran in alongside before the oars were unshipped, and the wind was thick with curses on their clumsiness. The landing between the rocks is a narrow one, and no more than two could come in at once. The others had to wait outside.

The rascals were beginning to tumble ashore, when Amice Le Couteur stood up and cried, "Stop there! If you land it is at your peril. We will not have it."

Those who were landing turned their black faces upwards in surprise, for they had not seen us. But from one of the waiting boats behind, half a dozen shots rang out in a sudden blaze of light, and the Séné-chal fell back among us, and our men began a hot fire at the boats from behind their rocks.

I ran to M. Le Couteur, as I had no weapons but a cutlass and pistols, and these were only for close work. He was bleeding in the head and chest, but said he thought the wounds were not serious.

"See that some of them don't slip away to the Creux or Dixcart while we're busy with the others here, Carré," he said, as I tied up his head with his own kerchief, and then dragged him down into a little hollow where no shots could reach him.

There was much cursing and shouting down below, and a satisfactory amount of groaning also, and our men fired and loaded without stopping and said no word. The landing-place and the rocks above were thick with smoke, which came swirling up in great coils, so that I could see nothing though I could hear enough and to spare.

I scrambled down the side of Pignon, bending among the rocks lest they should see me, and so came out on to the larger rocks, inside which lies the landing-place. I was thus in the rear of the Herm men, with the open sea behind me, and a glance told me that the Sénéchal's fears were justified. The two boats that had pushed in were alone there, and I heard the sound of oars working lustily down the coast.

I turned and tumbled back the way I had come, scrambling and falling, cutting and bruising myself on the ragged rocks, and so up to our men.

"There are only two boats there," I shouted. "The rest are off for the Creux."

"Good lad!" cried George Hamon. "Off after them, Phil, and keep them in sight. Fire your pistol if they stop. We'll divide and follow, and we'll not be far behind," and I ran on past Les Fontaines and Creux Belet.

I heard them pass Banquette as I stood in the gorse of the hillside, and followed them round to Grève de la Ville, where there was little chance of their landing, as the shore is not easy, and the climb not tempting.

From there I could have cut across into the Creux Road, and been at the harbour long before them, but I thought best to follow the cliffs and keep them in touch lest they should try any tricks.

They had to keep well out round Moie à Navet, but they came in again under Grande Moie, and so we came down the coast, they below and I above, till I ran across country, back of the Cagnons, and dropped into Creux Road just above the tunnel, and there found George Hamon with a good company come straight by the road from La Tour, and still panting hard from their rush.

"Ah, here you are, mon gars!" said Uncle George, "And where are they?"

"Coming along. I saw them past Les Cagnons. How are they at Eperquerie?"

"We left them at it, but they're scotched there. Will they try here, or go on?"

"Dixcart, if they know their business. It'll be all hands to the pumps there, Uncle George. Four of us could hold the tunnel here against fifty."

"Yes, we'll get on by Les Lâches and wait there and make sure. Do you stop here, Phil, with Godfray and De Carteret and Jean Brillot, until you are sure they have gone on, then come on and join us. Best barricade the tunnel with some of that timber."

He and the rest went on up the hillside to Les Lâches, and we four set to work hauling and piling till the seaward mouth of the tunnel leading from the road to the shore was barred against any possible entrance. And listening anxiously through our barrier, with the stillness of the tunnel behind us, we presently heard the sound of the toiling oars pass slowly on towards Dixcart. We waited till they died away and then climbed the hill to Les Lâches and sped across by the old ruins, with a wide berth to the great Creux at the head of Derrible Bay, and down over the Hog's Back into Dixcart Valley, where we knew, and they knew, their best chances lay. For in Dixcart the shore shelves gently, and the valley runs wide to the beach; fifty boats could land there in a line, and their crews could come up the sloping way by the streamlet ten abreast. It would be no easy place to defend if the enemy pushed his attack with persistence, and every man we had would be needed.

We tumbled into our men as they settled their plan

of defence.   We were twenty-one all told.   Ten were
to go along the Hog's Back cliff towards Pointe Château,
where they would overlook the point of landing, if the
enemy made straight for the valley.   They were to
begin firing the moment the boats touched shore, and
then to draw back into the valley.   The other ten
were to lie in the bracken on the slope of the opposite
hill, just where it gives on to the bay, and to pour in
their fire before the enemy had recovered from his
first dose.   Then, if he came on, the two bands would
meet him with volleys from both hillsides as he came
into the valley, and again retiring along the hillsides,
would continue to harass him till, at the head of the
valley, if he got that far, the united bands would meet
him hand to hand.   We judged he might be about
thirty strong, but hoped our first volleys might bring
us about even.

Uncle George asked me to go with himself and the
nine along Hog's Back.   As I had no gun, and only
one arm in full working order, I might be useful in
carrying any change of orders to the other party.

There was no sound of their coming yet, but the
pull round Derrible Pointe would account for that.
So we stole silently along to our appointed places.

The night was very dark and squally, but on this
side of the island we were sheltered.   On the other side
the white waves would be roaring and gnashing up the
black cliffs, but here in Dixcart they fell sadly on the
shingle and drew back into the depths with long-drawn
growls and hisses.

"V'la!" said Uncle George, as we lay on the cliff, and we heard the oars below in the bay, and all stood up ready.

They came in as close under the cliff as they dared, so close that we heard their voices clearly between the falling of the waves. And then, dimly, we saw the black bulks of their boats in the streaming surf as it ran back to the sea, and I started, for I could only see three, but could not be certain.

"Now!" said Uncle George, and our volley caught them full.

They roared curses and began snapping back at us as each man found his musket. But a step back took us under cover, for a black cliff two hundred and fifty feet high, and hidden in the night, offered no mark for them, and from the face of the opposite hill our other volley crashed into the marks their own fire offered.

"Again!" said Uncle George, as soon as our men were ready, and our ten guns spoke once more.

They were sadly discomfited, and furiously angry down below there. But those who were not wounded had tumbled ashore, and they replied to our second volley with a more concerted fire. And in the flash of their guns, I, craning over the scarp of the hill, saw clearly but three boats.

"Only three boats," I whispered in George Hamon's ear. "I'm off to look for the other," and before he could stop me I was gone. For he needed all his men and I believed I could manage alone.

Back across Hog's Back, past the old mill, through

the fields by La Forge, and along the hill-path by Les
Lâches, and down the hill, slipping and stumbling, and
into the Creux tunnel with only one fear — that I
might arrive too late.

And I was only just in time. As I ran in I heard
them on the seaward side hauling at the timbers of our
barricade, and with my chest going like a pump, and
my hands all shaking with excitement, I drew Peter
Le Marchant's cutlass and sent it lancing through the
openings wherever a body seemed to be.

Sudden oaths broke out, and the work stopped. I
pulled out one of my pistols, shoved the muzzle through
a hole and pulled the trigger, and still had wit enough
to wonder what would happen if it burst as Aunt
Jeanne had hinted.

It did not burst, however, and the discharge provoked a further outburst of curses. I drew the other,
and fired it likewise, and stood ready with my cutlass
for the next assault. But they had hoped to break
through unperceived, and possibly the violence of my
attack misled them into a belief in numbers. They
drew off along the shingle, and I leaned back against
the side of the tunnel and panted for my life.

I heard a discussion going on, and presently they were
at work at something, but I could not make out what.

I took advantage of the lull to strengthen my defences
with some boats' masts and any odd timbers I could
find, and lift, till I thought it impossible that any man
should get through.

But I was wrong.   There came a sudden roar outside

and a shot of size came crashing through my barricade, sending pieces of it flying wildly. They had a carronade, and had had to shift the boat to the end of the shingle to get the mouth of the tunnel into the line of fire.

Then I began to fear. Men I could fight, but carronades were beyond me.

Still, even when they had knocked my barrier to pieces, the men must come at last. The great iron shot could not reach me round the corners, though flying timbers and splinters might. They would fire again and again till the way was clear, and then they would come in a heap, and I must do my best with my cutlass. And it was not unlikely that the sound of the heavy guns might catch the ears of others and bring me help. So I drew back out of the tunnel on the land side and waited.

A stumble over a piece of timber set me to the hurried building of a fresh barricade at this end, outside the mouth of the tunnel. If it only stopped them for minutes, the minutes might be enough. It would in any case hamper men, and I did not believe they could train their guns upon it. So I groped in the dark, and dragged, and piled, and found myself using the wounded arm without feeling any pain, but also without much strength, till I had a not-to-be-despised fence which would at least give me chance of a few blows before it could be rushed.

Five times they fired, and the inside of the tunnel crashed with the fragments of the outer barricade, and then it was evidently all down.

There was a brief lull while they gathered for the rush. Then they came all together full into my later defence.

I stabbed through it and hacked at one who tried to climb. But they were many and I was one. The barrier began to sag and give under their pressure. I stabbed wildly through and through, and got groans for payment. And then of a sudden I was aware of another fighting by my side. He had come unperceived by me, and he spoke no word, but thrust and smote wherever opportunity offered, and his coming gave me new strength.

And then, with a shout, others came pouring down the Creux Road, and I knew that all was well, and I fell spent in the roadway.

CHAPTER XXXVIII

WHEN I recovered sufficiently to take notice of things, I was sitting in the tunnel with my back against the wall, a big fire of broken wood was burning brightly, and men were carrying in others from the harbour. The carried men were bound, and the others were strangers to me.

A flask was put to my mouth, and I took a pull at it, and turned to find Krok smiling his content at my recovery.

"Was it you, Krok?" and I shook both his hands heartily, while he held the flask between his knees.

"And my grandfather?" I asked. "Is he hurt?" And Krok nodded and then shook his head.

"Hurt, but not badly?" and he nodded quickly.

"And these are Guernsey men?"

He nodded again, and one of them came up and asked, "Feeling better? You had a tough job here all alone. We came ashore on the other side and were hurrying towards the firing lower down there where we heard the gun begin, and your friend here brought us down this road on the jump. He doesn't speak much, but he's got mighty good ears and sense."

"You were just in time. I was about done."

"Just in time is all right, but, in fact, it wouldn't have done to be much later."

"Can you tell me anything of my grandfather, Philip Carré?"

"Oh, you're young Phil Carré, who started all this business, are you?"

"I'm Phil Carré. What about my grandfather?"

"We had some warm work over there, and he got a shot through the leg. Not serious, I think. But we got the schooner and a lot of the rascals, and when we found the rest had come this way we came after them. But Torode himself got away. Maybe we'll find him here somewhere."

I had not given the man in George Hamon's cave a thought for hours past, but this sudden reminder brought my mind round to him, and me to my feet, with a jerk.

He was my father — I could not doubt it, though belief was horrible. He was a scoundrel beyond most. He lay there stricken by my hand. His life was sought by the law, and would certainly be forfeited if he was found. I must find George Hamon at once.

"Are they fighting still at Dixcart?" I asked the Guernsey man.

"There was firing over yonder as we came along," he said, pointing to the southwest. "But it is finished now."

"That was their chief attack. The Sénéchal was shot at Eperquerie. George Hamon is in charge

at Dixcart. We had better see how they have
fared."

"Allons! I know Hamon."

He left four of his comrades to guard the prisoners,
and the rest of us set off by the way I had already
passed twice that night, and came down over Hog's
Back into Dixcart.

They heard us coming, and George Hamon's quick
order to his men to stand by told me all was well, and
a shout from myself set his mind at rest.

"Mon Dieu! Phil, my boy, but I'm glad to see you
safe and sound. You've been on my mind since ever
you left. Who are — Why — Krok — and Henri
Tourtel? Nom d'Gyu! Where do you come from?"

"From Herm last. We came across after those
black devils. Old Carré said they would take a bite
at you as they passed. We landed on the other side,
and scrambled up a deuce of a cliff, and got to the
tunnel there just in the nick of time. Young Carré
here was fighting a dozen of them and a carronade
single-handed."

"Bon Gyu, Phil! We're well through with it. I
oughtn't to have let you go alone, but you were gone
before I knew, and we had all we could manage here.
There are ten of them dead, and the rest are in our
hands — about twenty, I think — and every man of
them damaged. They fought like devils."

"Many of ours hurt?" I asked.

"We've not come out whole, but there's no one
killed. Where's your grandfather?"

"Wounded on Herm, but not seriously, M. Tourtel says."

"Seen anything of Torode himself, Hamon?" asked Tourtel.

"Haven't you got him? Better look if he's among our lot. You would know him better than we would. They're all down yonder. I must go and see after Amice Le Couteur. We left him bleeding at Eperquerie. Get anything you want from our people, Tourtel. Krok, you come along with us," and we set off over the hill past La Jaspellerie to get to La Vauroque.

"Phil, my son," he said in my ear, "Your work is cut out for you this night. Are you good for it?"

"Yes."

"For her sake and your grandfather's and your own, we must get him away at once — now. To-morrow will be too late. We don't want him swinging in chains at Peter Port, and all the old story raked up. I wish to God you had killed him! — Mon Dieu! I forgot — you're you and he's your father. All the same it would have saved much trouble."

"What's to be done with him?"

"He may be dead. — Mon Dieu! I keep forgetting. — If he's alive, you will take him away in my boat —"

"Where to?"

"You want him to live?"

"I don't want to have killed him."

"Then you must get him to a doctor. You can't go to Guernsey, so that means Jersey. — And afterwards

— I don't know — you'll have to see what is best.
Wait a moment —" as we came to his house at La
Vauroque — "You'll need money, and take what you
can find to eat. I've got a bottle or two of wine some-
where. Before daylight you must be out of sight of
Sercq."

"Where will you say I've gone?"

"Bidemme! I don't know. . . . You can trust old
Krok?"

"Absolutely."

"Then, as soon as you have had the other patched
up and settled somewhere in safety, you'd better leave
him in Krok's care and get back here. And the sooner
the better. The people in Guernsey will want your
story from your own lips in this matter."

"How soon can we get into the cave?"

"Nom-de-dieu, yes! — . . . . Voyons donc! — About
two o'clock with a wet shirt. This wind will pile the
water up and the Race will be against us in the Gouliot.
The sooner we're off the better."

He handed me a sum of money, packed into a basket
all the eatables he could find and two bottles of wine,
and lit a lantern, and we set off through the gusty
night, past the deserted houses, past Beaumanoir all
dark and dead, and so down into Havre Gosselin where
the waves were roaring white.

We drew in Uncle George's small boat by its ropes,
and got aboard his larger one, and tied the smaller to
drag astern.

The west wind was still blowing strong, but it had

slackened somewhat with the turn of the tide. But when we tried to breast the Gouliot passage with that heavy boat, we found it impossible. Three times we nosed inch by inch into the swirling black waters, which leaped and spat and bit at us with fierce white fangs, and three times we were swept away down past Pierre au Norman, drooping over our oars like broken men.

"Guyabble! This is no good!" gasped Uncle George, as we came whirling back the third time. "We must go round." So we drew in the oars, and hoisted a bit of our lug, and ran straight out past Les Dents, whose black heads were sheets of flying foam, to make a long tack round Brecqhou. Then with the wind full on our port quarter, we made a quick, straight run for the Boutiques, and found ourselves not very far astray. Dropping the sail, and leaving Krok in charge, Uncle George and I pulled in the small boat to the channel into which his cave opened. It was still awash, but we could not wait. We dragged the boat up on to the shingle just showing at the head of the chasm, then wading out up to our shoulders to the leaning slab, we pulled down the rock screen and crawled into the tunnel.

The wounded man lay just as we had left him, breathing slowly and regularly, but showing no other sign of life. We dropped a little cognac into him, and took him by the shoulders and feet, and carried him into the tunnel. How we got him through I cannot tell, — inch by inch, shoving and hauling, till the sweat poured down us in that narrow place.

But we got him to the opening at last, and hauled the boat down and hoisted him in, soaked to the skin each one of us. Uncle George carefully closed his door, and we pulled out to Krok waiting in the lugger.

"Mon Dieu! I have had enough of him," said Uncle George, worn out, I suppose, with all the night's doings. "If he dies I shall not care much. He is better dead."

We laid him in the bottom of the boat and covered him with the mizzen sail.

"Keep well out round Bec du Nez," said Uncle George," "and run so for half an hour. Then run due east for two hours, and then make for Jersey. God keep you, my boy! It's a bitter duty, but you're doing the right thing."

He wrung my hand, and pushed off and disappeared in the darkness, and we ran up the lug and went thrashing out into Great Russel.

We turned and ran before the west wind straight for the French coast, till the sun rose and the cliffs of Sercq, about twelve miles away, gleamed as though they had but just been made — or had newly risen out of the sea. Then we turned to the southwest and made for Jersey.

As soon as it was light I saw Krok's eyes dwelling on our passenger with a very natural curiosity. Torode was unknown to him as to most of us, but there was a whole world of inquiry in his face as he sat looking down on the unconscious face below — studying it,

pondering it, catching, I thought, at times half glimpses
of the past in it.

I saw that I must tell him a part of the truth, at all
events, for I should need much help from him. My
mind had been running ahead of the boat, and trying
the ways in front, and it seemed to me that Jersey was
no safe refuge for a forfeited life.

Torode of Herm was a name known in all those
coasts. The news of his treacheries and uprooting
was bound to get there before long. Some long-
headed busybody might stumble on our secret and
undo us. My mind had been seeking a more solitary
place, and, ranging to and fro, had lighted on the
Ecréhou rocks which I had visited once with my grandfather and Krok and had never forgotten.

"Do you know who this is, Krok?" I asked, and he
raised his puzzled face and fixed his deep-set eyes on
mine.

He shook his head and sat, with his chin in his
hands and his elbows on his knees, gazing down into
the face below, and I sat watching him what time I
could spare from my steering.

And at last he knelt down suddenly and did exactly
as Uncle George had done — lifted the black moustache back off the unconscious man's mouth, and threw
back his own head to study the result. Then I saw
a wave of hot blood rush into his face and neck, and
when it went it left his face gray. He looked at me
with eyes full of wonder and pain, and then nodded
his big head heavily.

"Who, then?" and he looked round in dumb impatience for something to write with and quivered with excitement. But the ballast was bars of iron rescued from the sea and there was nothing that would serve.

Then of a sudden he whipped out his knife, and with the point of it jerkily traced on the thwart where I sat the word FATHER, and pointed his knife at me.

"Yes," I nodded. "It is my father come back when we all thought him dead. He comes in disgrace and, his life would be forfeited if they found him, so you and I are going to hide him for a time — till he is himself and can go away again."

Krok nodded, and he was probably thinking of my mother, for his fist clenched and he shook it bitterly at the unconscious man.

Then he knelt again, and looked at his wound, and shook his head.

"It was I shot him, not knowing who he was. And so I must save his life or have his blood on my hands."

From Krok's grim face I judged that the latter would have been most to his mind.

"I thought of trying the Ecréhous. We could build a shelter with some of the old stones, and he will be safer there than in Jersey. But I must get a doctor to him or he'll slip through our hands."

Krok pondered all this, and then, pointing ahead to the bristle of rocks in front and to himself, and then to me and the wounded man and to Jersey, I understood that he would land on the Ecréhous and build the shelter while I took the wounded man on to Jersey to find a doctor. And that chimed well with my ideas.

The sun had been up about three hours when we ran past the Dirouilles, with sharp eyes and a wide berth for outlying fragments, and edged cautiously in towards the Ecréhous. The sea was set so thick with rocks, some above and some below water, that we dropped our sail and felt our way in with the oars, and so came slowly past the Nipple to the islet, where once a chapel stood.

It was as lonely and likely a shelter for a shipwrecked soul as could be found, at once a hiding-place and a sanctuary. Sparse grass grew among the rocks, but no tree or shrub of any kind at that time. The ruins of the holy place alone spoke of man and his handiwork.

All around was the free breath of life, which, at times, indeed, might sound more akin to rushing death, and the sea and the voice of it; and the stark rocks sticking up through it like the fragments of a broken world. And above was the great dome of the sky — peaceful, pitiless, according to that which was within a man.

Krok scrambled ashore, and I handed him all that was left of our provisioning, then with a wave of the hand I turned and pulled clear of the traps and ran for Rozel Bay.

There was a little inn at the head of the bay, which had seen many a stranger sight than a wounded man. I had no difficulty in securing accommodation there, and the display of my money insured me fullest service, such at it was. I told them plainly that the unconscious man was related to me, and that he had received his wound at my hands. I let them believe it was an accident, and that we came from the coast of France. They were full of rough sympathy, and when I had seen him put into a comfortable bed and had dropped some more cognac into him, I started at once for St. Heliers to find a doctor.

There was no difficulty in that. I went to the first I was told of and fell fortunately. I described the nature of the wound, so far as I knew it, and told him the bullet was still there. He got the necessary instruments and we drove back to Rozel in his two-wheeled gig. Dr. Le Gros wore a great blue cloak, and his manner was brusque, but cloak and manner covered a very kind heart. Moreover, he had had a very large experience in gun-shot wounds, and he was a man of much discretion.

As soon as he set eyes on the wound he rated me soundly for not having it seen to before, and I bore it meekly. His patient was his only concern. He did not ask a single question as to how it was caused, or where we came from. It seemed, however, to puzzle or annoy him. He pinched his lips and shook his head over it and said angrily, "'Cré nom de dieu! It should have been seen to before."

"But, Monsieur," I said, "We have no doctor, else I would not have brought him here."

"But, nom de dieu! that bullet should have been got out at once. It is pressing on the brain. It may have set up inflammation, and what *that* may lead to the good God alone knows."

"Pray get it out at once, monsieur."

"Ay, ay, that's all very well, but the damage may be done, and now, 'cré nom de dieu, you expect me to undo it."

"I am sorry."

"Sorry won't set this right," — with a shake of the head like an angry bull — "No — 'cré nom de dieu!"

He was a rather violent old man, but skilful with his terrible little tools, and he worked away with them till I left him hurriedly.

He came out after a time with the bullet in his hand, "Le v'la," he said tersely. "And if that was all — bien! But —!" and he shook his head ominously, and talked of matters connected with the brain which were quite beyond me, but still caused me much discomfort.

He told me what to do and promised to return next day.

Torode — I never could bring myself to think of him as my father — came to himself during the night, for in the morning his eyes were open and they followed me with a puzzled lack of understanding. He evidently did not know where he was or how he got there. But he lay quietly and asked no questions, except with his eyes.

When the doctor came he asked, "Has he spoken yet?"

"Not yet," and he nodded.

"How long must he stop here, Monsieur le Docteur?"

"It depends," he said, looking at me thoughtfully. "Another week at all events. You want to take him home?"

"He is better at home."

"I must keep him for a week at all events."

So that day I took over some provisionings for Krok, and found him well advanced with his building. He had got the walls of a small cabin about half-way up, and had collected drift timber enough to roof it and to spare. I told him how things stood, put in a few hours' work with him on the house, and got back to Rozel.

"Has he spoken?" was the doctor's first question next day.

"Not a word."

"Ah!" with a weighty nod, and he lifted Torode's left hand, and when he let it go it fell limply.

And again, each day, his first question was, "Has he spoken?" And my reply was always the same. For, whether through lack of power or strength of will I could not tell, but certain it was that no word of any kind had so far passed between us.

One time, coming upon him unawares, I saw his lips moving as though he were attempting speech to himself, but as soon as he saw me he set himself once more to his grim silence, and the look in his eyes reminded me somehow of Krok.

On the seventh day, when the doctor asked his usual

question, and I as usual replied, he said gravely, " 'Cré
nom de dieu, I doubt if he will ever speak again.   You
see —" and he went off into a very full and deep explanation about certain parts of the brain, of which I
understood nothing except that they were on the left
side and controlled the powers of speech, and he feared
the bullet, and the inflammation it had caused, had
damaged them beyond repair.   And when I turned
to look at Torode, the dumb misery in his eyes assured
me in my own mind that it was so, for I had seen just
that look in Krok's eyes many a time.

Another whole week I waited, visiting Krok three
times in all, and the last time finding him living quite
contentedly in the finished house.   And then, Torode
having spoken no word, and the doctor saying he
could do no more for him, I had him carried down to
the boat and took him across to the Ecréhous.

He had been gaining strength daily, and, except for
a certain disinclination to exertion of any kind, and
his lack of speech, looked almost himself again.   Later
on, when he walked and worked, I noticed a weakness
in his left arm, and his left leg dragged a little.

At Krok's suggestion, I had bargained for a small
boat, and I took him also a further supply of provisions, and flour, and fishing-lines.   And before I left
them I thought it right to explain to Torode just what
had happened.

He listened in a cold, black fury, but fell soon into
a slough of despond.   His life was over, but he was not
dead.   For him, as for the rest of us, death would, I

think have been more merciful — and yet, I would not have had him die at my hands.

And so I left the two dumb men on the Ecréhous and returned to Sercq, and of my welcome there I need not tell.

My mother and Aunt Jeanne were full of questionings which taxed my wits to breaking point to evade, especially Aunt Jeanne's. She tried to trap me in a hundred ways, leading up from the most distant and innocent points to that which had kept me away so long. And since truth consists as much in not withholding as in telling, I was brought within measurable distance of lying by Aunt Jeanne's pertinacity, for which I think the blame should fairly rest with her.

I told them simply that I had been on matters connected with Torode, and would still be engaged on them for some time to come, and left it there.

Carette, of course, understood, and approved all I had done. She saw with me the necessity of keeping the matter from my mother, lest her peace of mind should suffer shipwreck again, and to no purpose. Her loving tenderness and thought for my mother at this time were a very great delight to me, and commended her still more to my mother herself.

My grandfather was still in Guernsey. His leg had taken longer to heal than it might have done, and, failing my information against the Herm men, his was of use to the authorities in preparing the charge against them.

There were near forty prisoners brought over from

Sercq, some of them so sorely wounded that it was doubtful if they would live until their trial. The rest had been killed, except some few who were said to have got across to France. To my great relief neither young Torode nor his mother were among the dead or the captives.

Krok was supposed in Sercq to be with my grandfather in Guernsey, and his absence excited no remark. For myself, in Sercq my absence was accounted for by the necessity for my being in Guernsey, — while in Guernsey an exaggerated account of the wound I had received on the Coupée offered excuse for my retirement; and so the matter passed without undue comment.

George Hamon had informed my grandfather of his recognition of Torode, and he told me afterwards that for a very long time the old man flatly refused to believe it.

My news of Torode's recovery was not, I think, over-welcome to Uncle George. He would have preferred him dead, and the old trouble buried forever, forgetting always that his death must have left something of a cloud on my life, though he always argued strongly against that view of the case.

"I find it hard to swallow, mon gars, in spite of George Hamon's assurances," said my grandfather when we spoke of it.

"I found it hard to believe. But Uncle George had no doubts about it. Krok, too, recognised him."

"Krok did? Ah — then —" and he nodded slow acceptance of the unwelcome fact.

Before I was through with the telling of my story, and signing it, and swearing to it before various authorities, I was heartily sick of the whole matter, and wished, as indeed I had good reason, that I had never sailed with John Ozanne in the *Swallow*.

But — "pas d'rue sans but" — and at last all that unpleasing business was over — except a little afterclap of which you will hear presently.

After many delays and formalities, all the prisoners were condemned to death, and I was free to go home and be my own man again.

Twice while in Guernsey I had taken advantage of the slow course of the law to run across to Jersey and so to the Ecréhous, and found Torode settled down in dumb bitterness to the narrow life that was left to him.

He was quite recovered in every way, save that of speech, but that great loss broke his power and cut him off from his kind.

I had never told him that his wound came from my hand, but he associated me with it in some way, and showed so strong a distaste for my company that I thought well to go no more.

He had taken a dislike to old Krok too. Their common loss had in it the elements of mockery, and on my second visit Krok expressed a desire to return to Sercq. Torode could maintain himself by fishing, as they had done together, and could barter his surplus at Rozel or Gorey for anything he required.

And so we left him to his solitude, and he seemed content to have us go. George Hamon, however, ran across now and again in his lugger to see how he was getting on, and to make sure that he was still there, and perhaps with the hope that sooner or later that which was in him still as strong as it had been any time this twenty years might find its reward.

CHAPTER XXXIX

"CARETTE, ma mie!" I asked, as we sat in the heather on Longue Pointe, the evening after I got home. "When shall we marry?"

"When you will, Phil. I am ready."

"As soon as may be then," and I drew her close into my arms, the richest treasure any man might have, and thanked God for his mercies.

It was a glorious evening, with a moon like a silver sickle floating over Guernsey. The sky was of a rare depth and purity, which changed from palest blue to faintest green, and away to the northwest, above the outer isles, the sun was sinking behind a bank of plum-coloured clouds which faded away in long, thin bands along the water line. The clouds were rimmed with golden fire, and wherever an opening was, the golden glory streamed through and lit the darkening waters between, and set our bold Sercq headlands all aflame. And up above, the little wind-drawn clouds were rosy red, and right back into the east the sky was flushed with colour. It was a very low tide too, and every rock was bared, so that from the white spit of Herm it seemed as though a long, dark line of ships sped northwards towards the Casquets. Brecqhou lay dark before us, and the Gouliot Pass was black with its coiling tide. A flake of light glimmered through the cave behind, and now and again came the boom of a wave under some low ledge below. Up above us the sky was full of larks, and their sweet sharp notes came down to us like peals of little silver bells. And down in Havre Gosselin the gulls were wheeling noisily as they settled themselves for the night.

I have always thought that view one of the most beautiful in the world, but all its glories were as nothing to the greater glory in our two hearts. We had had our cloudy days and our times of storm and strife; and now they were past, our clouds were turned into golden glories and our hearts were glad. We had been parted. We had looked death in the face. And now we were together and we would part no more.

We sat there in the heather till all the glories faded save our own, — till Guernsey and Herm and Jethou sank into the night — till Brecqhou was only a shadow, and the Gouliot stream only a sound; and then we went down the scented lanes close-linked, as were our hearts.

Jean Le Marchant was sitting in the kitchen with Aunt Jeanne. He was recovered of his wound, and Martin also, but, for the elder at all events, active life was over, and he would have to be content with the land, and his memories.

We came in arm in arm.

"Do you see any objection to our marrying at once, M. Le Marchant?" I asked. "We are of one mind in the matter."

"B'en!" said Aunt Jeanne, with a face like a globe of light. "We will have it on Wednesday. You can go over to the Dean for a license, mon gars, and I'll be all ready — Wednesday — you understand."

And Jean Le Marchant smiled and said, "At Beaumanoir Mistress Falla rules the roost. Every one does as she says."

"I should think so," said Aunt Jeanne, with an emphatic nod. "If they don't I know the reason why. So we'll say Wednesday. Have you had the news, Phil?"

"What news then, Aunt Jeanne?"

"Ah, then, you've not heard. George Hamon was in from Guernsey. He says you are to get the reward offered by the London merchants for the upsetting of Monsieur Torode."

"I?"

"And who better, mon gars? If it hadn't been for you, he'd be there yet gobbling their ships at his will. Now don't you be a fool, my dear. Take what the good God sends you with a good grace. You'll find a use for it when the babies begin coming, I warrant you. Little pigs don't fatten on water. Ma fé, non!" — at which bit of Aunt Jeanne, Carette only laughed, with a fine colour in her face.

And to make an end of that, in due time the £5000 was indeed sent to me, and I put it in the bank in Guernsey for the use of Carette "and the children," as Aunt Jeanne said — and of the interest I reserved a portion for the provision of such small comforts as were possible to the lonely one on the Ecréhous.

And so, by no merit of my own, I became a man of substance and not dependent on Aunt Jeanne's bounty, which I think she would have preferred.

We were married in the little church alongside the Seigneurie, at the head of the valley, by M. Pierre Paul Secretan, and Aunt Jeanne's enjoyment therein and in the feast that followed was, I am certain, greater than any she had felt when she was married herself.

We continued to live with her at Beaumanoir, and she gave me of her wisdom in all matters relating to the land and its treatment, as she did also to Carette in household matters and the proper bringing up of a family, about which latter subject she knew far more than any mother that ever was born.

In me she found an apt pupil, and so came to leave matters more and more in my hands, with sharp criticism of all mistakes and ample advice for setting things right.

Carette drank in all her wisdom — until the babies came, and then she took her own way with them, and judging by results it was an excellent way.

George Hamon still brought me word from time to time of the exile on the Ecréhous.

We were sitting over the fire one cold night in the spring, Carette and I, Aunt Jeanne having gone to bed to get warm, when a knock came on the door, and when I opened it George Hamon came in and stood before the hearth. He looked pinched and cold, and yet aglow with some inner warmth, and his first word told why.

"He is dead, Phil. I found him lying in his bed as if asleep, but he was dead."

I nodded soberly. He was better dead, but I was glad he had not died by my hand.

"I have got him here —" said Uncle George.

"Here?" and I jumped up quickly.

"In my boat down in Port du Moulin."

"But why?"

"Because —" and he stood looking at us, and Carette nodded understandingly. And at that he went on quickly — "Because I have waited over twenty years, Phil, and I am going to wait no longer," and I understood.

"You are going to tell her?" I asked.

"Yes — now. I must. But not all, I think. We will see. But not all if we can help it. It will open the old wound, but, please God, I will heal it and she shall be happy yet."

"Yes," I said. "I think you can heal the wound, Uncle George. What do you want me to do?"

"Come with me, if you will," and I kissed my wife and followed him out.

"You understand," he said, as we went across the fields to Belfontaine. "He was among Torode's men. I recognized him, and we smuggled him off so that he should not be hanged," and on that understanding we knocked on the door and went in.

My grandfather was reading in one of his big books, my mother was at her knitting, and Krok was busy over a fishing-net.

"Ah, you two!" said my mother. "What mischief are you plotting now? It is like old times to see you with your heads together. But, ma fé, you seem to have changed places. What trouble have you been getting into, George?"

"Aw, then, Rachel!—It is out of trouble I am getting. I bring you strange news," and she sat looking up at him with deep wonder in her eyes.

Perhaps she saw behind his face into his thoughts — into his heart. For, as she gazed, a startled look came over her, and her face flushed and made her young again.

"What is it?"

"Paul Martel died yesterday."

"Paul?" and her hand went quickly to her heart, as though to still a sudden stab of pain, and for the moment her face whitened and then dyed red again.

Krok had eyed Uncle George keenly from the moment he entered. Now he did a strange thing. He got up quietly and took down a lantern and went to the fire to light it. Perhaps it had been an understood thing between them. I do not know.

My mother looked at Krok and then at Uncle George, and my grandfather stood up.

"Yes," said Uncle George with a grave nod. "I have got him here — in my boat in Port du Moulin, for I knew you could not credit it unless you saw him yourself."

"But how —" she faltered.

"He was among Torode's crew — He was wounded.

I recognised him and we got him away lest — well, you understand? He has been living on the Ecréhous and he died there yesterday. Will you see him?" and he looked at her very earnestly, and she knew all that his look meant.

Her silence seemed long, while Uncle George looked at her entreatingly, and she looked at the floor, and seemed lost in thought.

"Yes," she said at last, and went towards the door.

"Put on a shawl. The wind is cold," said Uncle George, and it seemed to me that there was something of a new and gentle right in his tone, something of proprietorship in his manner.

And so we went along the foot-paths past La Moinerie and down the zig-zag into Port du Moulin, the only bay along that coast into which my mother could possibly have gone by night, and that was why Uncle George had brought him there.

I do not think a word was spoken all the way. Krok held the lantern for my mother's feet. Uncle George walked close behind her, and at times before her, in the descent, and helped her down, and so we came at last to the shingle and crunched over it to the boat.

Krok put down his lantern on a rock, and he and Uncle George got in and pulled out to the lugger which was anchored about twenty yards out.

They came back presently, and lifted out the body and laid it gently on the stones, and Krok brought his lantern. My mother's face was very white and pinched as she knelt down beside it, and at first sight she started and looked quickly up at Uncle George as though in doubt or denial. And presently Uncle George bent down and with his hand lifted the moustache back form the dead man's mouth, and my mother gazed into the dark face and said quietly:

"It is he"; then she seized my grandfather's arm suddenly and turned away. They were stumbling over the rough stones when Krok ran after them with the lantern and came back in the dark.

We laid the body in the boat again, and Krok lifted in some great, round stones, and we rowed out to the black loom of the lugger. Uncle George lit his own lantern, and by its dim light Krok set to work preparing my father's body for its last journey.

Whether he was simply anxious to get done with the business, or whether he felt a gloomy satisfaction in performing these last rites for a man whom he had always hated for his treatment of my mother, I do not know. But he certainly went about it with a grim earnestness which was not very far removed from enjoyment.

He stripped the mizzen mast of its sail and Uncle George said no word against it. If Krok had required the lugger itself as a coffin he would not have said him nay.

He wrapped the body carefully in the sail, with great, smooth stones from the beach, and with some rope and his knife he sewed it all tightly together, and pulled each knot home with a jerk that was meant to be final, and his hairy old face was crumpled into a frown as he worked.

We ran swiftly up Great Russel under the keen east wind, until, by the longer swing of the seas, we knew we were free of the rocks and islands to the west.

Then Uncle George turned her nose to the wind, and under the slatting sail, with bared heads, we committed to the seas the body of him who had wrought such mischief upon them and in some of our lives.

"Dieu Merci!" said Uncle George, as the long white figure slipped from our hands and plunged down through the black waters. Then he clapped on his cap and turned the helm, and the lugger went bounding back quicker than she had come, for she and we were lightened of our loads.

We ran back round Brecqhou into Havre Gosselin, and climbed the ladders and went to our homes.

Uncle George and my mother were married just a month after our little Phil was born, and I learned again, from the look on my mother's face, that a woman's age is counted not by years but by that which the years have brought her.

They have been very happy. There is only one happier household on the island, and that is ours at Beaumanoir, for it is full of the sound of children's voices, and the patter of little feet.

THE END

THE FORTY MEN OF SERCQ IN THE YEAR 1800.

EAST SIDE

NO.	NAME OF HOUSE	TENANT
1.	Le Fort	Thomas Hamon
2.	Le Grand Fort	Jean Le Feuvre
3.	La Tour	Amice Le Couteur (Sénéchal)
4.	La Genêtière	Philippe Guille
5.	La Rade	Thomas Mauger
6.	La Ville Roussel	Pierre Le Feuvre
7.	La Ville Roussel	Abraham De Carteret
8.	La Ville Roussel	Jean Vaudin
9.	La Ville Roussel	Philippe Guille
10.	La Ville Roussel	Jean Drillot
11.	Le Carrefour	Elie Guille
12.	La Valette du Bas	Elie Guille
13.	La Valette	Robert De Carteret
14.	Vaux de Creux	Pierre Le Pelley (Seigneur)
15.	La Friponnerie	Martin Le Masurier
16.	La Colinette	Jean Falle
17.	La Manoir	Pierre Le Pelley (Seigneur)
18.	La Vauroque	Thomas De Carteret
19.	La Forge	Thomas De Carteret
20.'	La Pomme du Chien	Pierre Le Pelley (Seigneur)
21.	Dixcart	Thomas Godfray
22.	Grand Dixcart	Henri Le Masurier
23.	Petit Dixcart	Eliza Poidestre
24.	La Jaspellerie	William Le Masurier
25.	Clos Bourel	Abraham Guille

PETIT SERCQ

NO.	NAME OF HOUSE	TENANT
26.	La Sablonnerie	Philippe Guille
27.	La Moussie	Nicholas Mollet
28.	La Friponnerie	Philippe Baker

417

WEST SIDE

Petit Sebcq

29.	Du Vallerie	Jean Hamon
30.	La Pipetterie	Helier Baker

Sebcq

31.	Dos D'Ane	Abraham Guille
32.	Beauregard	Philippe Slowley
33.	Beauregard	Pierre Le Masurier
34.	Le Vieux Port	Philippe Tanquerel
35.	Le Port	Edouard Vaudin
36.	La Moignerie	Jean Le Feuvre
37.	La Rondelrie	Thomas Mauger
38.	La Moinerie	Abraham Baker
39.	L'Ecluse	William De Carteret
40.	La Seigneurie	Pierre Le Pelley

And for the purposes of this story —

Belfontaine	Philip Carré
Beaumanoir	Peter Le Marchant (Jeanne Falla)

152

152

3 2044 0